Transformative Justice

Transformative Justice

Critical and Peacemaking Themes Influenced by Richard Quinney

EDITED BY
JOHN F. WOZNIAK, MICHAEL C. BRASWELL,
RONALD E. VOGEL, AND KRISTIE R. BLEVINS

LEXINGTON BOOKS

A division of
ROWMAN & LITTLEFIELD PUBLISHERS, INC.
Lanham • Boulder • New York • Toronto • Plymouth, UK

LEXINGTON BOOKS

A division of Rowman & Littlefield Publishers, Inc.
A wholly owned subsidiary of The Rowman & Littlefield Publishing Group, Inc.
4501 Forbes Boulevard, Suite 200
Lanham, MD 20706

Estover Road
Plymouth PL6 7PY
United Kingdom

British Library Cataloguing in Publication Information Available

Library of Congress Cataloging-in-Publication Data

Transformative justice: critical and peacemaking themes influenced by Richard Quinney / edited by John F. Wozniak . . . [et al.].
p. cm.
ISBN-13: 978-0-7391-0932-8 (cloth : alk. paper)
ISBN-10: 0-7391-0932-4 (cloth : alk. paper)
ISBN-13: 978-0-7391-3165-7 (ebooks)
ISBN-10: 0-7391-3165-6 (ebooks)
1. Restorative justice. 2. Quinney, Richard. 3. Criminology. 4. Reconciliation. I. Wozniak, John F. (John Francis), 1951–
HV8688.T73 2008
364.601–dc22 2008031240

Printed in the United States of America

™ The paper used in this publication meets the minimum requirements of American National Standard for Information Sciences—Permanence of Paper for Printed Library Materials, ANSI/NISO Z39.48–1992.

Dedication

For the love and joy that mean so very much in our lives, we dedicate this book to our families—

To Margaret Wozniak, Melinda Bickel, Eric, Laura, and Martin Wozniak

To Susan, Matt, and Scott Braswell

To Brenda and Hailey Vogel

To Sharon and Luther Blevins and Jason Dahms

Contents

Part II Peacemaking Themes

Chapter 1

Introduction to Transformative Justice: Critical and Peacemaking Themes Influenced by Richard Quinney

John F. Wozniak

> *Can you imagine a world without crime? What would our lives be like without criminals and criminal justice? With all the policies and programs, the political words and deeds, the rhetoric on law and order steadily belaboring it, completely eliminating crime would deny part of our experience. Crime and its control are basic to the way of life in the United States.*

These words were presented in the first chapter of Richard Quinney's (1979, p. 1) *Criminology* textbook which also suggested that:

> We should see what it is about crime that interests us. For some of us crime may have taken concrete form — we may have been the object of criminal laws and the system that administers criminal justice. Or we may have been the victims of violent or exploitative acts of a criminal nature. Then too, crime has entered our imaginations in one way or another all our lives. We have grown up in a world of crime.

Along with providing these introductory imageries, Richard Quinney indicated that one of his key textbook goals was to furnish critical ideas about crime that *aim toward a transformation of society*.

It is instructive to further point out that Richard Quinney's contributions to the fields of criminology and criminal justice have extended well beyond the ideas expressed in his criminology textbook. According to Randy Martin and colleagues (1990, p. vii), Richard Quinney is one of fifteen pioneers in criminology who have helped to shape the discipline and have influenced thinking about criminal behavior.

As will be shown in more detail later, Richard Quinney's legacy within criminology and criminal justice is that he is one of the people in these fields who has consistently encouraged a general questioning of how crime and criminal justice are commonly experienced and controlled within contemporary society. In this spirit, criminology and criminal justice as disciplines of teaching, research, and service have increasingly attracted more and more scholars and practitioners over the last three decades.

Year after year, a plethora of criminology and criminal justice textbooks have endeavored to provide up-to-date information about the varied social contexts of unlawful behavior and its control. As in the past, criminologists and criminal justice specialists working today have examined crimes, criminals, and criminal justice from a diverse set of angles.

One illustration of the multi-dimensional nature of current crime studies can be seen in the diverse topics covered in readings within criminology and criminal justice in the past fifteen years. That is, such collections of readings have been published on: criminological theories (Cordella and Siegel, 1996; Cullen and Agnew, 2006; Paternoster and Bachman, 2001; Renzetti et al., 2003; Williams and McShane, 1998); crime controversies (Fuller and Hickey, 1999; Monk, 2001; Moriarty, 2003; Potter, 2002; Schwartz and Hatty, 2003); juvenile delinquency (Bartollas, 2003; Berger, 1996; Weis et al., 2001); gangs (Egley et al., 2006; Esbensen et al., 2004; Huff, 2002); gender and crime (Renzetti and Goodstein, 2001; Renzetti et al., 2006; Schram and Koons-Witt, 2004); corrections (Latessa and Holsinger, 2006; Petersilia, 1998; Schwartz and Travis, 1997); white-collar crime (Geis et al., 1995; Shichor et al., 2002; Shover and Wright, 2001) and corporate crime (Ermann and Lundman, 2002; Lofquist et al., 1997; Pearce and Snider, 1995).

With the publishing of this present book that you are now reading, another collection of readings about crime is added to the above-mentioned sets of literature. One might become curious and ask why publish another book of readings about crime? In other words, aren't there already enough crime-related readings available in these fields of study?

What makes this present book of readings unique is that it is very unlike all the others mentioned just above. That is, this present book of readings has two central dimensions that have not been provided together before within criminology and criminal justice literature. First, each of its chapters have been inspired by the general content and challenge of Richard Quinney's socially progressive writings (such as those about critical and peacemaking criminology) within criminology and criminal justice. Second, each of these chapters represent crime-related analyses that promote the growth and development of *transformative justice* in terms of what Harris (2006, p. 556) has identified as a combination of a paradigm, philosophical approach, social movement, and "way of life" within criminology and criminal justice.

In this light, the upcoming discussion in this introductory chapter has three main parts. First, it will be illustrated how each chapter in this book of readings has drawn inspiration from the crime-related writings of Richard Quinney. Second, core assumptions of critical criminology and peacemaking criminology will be identified and linked to these chapters with particular regard to critical and peacemaking criminology. Third, the meaning and application of transformative justice as a concept and approach to the study of crime will be discussed in relation to these chapters as well. Hence, upon reading the next sections of this introductory chapter, it will be made clear how this book of readings has been designed to focus on transformative justice especially in keeping with crime-related writings of Richard Quinney.

Chapters Inspired by the Work of Richard Quinney

At the book exhibit of the American Society of Criminology conference of 2000 in San Francisco, Michael Braswell and I were discussing new books about crime and justice and shared ideas about Richard Quinney's book about his scholarly and autobiographical writings titled *Bearing Witness to Crime and Social Justice*. The feature of this book that we were both drawn to was how it clearly illustrated the various ways that Richard Quinney has challenged status quo thinking about crime and its control during the past three decades.

Hence, we decided to organize a group of authors to write essays in honor of Richard Quinney for a special issue (Volume 48–2) of *Crime & Delinquency* (April 2002). We asked each of the invited authors to reflect on *Bearing Witness to Crime and Social Justice* in a manner that either illustrated the progression of Richard Quinney's thinking and writing or offered a type of analysis that was compatible with Richard Quinney's scholarly writings.

We titled this special issue "Criminology at the Edge" because we viewed Richard Quinney's body of work as pivotal in bringing about many key paradigm shifts within criminology/criminal justice as a field of study. Notably, in the preface to *Bearing Witness to Crime and Social Justice*, Richard Quinney (2000a, pp. x–xi) observed:

> My own travels through the 1960's, the 1970's, the 1980's, and the 1990's were marked by a progression of ways of thinking and acting: from the social constructionist perspective to phenomenology, from phenomenology to Marxist and critical philosophy, from Marxist and critical philosophy to liberation theology, from liberation theology to Buddhism and existentialism. And then to a more ethnographic and personal mode of thinking and being. It is necessary to note that in all these travels nothing was rejected or deleted from the previous stages; rather, each new stage of development incorporated what had preceded it. Each change was motivated by the need to understand crime in another and more complex way, in a way excluded from a former understanding. Each stage incorporated the changes that were taking place in my personal life. There was to be no separation between life and theory, between witnessing and writing.

In this context, the eight articles in that special issue of *Crime & Delinquency* were not written to evaluate or critique Richard Quinney's past and present writings. Instead, each of these articles endeavored to build on the socially progressive theoretical and philosophical thrusts that Richard Quinney accentuated about crime, criminals, the criminal justice system, and society on the whole.

The most compelling quality of Richard Quinney's work is that he is not only an innovative thinker but also an innovative teacher. That is, within his general body of writings, Richard Quinney set his sights on broadening the theoretical discourse underlying criminological and criminal justice research as well as on heightening ways of teaching students about the relevance of sociology and moral philosophy to crime and its control. In this regard, Richard Quinney's (2000a, p. 194) following remarks are useful to examine:

> Whatever else we do as criminologists, we are engaged in a moral enterprise. Simply stated, our underlying questions are these: How are human beings to live? Who are we, and of what are we capable? And how could things be different? The criminologist, although not likely educated as a moral philosopher, operates with an implicit moral philosophy, and is engaged in the construction of a moral philosophy. The many and varied issues surrounding crime and criminal justice are ultimately about how we humans might live. And at the same time, what we criminologists are doing—in addition to the other things we are doing—is *witnessing* to all that is associated with crime and criminal justice.

The original eight articles within that special issue of *Crime & Delinquency* were framed in a way to likewise bear witness to issues about crime emerging in these beginning years of the twenty-first century. Moreover, these articles are similar to Richard Quinney's writings in several ways. They were: designed to advance socially progressive thinking about crime and justice, concerned with the human suffering involved in crime and its victims, and predicated on the development of innovative ideas about lessening crime and bettering our social existence now and in the future.

Since publishing this special issue of *Crime & Delinquency*, Michael Braswell and I decided (along with our other two co-authors) that it would be fruitful to add four articles (see Chapters 7, 9, 12, and 13) with the original eight articles (of that special journal issue) to expand the general scope of this present book. Thus, as seen in the table of contents of our present book, it became possible to divide chapters into two main parts: *critical themes* and *peacemaking themes*. Here, we determined that our book could be generally organized in terms of two theoretical frameworks commonly employed by Richard Quinney in his analyses of crime and criminal justice.

However, it is important to note that at present, there are wide-ranging conceptions and interpretations among criminology and criminal justice analysts of the general nature and meanings of what is meant by the terms, "critical criminology" and "peacemaking criminology." For example, some authors conceive of peacemaking criminology as one of many types of critical criminology (Akers and Sellers, 2004; Arrigo, 1999; Bohm, 2001; Cullen and Agnew, 2006; Maclean and Milovanovic, 1991; Schwartz and Hatty, 2003). Other authors designate peacemaking criminology as a type of social conflict theory (Lilly et al., 2007; Miller et al., 2006; Schmalleger, 2006).

Nonetheless, Richard Quinney's conceptualizations of critical and peacemaking criminology are helpful guideposts to explore the analyses of crime and criminal justice provided in the other twelve chapters of this present book as well be illustrated in the next section.

Core Assumptions of Critical Criminology and Peacemaking Criminology

Like other analysts mentioned above, Richard Quinney, along with his colleague, John Wildeman (1991, p. 79) viewed peacemaking criminology as one of four new directions (along with left realism, feminism, and postmodernism) that critical criminology had been moving in the 1990s. Be that as it may, within Richard Quinney's collected works, basic thrusts of critical and peacemaking criminology were demarcated.

That is, according to Quinney and Wildeman (1991, p. 72), critical criminology is "a radical questioning of the justness and effectiveness of all our social institutions." They (1991, p. 73) further observe:

> The critical criminology that began to flourish in the 1970's essentially tried to realize two goals: first, to analyze crime in American life through a critical inspection of the contradictions of our master institutions and, second, to define crime as more than just behavior in violation of the law of the state but also as behavior that causes social harm and social injury to great numbers of people. Crime was not conceptualized as institutionalized behavior in violation of basic human rights.

Similarly, it has been observed that critical criminologies:

> prefer to define crime as social harm and/or as violations of human rights . . . oppose the existing social order of power based on inequality . . . usually demand a radical transformation, not just of criminal justice, but of the total social and political organization of society (Einstadter and Henry, 1995, p. 227) and regard major social structural and cultural changes within society as essential steps to reduce criminality and to promote social justice (DeKeseredy and Perry, 2006).

Moreover, Francis Cullen and Robert Agnew (2006, pp. 295–296) contend there are five central themes of critical criminology as follows:

- The concepts of inequality and power are integral to any understanding of crime and its control.
- Crime is a political, not a value-free concept; what is and is not outlawed reflects the power structure in society.
- The criminal justice system ultimately serves the interests of the capitalist class and is largely set up to process poor and minority offenders, while ignoring the illegalities of rich and corporate offenders.

- Capitalism is the root cause of criminal behavior; under capitalism, the human needs of the poor are ignored and a fertile environment is created for crimes by corporations.
- The solution to crime is the creation of a more equitable society; the ways in which capitalist-based exploitation creates crime and victimization should be unmasked.

In Robert Bohm's (2001, p. 103) view, critical criminology is "a product of the demystification of American society that began toward the end of the 1950's. *Demystification* is the correcting of conceptions or 'setting the record straight'" (italics in original). Bohm (2001, p. 104) further asserts that critical criminology assumes humans are both determined and determining such that "Human beings are the creators of the institutions and structures that ultimately dominate and constrain them. Furthermore, as creators, they are capable of changing institutions and structures" and "conflict is the norm, that society is characterized primarily by conflict over moral values."

In fact, critical criminology, according to Piers Beirne and James Messerschmidt (2006, pp. 427–428) uniformly questions the following:

- the usage of the legalistic definition of crime—dominant conceptions of the "violent" offender that exclude many other agents of social injuries
- prevailing usages of linear, non-dialectical notions of "causation"
- "correctional" penal policy
- the increasing investment of energy in more punitive responses to crime
- the limited attention paid to political economy in the contribution to crime
- the targeting of selected groups, informally or formally, for official police intervention
- the resistance to entertaining gross inequalities in living standards, alienating working conditions, and dilapidated communities
- the continued and often systematic practices of sexism, racism, classism and their intersecting effects often disguised as neutral and objective or factual categories (emphases in original)

Likewise, Michael Lynch and Raymond Michalowski (2006, pp. 14–15) assert that critical criminology is comprised of different criminologies of resistance (i.e., feminists, critical race theorists, political economists, postmodernists) that "share a commitment to understanding the deeper social forces that shape the definition, commission, and punishment of crime" and tend to emphasize that "the social reality of crime is a fluid one, arising from the interplay among social forces, particularly gender, class, race, and culture."

It would be remiss to fail to point out that critical criminology is especially oriented toward analyzing ways in which social inequalities in capitalist society have impacts upon crime. In this regard, Martin Schwartz and Suzanne Hatty (2003, p. X) stress that within critical criminology:

> Race has been important to many theorists, and increasingly scholars in this area take gender into account when developing their theories. The most cutting-edge work today not only includes race, class, and gender, but also specifically attempts to locate the intersections between these identities and experiences. . . . For example, in some circumstances being an African-American might be the primary influence on a person's behavior, but in others it might be the fact of being a woman, or being an African-American woman, or being a poor African-American woman or even just being a poor woman. She is the same woman, but in different circumstances she may call upon difference resources. The same applies, of course, to rich white men, or any other combination.

Indeed, it can be very reasonably argued that peacemaking criminology has these same concerns about crime in relation to capitalist society. However, Richard Quinney (1991, p. 4) set the stage for the emergence and growth of peacemaking criminology, with these often-cited wordings, that it is a: "nonviolent criminology of compassion and service": which "seeks to end suffering and thereby eliminate crime." In this vein, Richard Quinney (1991, p. 9) proposes that *peacemaking criminology* must "search for the reasons that make us suffer." Similarly, Harold Pepinsky (1989, p. 6) observes that an aim of the peacemaking perspective is to "figure out how we can get along without criminalizing and victimizing one another."

Within Richard Quinney's (2000b, p. 28) peacemaking criminology construct, two central concepts are *negative peace* and *positive peace*, which differentiates in the following:

> Punishment is not the way of peace. Responses to crime that are fueled by hate, rather than generated by love, are necessarily punitive. Such responses are a form of violence, a violence that can only beget further violence. Much of what is called" criminal justice" is a violent reaction to, or anticipation of, crime. The criminal justice system, with all of its procedures, is a form of *negative peace*, its purpose being to deter or process acts of crime through the threat and application of force. *Positive peace*, on the other hand, is something other than the deterrence or punishment of crime. Positive peace is more than merely the absence of crime and violence—and of war. Positive peace exists when the sources of crime—including poverty, inequality, racism, and alienation—are not present. There can be no peace—no positive peace—without social justice. Without social justice and without peace (personal and social), there is crime. And there is, as well, the violence of criminal justice. The negative peacemaking of criminal justice keeps things as they are. Social policies and programs that are positive in nature—that focus on positive peacemaking—create something new. They eliminate the structural sources of violence and crime. Positive peace is the objective of a critical, peacemaking criminology (italics in original).

Related to Richard Quinney's peace-oriented themes of social justice, John Fuller (1998) formulated primary tenets of peacemaking criminology to be ideally implemented into our current system of criminal justice. According to John Fuller (1998), the foundation of peacemaking is *nonviolence*, upon which five tenets of peacemaking need to be extended toward crimes, criminals, and criminal justice. Ronald Hunter and Mark Dantzker (2002, p. 126) summarize these five tenets of peacemaking in this way:

- *Social justice*—social injustices such as sexism, racism, and ageism must be dealt with to provide equity and harmony within society.
- *Inclusion*—attempts must be made to involve both the victim and the offender in the dispute resolution process rather than just imposing governmental edicts upon them. Deterrence and punishment goals should be subverted to the mutual needs of victims and offenders.
- *Correct means*—the process by which justice is attained must be addressed, and the legal safeguards of due process must be accorded to offenders.
- *Ascertainable criteria*—the justice process must be conducted in a manner that all participants understand and have confidence in.
- *Categorical imperative*—the decisions and outcomes of the justice process must be based on moral precepts (reasoning) that are universally applicable to all situations and all persons.

Hence, according to John Fuller (2003, p. 88):

> By employing this peacemaking perspective in the criminal justice system, it is suggested that the problems of crime will be reduced. As opposed to the war on crime perspective, the peacemaking perspective has the potential to provide lasting solutions to the problems that lead individuals to commit violations of the law. The war on crime perspective with its emphasis on punishment and retribution ensure that offenders will strive only to commit their crimes in a more efficient manner so as not to get caught. The peacemaking perspective on the other hand, seeks to address the conditions of society that foster crime and to address the problems of the individual offender. Additionally, the peacemaking perspective seeks to understand and respond to the concerns of victims.

Various other criminological analysts have endeavored to sketch core thrusts of peacemaking criminology such as Larry Siegel (2007) who wrote:

> To members of the peacemaking movement, the main purpose of criminology is to promote a peaceful, just society . . . . Peacemakers view the efforts of the state to punish and control as crime-encouraging rather than crime-discouraging . . . . Today, advocates of the peacemaking movement . . . try to find humanist solutions to crime and other social problems. Rather than punishment and prison, they advocate such policies as mediation and conflict resolution.

In the conclusion to the peacemaking criminology reader (1991) that he co-edited with Richard Quinney, Harold Pepinsky (1991) presented an overview of the three major intellectual perspectives of peacemaking criminology. These three perspectives (Fuller and Wozniak, 2006, p. 255) include: religious/humanist traditions (i.e., the root of each of the major religions is teaching of peace and harmony); feminist traditions (i.e., a rational, humane, and ultimately effective criminal justice system must treat individuals the same regardless of their gender or race and class for that matter) and critical traditions (i.e., critique of power arrangements in contemporary society that produce a working environment where fair compensation for one's labor becomes problematic).

Relatedly, Ronald Berger, Marvin Free, and Patricia Searles (2005, p. 166–167) present central emphases of peacemaking as follows:

- Crime may be understood as an act of power that inflicts suffering and denies the humanity of another.
- The most fundamental cause of crime may be seen as *any* social process that equates differences among people with evaluations of worth and that allows people the "delusion that they are unconnected to those whom they interrelate" (Henry and Milovanovic, 1994, p. 124).
- Crime is not something apart from ordinary social life but is an integral part of society, for the ability to subject one to the power of another is much of what passes for family life, business practice and governmental authority.
- Instead of waging war on crime, peacemaking criminologists search for a way of peace which entails strategies of negotiation and conflict resolution, redemption and reconciliation, and nonviolent resistance to social injustice.
- Peacemaking solutions to crime focus on the *prevention* rather than on the repression of crime.

Stemming from this framework of analysis, Ronald Berger and his colleagues (2005, p. 167) delineate three general approaches of crime prevention linked with peacemaking criminology as they further state:

> *Primary prevention* attempts to keep criminal behavior from arising in the first place; it is directed at the entire community and not just at individuals who are seeking or need rehabilitative treatment. *Secondary prevention* concentrates on early identification and treatment of vulnerable or at-risk youths, and *tertiary prevention* entails interventions that protect society from offenders and that reduce the likelihood of recidivist behaviors. Clearly the most effective prevention strategy is one that combines all three modalities.

Chapters with Critical Criminology Themes

Given these descriptions of the core assumptions of critical and peacemaking criminology, attention can now be drawn to the fact that in this present book, six chapters generally fall within the parameters of "critical criminology" and six other chapters represent work within the "peacemaking criminology" approach.

It is acknowledged, of course, that there is an overlapping of theoretical and policy concerns arising from critical and peacemaking criminology. Nonetheless, in our way of thinking, the chapters designated as "critical" or "peacemaking" writings are very appropriately distinguished within this present book.

The rationale to support this latter contention becomes apparent upon basic comparison and contrast of critical criminology and peacemaking criminology. Given the discussion presented so far in this chapter, both of these latter approaches in criminology are not content to address the study of crime in terms of a mainstream criminology approach. Unlike mainstream criminology, both critical and peacemaking criminology do not unequivocably accept legalistic, government supported definitions of crime. Further, critical and peacemaking perspectives of crime are not predicated upon carrying out a criminology to facilitate the placement of offenders more and more into the criminal justice system. As such, both critical and peacemaking criminology are on similar paths, but carry out travels in regard to criminology and criminal justice in several distinctive ways.

First, critical criminology has generally been in existence for a longer duration than peacemaking criminology. As a result, critical criminology has a greater number of inter-related orientations in its paradigm than peacemaking criminology. For example, critical criminology has been found to consist of perspectives ranging from anarchism to Marxism to left realism to feminism to postmodernism to constitutive criminology to cultural theory to queer theory to semiotics to critical race theory to chaos theory to restorative justice to peacemaking criminology (Arrigo, 1999; Einstadter and Henry, 1995; Lilly et al., 2007). While often being conceptualized as a form of critical criminology, peacemaking criminology since its formal emergence in the 1990s has included, for the most part, three major traditions—religious/humanist, feminist, critical—again, as indicated earlier in this chapter.

Second, critical criminology and peacemaking criminology are similar in approach to the study of crime but are distinctive in terms of some central thrusts. That is, as stated earlier, critical criminology is a criminology of resistance that tends to view crime as a social harm and violation of human rights and it generally seeks to demystify the contradictions arising from the institutional arrangements in contemporary society. For peacemaking criminology, crime is viewed as a form of human suffering and thereby it is predicated upon a goal to search for the reasons human suffering comes about in the context of society. And there is a major orientation in peacemaking criminology to build a foundation of nonviolence at all levels of society as an alternative to war and violence that tend to permeate the social structure of current society. In essence, a peaceful, just society is to be promoted and be the purpose of criminology.

Third, again each approach is similar but critical criminology and peacemaking criminology envision the causes of crime in these respective ways. Ultimately, within critical criminology, there is over-riding tendency to draw attention to capitalism as the root cause of crime. Within peacemaking criminology, the cause of crime stems from the misconception that we are unconnected to each other and the social process that equates differences among people with evaluations of worth.

Fourth, within critical criminology, there is a common stance expressed that the criminal justice system, in the long run, generally serves the interests of the upper class rather than all members of society as a whole. Peacemaking criminology, however, views the criminal justice system as generally engaging in "negative peace" —which again involves the process of deterring and processing acts of crime through acts of force and physical threat.

Fifth, the solution for crime in critical criminology is to work toward bringing about a more equitable society so that inequalities of race, class, and gender violations of basic human rights are all alleviated. The solution for crime in peacemaking criminology is to promote a peaceful, just society through an implementation of mediation, conflict resolution, reconciliation and community-oriented prevention as alternatives to punishment of offenders and the use of prison as the main correctional strategy.

Bearing these distinctions just made in regard to critical criminology and peacemaking criminology, readers of this present book are encouraged to view Chapters 2 to 7, 8 to 13 as generally addressing the concerns of critical criminology and peacemaking criminology, respectively. Before we discuss the meaning and application of transformative justice, let us now turn to a brief illustration of some ways the chapters of this present book link to critical criminology and peacemaking criminology.

Kevin Anderson's chapter is particularly linked with critical criminology's stance that capitalism is the root cause of crime. By exploring Richard Quinney's extension of Marxist themes into other theoretical/philosophical realms, he is endeavoring to provide novel insights about the multi-dimensional linkages between capitalism and crime in a social process in which humans are determined and determining.

As such, the "Marxist Dimension" chapter addresses a central question: "What is one to make of Richard Quinney's journey to, through, and beyond Marxism?" In an appreciative discussion of Richard Quinney on this matter, Kevin Anderson maintains that important continuities can be discerned on examination of the Marxist dimensions of Richard Quinney's writings which commonly draw attention toward the creation of institutions by humans that ultimately dominate and constrain them. Kevin Anderson thereby illustrates the logic and assumptions in Richard Quinney's writings that connect Marxism, Eastern thought, existentialism, and the work of Erich Fromm to criminology. The important contribution of Kevin Anderson's chapter for our purposes here is that it aptly demonstrates that Richard Quinney's well-known theoretical writings are shaped by his experiential roots and life experiences.

Along with addressing the essential relationship between capitalism and crime, Larry Tifft's chapter evokes another core critical criminology theme. That is, his concern with the political economy of crime can be seen as a radical questioning of the justness and effectiveness of social institutions in present day capitalist society.

In more specific terms, Larry Tifft focuses upon two prominent directions within Richard Quinney's writings: "A path of critical analysis, of sociological imagination; and a path of transformative being, of social change." In this writing, five path markers become apparent in Richard Quinney's critical analysis of the political economy of crime. Also in relation to critical analysis, Larry Tifft discusses how definitions of crime and questions about usage of legalistic definitions of crime are parts of Richard Quinney's radical analysis of crime and justice. The final section of this chapter explores the implications of Richard Quinney's work for a path of peace involving personal and collective transformation which brings to mind critical criminology's imagery that violation of human rights and power based upon inequality "demand a radical transformation".

Ronald Kramer, Raymond Michalowski, and David Kauzlarich evoke a critical criminology theme that capitalism provides a fertile environment for crimes committed by corporations. In effect, their chapter broadly depicts how taking a critical criminology perspective enables one to demystify how crime at top levels of society comes about. That is, reading their chapter enables one to contemplate how members of the corporation are not only dominated but also constrained by the illegal and socially harmful social relations which emerge when a state-corporate crime unravels over time and across a nation and the world.

More directly, this writing of Ronald Kramer and his colleagues outlines the contributions of Richard Quinney in "setting the record straight" for the study of white collar and corporate crime as well as for the sociology of law, crime, and justice in the 1970s. They also illustrate how Richard Quinney's book, *The Social Reality of Crime* (1970), has influenced their concept of state-corporate crime. These latter authors then discuss the creation of the concept of state-corporate crime, distinguish between state-initiated and state-facilitated corporate crime, provide a theory of state-corporate crime, review research on state corporate crime, and draw conclusions on the potential directions of future research in this area of study.

The chapter of Joan McDermott about "Criminology as a Moral Enterprise" can be seen as an attempt to advance a critical criminology theme raised by Robert Bohm (2001) earlier in this chapter. That is, the ways that institutions and structures come to dominate and constrain people are often linked to a social context in which "conflict is the norm" . . . "society is characterized primarily by conflict over moral values." Parenthetically, Joan McDermott's chapter is intertwined with critical criminology's concern with ways in which social inequalities (such as race, class, and gender) have impacts upon crime. It should also be noted that the discussion in her chapter overlaps into peacemaking criminology foci of interests in respect to: religion, theology, and Buddhism and linkages between feminist-pragmatism and peacemaking criminology.

So what does Joan McDermott specifically write about for this present book? Her chapter begins by noting the ways in which Richard Quinney has affected her thinking about crime and justice. She next draws on John Dewey's classical pragmatism to convey a link between pragmatism, feminism, and feminist criminology. These latter three perspectives are then considered in respect to sources of oppression and the goal of liberation, epistemology and methods, social responsibility, and the integration of theory and practice. In her conclusion, Joan McDermott depicts the conceptual linkages between pragmatist feminism and Richard Quinney's criminology.

Alan Mobley, Harold Pepinsky, and Chuck Terry's chapter addresses paradoxical relations of criminologists to the work of Richard Quinney. Here, it is important to note that Harold Pepinsky's coauthors are ex-convicts who are now part of a new perspective referred to as "Convict Criminology." Rather than providing a chapter in a more customary way, Alan Mobley and his colleagues "take turns in conversation" about Richard Quinney's writings, and the results of these conversations are presented herein.

Thereby, their chapter intertwines Richard Quinney's writings, views of convict criminologists, and topics and concepts ranging from peacemaking theory, underclass prisoners, Buddhist cosmology, governing prisons, American corrections, organizational management, logic of commodities, spiritual journey, inner self, providence, enemies of the state, allegory of the offender, social existence, Taoist thought, Marx, reconciliation, Koan (a paradox in Buddhist terms), and "right" ethical practice. Like Richard Quinney's work in general, the Mobley et al. chapter touches on themes not usually addressed within commonplace textbooks and journal articles within the current field of criminology/criminal justice.

In this light, how does their chapter link with the perspective of critical criminology? Again, as noted earlier, convict criminology has been identified as one of the current variants of critical criminology (Lilly et al., 2007, pp. 203–204). One of the emphases of critical criminology is to unmask how capitalist-based exploitation creates crime and victimization. Hence, as noted by Lilly et al. (2007, p. 203), convict criminologists, as also expressed in the Mobley-Pepinsky-Terry chapter, strive to give voice and "relevance to the victims of the criminal justice system" as they engage in discourses and research writings about their experiences as clients within the criminal justice system. It also is reasonable to suggest that convict criminologists are very likely to question and perhaps directly investigate "the targeting of selected groups, informally or formally, for official police intervention" (Beirne and Messerschmidt, 2006, p. 428)—which was identified earlier as one of the tenets of critical criminology.

Randall Shelden's chapter focusing on "Why the Prison Industrial Complex Needs Crime" calls to mind several aforementioned themes of critical criminology. That is, one of this chapter's intents is to radically question the justice and effectiveness of prisons as a form of a total institution in contemporary society (e.g., Welch, 2004, p. 108). Randall Shelden's analysis here also can be seen as "setting the record straight" about the actual operations of U.S. prisons over the past few decades. This chapter further exemplifies critical criminology's notion that the criminal justice system is generally set up to process the poor and minorities within society.

In the introduction to his chapter, Randall Shelden brings to attention that Richard Quinney similarly used the term "social-industrial complex" in his *Class, State, and Crime* book of 1977. Shelden's chapter builds upon this theme by asserting that within the United States, the prison industrial complex "represents an interconnection among the criminal justice system, the political system and the economic system—just like the military represents a connection with the political and economic system."

Upon illustrating increasing U.S. incarceration data, this analysis then addresses ways that prisons serve as a "market," for capitalism—again suggesting a critical criminology theme of a desire to examine the root causes of capitalism in order to unmask capitalist-based exploitation. Randall Shelden's chapter moves on to identify developments in ways the criminal justice system is becoming structured such as: the system emergence of influence on prisons of the American Legislative Exchange Council (ALEC), whose mission is to promote "free markets" and privatization; recycling prisoners through the "perpetual prisoner machine"; uplifting rural economies through more usage of rural prisons; and exploiting prisoners to enhance rural populations.

Chapters with Peacemaking Criminology Themes

One way to demarcate Chapters 8 to 13 of our book as oriented toward peacemaking criminology is to note, of course, that each of these writings has "peacemaking" in its title. Again, as will be discussed ahead, these latter six chapters commonly address various core elements of peacemaking criminology very much in keeping with the peacemaking-oriented notions of Richard Quinney.

Chapter 8 of John Wozniak is aligned with the peacemaking theme "to search for reasons that make us suffer" by undertaking a content analysis of previous peacemaking criminology research in respect to a survey of peacemaking authors. This chapter also is designed to help facilitate a key peacemaking criminology goal to promote a peaceful, just society. In this light, John Wozniak's chapter illustrates and explores elements of a peacemaking criminology theoretical model that examines the connections between social structure, crimes, social harms, the criminal justice system, and peacemaking alternatives. As such, this chapter complements John Fuller's pyramid model of peacemaking criminology (Fuller, 1998; Fuller and Wozniak, 2006) and together these models have the potential to further stimulate interest and participation in the peacemaking criminology paradigm/social movement which has come about since the early 1990s.

John Wozniak's other chapter observed that at present, there has not been a systematic analysis of Richard Quinney's collection of writings about peacemaking criminology. Thus, this second chapter of John Wozniak provides such a synthesis of Richard Quinney's peacemaking criminology writings. This chapter's link to core assumptions of peacemaking criminology is seen in its attempt to pull together Richard Quinney's ideas about the peacemaking perspective in criminology such as: his views of crime as suffering, the social context this suffering is connected to in today's society, and his views of religious and spiritual themes applicable to peacemaking criminology.

A further contribution of this latter chapter is that it identifies some of Richard Quinney's writings that are precursors or building blocks for his theoretical conceptions of peacemaking criminology. Chapter 9 also points out that when Richard Quinney's peacemaking criminology writings are examined together, it is possible to gain further insights concerning peacemaking ways to bring about personal and social transformation and to be a peacemaking teacher, researcher, and policy-maker.

Polly Radosh's chapter on women's crime and women in prisons expounds upon notions within the feminist tradition of peacemaking as identified by Harold Pepinsky (1991). Her chapter can also be read as an example of the negative peace experienced by women as criminal offenders and prison inmates. Moreover, she reported nearly all of women's crime is related to sexual exploitation, abuse, poverty, and structural inequality. These imageries recall that one of peacemaking criminology's central emphases is to discern crime as an act of power that inflicts suffering and denies the humanity of another and that it is important to seek ways to respond to these concerns of victims.

In the introduction of her chapter, Polly Radosh indicates how Richard Quinney's work on peacemaking had an effect on her thinking about crime and justice. For example, Radosh states that "Quinney's work helps us to see that women's crime is a reflection of social injustice. When we see the world as it is, rather than as we are conditioned to see it, women's crime has new meaning." She then illustrates this point by reviewing arrest patterns and incarceration trends of female offenders, along with unique characteristics of female inmates and inmate mothers. Other pertinent topics addressed in the Radosh chapter include punishment, women's crime and parenting, prison programs for mothers, and the effectiveness of mother-infant programs. This chapter concludes with a consideration of how Richard Quinney's views might be used to better support female offenders to move away from a life of crime and violence.

Michael Braswell and John Whitehead's chapter contributes further perspective into the ongoing emphasis within peacemaking criminology of not only striving for the highest quality of teaching about crime and criminal justice but also seeking effective ways to teach about the social advantages of nonviolence as a guiding principle of social interaction (see for example, Wozniak, 2000, 2005; Sanzen, 1991; Caulfield, 2000; McCarthy, 2002). In particular, this chapter delineates the peacemaking criminology theme of Ronald Berger et al. (2005) that there is a "delusion that we are all unconnected to those we interrelate," particularly in regard to relations between the student and teacher in a university classroom. Importantly, Michael Braswell and John Whitehead have called for lessening of the gap developing expertise and experiencing learning and advocate instead bringing the teacher and student together in the process of learning, especially about crime and the value of nonviolence. Moreover, like peacemaking criminologists who try to find humanist solutions to crime, Michael Braswell and John Whitehead portray the pedagogical worth of teachers and students striving together to arrive at humanist understanding of crime and its control.

At the beginning of their chapter, Michael Braswell and John Whitehead state, "This essay is written in the spirit of Richard Quinney's contributions to teaching as an exploration into the contradictions, ironies, and connections (both obvious and hidden) that allow learning to unfold and show itself to both teachers and students." Given these latter thrusts, they observe how teaching and learning for teachers and students often become affected by experience and expertise, feelings and intuition, thinking and knowledge, and imagination and creativity. This chapter concludes by bringing attention to the possibility of "experiencing whole sight" (synthesis of our heart and our mind), which is to be worked on together by teachers and students. Essentially, Braswell and Whitehead's chapter offers frameworks to improve the teaching and learning of peacemaking and justice issues. Hence, it is writings such as this chapter and similar works (Brock-Utne, 1985; Caulfield, 2000; Pepinsky, 2000, 2006, pp. 109–142; Sanzen, 1991; Wozniak, 2000, 2006) that facilitate the possibility of teaching nonviolence and peacemaking as a fourth tradition of peacemaking criminology (i.e., Pepinsky, 1991).

John Fuller and Amy Hembree's chapter is designed to show that "peacemaking ideas exist in the real world." Thereby, in "Peacemaking and Crime: Advocating Reform on the Internet," they provide numerous examples of websites that promote "positive peace" on a national and international basis. Their chapter and their peacemaking website are organized around elements of John Fuller's earlier mentioned pyramid model of peacemaking and his original peacemaking textbook (1998). Notably, the Fuller-Hembree chapter and peacemaking website call to mind peacemaking criminology's core goal to work toward bringing about a peacemaking movement that promotes a peaceful, just society. All in all, this chapter is geared toward: developing Richard Quinney's peacemaking stance that there is a need to search for reasons that crime makes us suffer and creating knowledge in respect to Harold Pepinsky's peacemaking assertion that we need to "figure out how we can get along without criminalizing and victimizing one another."

In their chapter, John Fuller and Amy Hembree discuss how they got started in devising and maintaining their "peacemaking and crime" website, including formulating salient peacemaking themes and providing ongoing organizational features (such as In the News, Links, and Did U Know?) Their chapter depicts examples of peacemaking criminology-oriented items which commonly can be obtained through these three organizational features of their "peacemaking and crime" website. In addition, their chapter informs its readers of possible e-mail discussion lists and links of sites to view pertinent crime-related publications (some paper, others online only).

In the final chapter, John Whitehead, Wayne Gillespie, and Michael Braswell conjecture about the future of the peacemaking perspective. This chapter is linked to a central peacemaking theme of presenting analyses of crime and its control in keeping with the religious/humanist tradition. As they state, one area of concern is the relationship of peacemaking to secular humanism. Their chapter also examines current problems with capitalism—which is coordinated with peacemaking criminology's emphasis upon the importance of endeavoring to critique a power arrangement, such as capitalist economy, which "produces a working environment where fair compensation for one's labor becomes problematic."

In John Whitehead and colleagues' chapter, the directions that peacemaking criminology might take in the future are contemplated in respect to secular humanism, (including the writings of Erich Fromm, Karl Marx, and Jurgen Habermas). This chapter then raises concerns about the need to develop more explicit guidelines for peacemaking criminology, including a consideration of often-used peacemaking principles of mindfulness, caring, and connectedness. After that, the Whitehead et al. chapter also unprecedentedly discusses individual, systemic, and cultural contexts of peacemaking in relation to the functionalist perspective of Talcott Parsons again in relation to these three latter peacemaking principles. The final section of this chapter illustrates "How the peacemaking model differs from the system of globalized capitalism that is currently in place" and mention is made of Richard Quinney's writings which critique capitalism as a "system of exploitation."

To sum up this section, there is not an intent here to provide an encompassing review of what is meant by the perspectives of critical criminology and peacemaking criminology. Rather, this latter discussion of these two criminological perspectives was done to facilitate understanding why these diverse set of chapters were grouped in terms of critical and peacemaking themes. Granted, there is much overlap between these criminological perspectives. But more important for our purposes is to consider that critical criminology and peacemaking criminology perspectives and analyses very readily coincide and are much attuned with goals of gaining *transformative justice* in our society. The final section of this introduction addresses this latter point in various ways.

Conceptions of Transformative Justice

Before reading the twelve chapters in this volume, it is beneficial to note that, within literature on this topic, there is common usage of two inter-related concepts: *social transformation* and *transformative justice*. Space limitations do not permit an extended overview of these two concepts in respect to their various conceptualizations and applications (see, for example, the discussion of Austin Turk's principles of structural transformation in Lanier and Henry, 2004, pp. 273–274). Nevertheless, it is instructive to consider the ideas arising from three sets of authors on *social transformation* (Quinney and Wildeman, 1991; Braswell et al., 2001; Sullivan and Tifft, 2005) and four authors on *transformative justice* (Barak, 2003b; Morris, 2000; Harris, 2006; Barak et al., 2007).

As touched upon at various points in Chapter 9 of this present book, Richard Quinney has written on various occasions about personal and social transformation in relation to peacemaking criminology. For instance, in his *Problem of Crime* textbook (Quinney and Wildeman, 1991), a chapter was titled "Peace and Social Justice" and it reveals various dimensions involved in the notion of social transformation in respect to peacemaking criminology. For example, this writing (Quinney and Wildeman, 1991, p. 110) maintains that:

> The peace and social justice perspective continues to develop in criminology. There are proposals and programs on mediation, conflict resolution, and reconciliation; there is the movement to abolish the death penalty; and there are humanist programs of rehabilitation and community organization. These are the practices of a criminology of peacemaking, a criminology that seeks to alleviate suffering and thereby reduce crime . . . . This is a criminology that is based necessarily on *human transformation* in the achievement of peace and justice. Human transformation takes place as we change our social, economic, and political structure. And the message is clear: Without peace within us and in our actions, there can be no peace and justice in our results. Peace is the way (my italics).

According to Richard Quinney and John Wildeman (1991, p. 113), social transformation involves more than changing the larger social structure. That is, upon their discussing the importance of the awareness of human suffering, right understanding, and compassion and service (i.e., as central principles of peacemaking criminology), they encourage their readers to also recognize the importance of social transformation at the personal level. Hence, they (1991, p. 117) state:

> Without *inner* peace in each of us, without peace of mind and heart, there can be no *social* peace between people and no peace in societies, nations, and in the world. To be explicitly engaged in this process, of bringing about peace on all levels, of joining ends and means, is to be engaged in *peacemaking*. In peacemaking, we attend to the ultimate purpose of our existence—to heal the separation between all things and to live harmoniously in a state of unconditional love. The radical nature of peacemaking is clear: No less is involved than the transformation of our human being. Indeed, we will be engaged in action, but action will come out of our transformed being. Rather than attempting to create a good society first and then trying to make ourselves better human beings, we have to work on the two simultaneously. The inner and the outer are the same. . . . The transformation of ourselves and the world becomes our constant practice, here and now (italics of original).

Additionally, on social transformation, Quinney and Wildeman (1991, pp. 118–119) conclude:

> All of this is to say, to us as criminologists, that crime is suffering and that the ending of crime is possible only with the ending of suffering. And the ending both of suffering and of crime—the establishing of justice—can come only out of peace, out of a peace that is spiritually grounded in our very being. To eliminate crime—to end the construction and perpetuation of an existence that makes crime possible—requires a transformation of our human being. We as human beings must *be* peace if we are to live in a world free of crime, in a

> world of peace. We are fully aware by now that the criminal justice system in this country is founded on violence rather than on peace. It is a system that assumes that violence can be overcome by violence, evil by evil. Criminal justice at home and warfare abroad are of the same principle of violence. This principle sadly dominates much of our criminology. Fortunately, more and more criminologists are realizing that this principle is fundamentally incompatible with a faith that seeks to express itself in compassion, forgiveness, and love. Recognizing that the criminal justice system is the moral equivalent of the war machine, resistance to one goes hand in hand with resistance to the other. . . . When our hearts are filled with love and our minds with willingness to serve, we will know what has to be done and how it is to be done. Such is the basis of a nonviolent criminology. . . . where. . . . everything is done out of compassion to lessen the suffering of others (italics of original).

These latter three sets of quotes are expressed in detail for two reasons. First, these wordings illustrate the type of sociological reasoning that has drawn peacemaking scholars and practitioners to this perspective in the first place. Second, these wordings indeed make it clear about the type of social transformation that is of concern here and in keeping with each of the chapters in this present book.

In *Corrections, Peacemaking, and Restorative Justice*, Michael Braswell, John Fuller and Bo Lozoff (2001) utilize a subtitle: "Transforming Individuals and Institutions." In essence, the work of Michael Braswell and his colleagues (2001) parallels Richard Quinney's imageries about what is to be involved in personal and social transformation.

For example, in their introduction, Braswell et al. (2001, p. 5) suggest that personal transformation involves a "growing sense of 'connectedness' of how we are connected to each other and our physical environment in community." Like Richard Quinney, they (2001, pp. 6–7) characterize social transformation as involving community struggles to be inclusive rather than exclusive about crime (i.e., human kindness foundation, the prison fellowship, teaching citizens and inmates about peacemaking) as well as a community of peacemaking individuals who strive to reach out to social institutions.

Very relatedly, Michael Braswell and his colleagues (2001) advance the idea of social transformation through utilization of the peacemaking perspective very directly to all levels of the criminal justice system (i.e., police, courts, and corrections). As they note (2001, p. 72), the goal of corrections especially can be predicated upon "repairing the social fabric of society that was damaged by crime." In their view (Braswell et al., 2001, p. 76) the social transformation involved in a movement toward peacemaking in corrections would systematically incorporate each of the following into corrections settings:

- Opposition to capital punishment
- Limitation of solitary confinement
- Opportunities for rehabilitation
- Restorative justice processes

- Dignified and humane treatment
- Sense of personal safety and security from other inmates.

Michael Braswell and colleagues (2001) further emphasize the "promise of community" in efforts to bring about social transformation in regard to crime, particularly in respect to the value (i.e., social capital) of implementing restorative justices process. More specifically on this theme, they (2001, p. 146) contend:

> What is unique about the contemporary attempts to use the community in resolving conflicts is the partnering of the community with the government. It is easy to forget that in the larger context, government officials and community members live in the same neighborhoods. In traditional societies, the community performed the functions of government. Today, the social institutions of government have encroached into many of the arenas of the family and community to the point where the influence of the community has lost much of its relevance. The goal of restorative justice programs is bringing the community back into the conflict-resolution process. This involves looking at criminal acts in a more comprehensive and inclusive way. It expands the scope of focus beyond the conflict between the offender and the government by including the victim, other interested parties such as the families of the victim and the offender, and the community itself.

Perhaps, recognizing the possibility of criticism of their peacemaking thrust in crime policy, Michael Braswell and colleagues (2001, p. 146) assert further about this type of social transformation process that:

> Restorative justice in the community is superior to the traditional criminal justice system because of the responsibility it places on the offender. Rather than having something done to him or her, the offender must actively participate in the healing process of the community, the victim, and ultimately him or herself. This healing process might be as simple as an apology to the victim, or it might mean paying restitution to recompense the victim's loss. The offender might be required to perform some type of community service to repay the damage done to public property or the social order. But, most importantly, from a restorative justice perspective, the offender must willingly and actively participate in his or her own healing. This might include traditional treatment methods such as drug and alcohol programs, or it could include having offenders publicly take responsibility for their actions and engage in community education programs designed to prevent others from making the same mistakes.

Consistent with the perspectives of Richard Quinney and Michael Braswell and colleagues (2001), Dennis Sullivan and Larry Tifft (2005) designed their book about restorative justice, in part, about whether personal and social transformation is possible in present day society. Overall, this restorative justice book is broad in scope. As a foundation for their concluding observations about personal and social transformation, they (2005) draw attention to various issues linked with the provision of restorative justice into communities.

That is, chapters in Sullivan and Tifft's (2005) book explain what restorative justice is all about; overview requirements of effective restorative justice practices; consider key types of restorative justice; explore basic dimensions of a needs-based justice in regard to delivery of restorative justice responses to crime; and provide a critical criminology perspective on crime and social harm. These latter points are raised to illustrate the extended layering of societal concerns that has led up to their consideration of the personal and social transformation called for to lessen the social harms of interpersonal violence within our society.

Like Michael Braswell and colleagues (2001), Dennis Sullivan and Larry Tifft's (2005) call for personal and social transformation is most inclusive of people in society, with a persistent emphasis upon the "needs of all" in the community to be ideally taken into account. For example, in their vision of effective restorative justice, they (2005) suggest people will need to be in the personal transformation process of learning how to "strip away" and "empty" a sense of self that might be "infatuated" with a sense of power. Why do that, exactly? For these latter authors, a personal transformation is best served when the restorative justice process requires one to give up on power as a means to an end.

Dennis Sullivan and Larry Tifft, like Richard Quinney and Michael Braswell and colleagues, treat personal and social transformation as inextricably related. In other words, both social goals cannot truly come about without the other also taking place on a broad level among members of society. However, in direct respect to social transformation, Dennis Sullivan and Larry Tifft (2005, p. 169) stress: "the possibilities for growth, healing, and transforming social arrangements exist on all levels, from the most personal up through the most global." Thereby, social transformation begins with our loved ones and in child care and extends to possibilities of restorative places of work, restorative schools, and restorative school environments, along with the types of correctional setting restorative justice programs revealed in their book.

Most importantly, these three considerations of social transformation are stated in this introduction to explicitly illustrate a central underlying thrust of each chapter in this present book. That is, each analysis here is not provided to support status quo, punitive-oriented, and often non-inclusive practices of the criminal justice system in controlling individuals found to have broken the law in society. Instead, these twelve chapters in our present book can be seen as working toward personal and social transformation of the general social context in which we all live. This social context is not more of the same in our society, especially in regard to crime and criminals. Rather, the social context to be worked toward involves a peaceful and just social transformation of how we interact with each other and especially how those accused of crime are included within the social interactions of our everyday life.

There is another principle guiding each of the chapters in this present book that is closely linked with social transformation. This is the social belief of the far-reaching need to work more toward a process of transformative justice within contemporary society. Again, as noted above, we will consider four sets of writings about the nature of the term, transformative justice. In particular, we will explore what it might mean for our social world if steps were taken to move toward that version of justice instead of the punitive-oriented and non-inclusive type of social justice now commonly applied within the criminal justice system and the general social institutions of today's society.

To set the stage for authors who specifically provided analyses that incorporated the term "transformative justice," it is useful to consider how Gregg Barak, Paul Leighton, and Jeanne Flavin (2007) have summarized the ideas of criminological analysts who are writing about this alternative view of justice. For example, in their conclusion of their latest edition of *Class, Race, Gender, and Crime*, Gregg Barak and his colleagues (2007, pp. 270–272) stipulate social justice (albeit transformative justice) involves the following:

- Social justice systems venture beyond the immediate conflicts between particular offenders and their victims.
- Social justice models expand the notions of conflict and injury beyond what the law recognizes to include those harms identified as part of an evolving set of human rights.
- Social justice models also view crime as something more than in interpersonal violation weighed against a particular nation-state's legal order.
- Crimes are not merely personal expressions, they are institutional and structural expressions of fundamental political and economic arrangements.
- Social justice models recognize the indivisible relations between, for example, the crime of homelessness in an affluent society and the crimes by and against the homeless as rooted in a violence of poverty and the so-called dependent classes of people.
- Social justice stresses the importance of public policies of crime control that go beyond the confines of the criminal justice system and the crimes of the poor and powerless.
- In social justice models, attention and care should also be given not only to the crimes of the rich and powerful, but also more generally to corporate deregulation, the formation of social capital, and the marginalization of the multi-ethnic underclass.
- Social justice models believe in the eradication of social subjugation, oppression, and exploitation of people and in the establishing of fundamental human rights of all.

Notably, these general tenets of "social justice" are much in keeping with what Gregg Barak wrote about "transformative justice" in the conclusion of his book about violence and nonviolence. That is, in a section titled "Transformative Justice and Pathways to Violence and Nonviolence," Barak (2003b, p. 323) argued that:

> *Transformative justice* is about dealing with both the injustice of being victimized and with the injustice of distributive justice. Transformative justice departs from the adversarialism of repressive, retributive, vengeful, and even restorative justice on the grounds that these forms of justice serve to perpetuate and reproduce the marginal and disempowering conditions of the victimized and the enraged. Instead, policies of nonviolence are called for that seek to transform the dominant practices of our penal-justice systems and of the larger systems of distributive injustice throughout society. At the same time, transformative justice seeks to move victims from vengeance to forgiveness, from defensive hatred and alienation to altruistic empathy and protectiveness, as it seeks to respond to the needs of the most vulnerable and harmed in our society who require at a minimum four things: (a) answers to why they were victimized, (b) recognition of the wrongs they incurred, (c) restitution for the injuries they received, and (d) the restoration or establishment of peace and security lost or never obtained (italics of original).

Very similarly, Ruth Morris (2000, p.21) presents imageries of transformative justice in the following:

> Transformative justice sees crime as an opportunity to build a more caring, more inclusive, more just community. Safety doesn't lie in bigger fences, harsher prisons, more police, or locking ourselves in till we ourselves are prisoners. Safety and security—real security—come from building a community where because we have cared for and included all, that community will be there for us, when trouble comes to us. For trouble comes to us all, but trouble itself is an opportunity.

In support of her conception of transformative justice, Ruth Morris (2000) identifies seven paths to be taken toward transformative justice as follows:

- Tuning Up our Individual Lifestyles
- Using our Consumer Power
- Disseminating our Awareness Everywhere
- Transforming our Sources of Information
- Changing our Political Systems to Achieve Democracy
- Regaining Control of Corporations
- Building International Networks for Compassion

In her conclusion, Ruth Morris (2000, p. 256) offers further descriptions of transformative justice such as:

> Retributive justice rests on the security of bars and locks and separations. Transformative justice rests on the security of a caring community that includes all and never deserts those in trouble. Transformative justice uses the power of community to heal wrongs, and to change the world. It challenges unhealthy barriers of race, class, and status. It rebuilds community where community has broken down. It heals the broken-hearted, because it listens to and cares about pain of all kinds. No wonder transformative processes are so much more satisfying to all of us! Transformative justice is the way of the future.

One of the most definitive reviews and summations of research about transformative justice is provided by Kay Harris (2006, p. 255) who found "there is no simple, universally accepted definition for either transformative justice or restorative justice." Nonetheless, she (2006, p. 556) indicates that the term, transformative justice has involved a range of usages. That is, it has been treated as a paradigm, general philosophical approach, a social movement, a way of life, and a "means to conflict resolution that results in changed relationships among those involved" (Harris, 2006, p. 556).

Furthermore, Kay Harris (2006, pp. 558–559) posits that transformative justice moves beyond restorative justice in these ways:

- It is concerned with justice issues wherever they arise such as in relation to conflicts in families, schools, neighborhoods, workplaces, or on a national or international level.
- It extends the scope of inquiry beyond the immediate situation into what are often unrecognized and unchallenged assumptions and paradigms underlying current economic, political, criminal justice and social arrangements.
- It seeks to effect change on a structural level while helping those whose lives were affected by interpersonal harms.

Kay Harris (2006) also reports that there have been debates about whether transformative justice and restorative justice are two distinct orientations or not. More importantly, for the purposes of our present book, it seems reasonable to suggest that conceptions of social transformation and transformative justice are aptly considered elements of what Gregg Barak (2003a) termed as "visionary criminology." As such, Barak (2003a) claims this type of criminology tends to see things that most people don't see and works against general acceptance of prevailing hierarchies of social inequality that contribute to the conditions of structural crime and tend to depart from adversarial and repressive notions of justice.

In sum, notions of social transformation and transformative justice, as just expressed in this introduction, tend to complement the analyses of crime provided within the various chapters in our present book. We invite readers of these chapters to keep in mind the aspects of criminology outlined in this introduction: the influence of Richard Quinney's work; core assumptions of critical criminology and peacemaking criminology; and the social policy applications of movements toward social transformation and transformative justice within society. It is hoped that these themes presented in this introduction will augment understanding and further dialogue/research/practice in keeping with the spirit of the criminological work of Richard Quinney (1991, p. 2), whose words of relevance here are: "When our hearts are filled with love and our minds with willingness to serve, we will know what has to be done and how it is to be done. Such is the basis of a nonviolent criminology." Consider also these musical lyrics in your reading of chapters of this present book.

Violence springs one thing
more and more of the same
military madness
smell of flesh and burning pain
so I sing out to the masses
stand up if you are still sane
all of us gone crazy
sing this one refrain

we can chase down all our enemies
bring them to their knees
we can bomb the world to pieces
but we can't bomb it into peace
we may even find a solution
to hunger and disease
we can bomb the world to pieces
but we can't bomb it into peace
power to the peaceful, love to the peaceful
power to the peaceful, love to the peaceful
(Michael Franti, hip hop musician and social activist, from
San Francisco, California)

What if love was everywhere
what if love were free
what if love reached every heart
from me to you to me
what if there was so much love
everyone could share
every heart and every voice
and love was everywhere

what if there was so much love
rising like a tide
more than stars you've ever seen
more than tears you've cried
what if oceans full of love
washed across the land
heart to heart to hungry heart
and hand to hand to hand

what if you loved all of me
what if I loved you
what if love was all we had
and all we had to do
what if we could really give

all our hearts could hold
heart to heart to hungry heart
and soul to soul to soul

what if love was here to stay
here to make us free
what if love could heal the earth
and me and you and me
what if love could heal a heart
nothing could repair
what if we gave up on love
and love would still be there
and love would still be there
(Carol Denney, folk musician from Berkeley, California)

References

Akers, R. L., & Sellers, C. S. (Eds.). (2004). *Criminology theories: Introduction, evaluation, and application* (4th ed.). Los Angeles, CA: Roxbury.

Arrigo, B. A. (Ed.). (1999). *Social justice/criminal justice: The maturation of critical theory in law, crime, and deviance.* Belmont, CA: Wadsworth.

Barak, G. (2003a). Revisionist history, visionary criminology, and needs-based justice. *Contemporary Justice Review* 6(2): 217-225.

Barak, G. (2003b). *Violence and nonviolence: Pathways to understanding.* Thousand Oaks, CA: Sage.

Barak, G. (2005). A reciprocal approach to peacemaking criminology: Between adversarialism and mutualism. *Theoretical Criminology* 9(2): 131-152.

Barak, G. Leighton, P., & Flavin, J. (2007). *Class, race, gender, and crime: The social realities of justice in America.* (2nd ed.). Lanham, MD: Rowman and Littlefield.

Bartollas, C. (Ed.). (2003). *Voices of delinquency.* Boston, MA: Allyn and Bacon.

Beirne, P., & Messerschmidt, J. W. (2006). *Criminology* (4th ed.). Los Angeles, CA: Roxbury.

Berger, R. J. (Ed.). (1996). *The sociology of juvenile delinquency.* (2nd ed.). Chicago, IL: Nelson-Hall.

Berger, R. J., Free, Jr., M. D., & Searles, P. (2005). *Crime, justice, and society: An introduction to criminology* (2nd ed.). Boulder, CO: Lynne Rienner.

Bohm, R. M. (2001). *A primer on crime and delinquency theory* (2nd ed.). Belmont, CA: Wadsworth/Thomson.

Braswell, M., Fuller, J., & Lozoff, B. (2001). *Corrections, peacemaking, and restorative justice: Transforming individuals and institutions.* Cincinnati, OH: Anderson.

Brock-Utne, B. (1985). *Educating for peace: A feminist perspective.* New York: Pergamon Press.

Caulfield, S. L. (2000). Creating peaceable schools. *The Annals of the American Academy of Political and Social Science 567* (January): 170-185.

Cordella, P., & Siegel, L. (Eds.). (1996). *Readings in contemporary criminological theory.* Boston, MA: Northeastern University Press.

Cullen, F. T., & Agnew, R. (Eds.). (2006). Criminological theory, past to present: Essential readings. (3rd ed.). Los Angeles, CA: Roxbury.

DeKeseredy, W.S. and Perry, B. (2006). Introduction: The never-ending and constantly evolving journey. In W. S. DeKeseredy and B. Perry (Eds.), *Advancing critical criminology: Theory and application* (pp. 1-8). Lanham, MD: Lexington.

Egley, Jr., A., Maxson, C. L., Miller, J., & Klein, M. W. (Eds). (2006). *The modern gang reader.* (3rd ed.). Los Angeles, CA: Roxbury.

Einstadter, W., & Henry, S. (1995). *Criminological theory: An analysis of its underlying assumptions.* New York: Harcourt Brace.

Ermann, M. D., & Lundman, R. J. (Eds.). (2002). *Corporate and governmental deviance: Problems of organizational behavior in contemporary society.* (6th ed.). New York: Oxford University Press.

Esbensen, F-A., Tibbetts, S. G., & Gaines, L. (Eds.). (2004). *American youth gangs at the millennium.* Long Grove, IL: Waveland Press.

Fuller, J. R. (1998). *Criminal justice: A peacemaking perspective.* Boston, MA: Allyn and Bacon.

Fuller, J. R. (2003). Peacemaking criminology. In M. D. Schwartz & S. E. Hatty (Eds.), *Controversies in critical criminology* (pp. 85-95). Cincinnati, OH: Anderson.

Fuller, J. R., & Hickey, E. W. (Eds.). (1999). *Controversial issues in criminology.* Boston, MA: Allyn and Bacon.

Fuller, J. R., & Wozniak, J. F. (2006). Peacemaking criminology: Past, present, and future. In F. T. Cullen, J. P. Wright & K. R. Blevins (Eds.), *Taking stock: The status of criminological theory advances in criminological theory* (pp. 251-273), Volume 15. New Brunswick, NJ: Transaction.

Geis, G., Meier, R. F., & Salinger, L. M. (Eds.), (1995). *White-collar crime: Classic and contemporary views*. (3rd ed.). New York: Free Press.

Harris, M. K. (2006). Transformative justice: The transformation of restorative justice. In D. Sullivan & L. Tifft (Eds.), *Handbook of restorative justice: A global perspective* (pp. 555-566). New York: Routledge.

Henry, S., & Milovanovic, D. (1994). The constitution of constitutive criminology: A postmodern approach to criminological theory. In D. Necken (Ed.), *The Futures of criminology* (pp. 110-133). London: Sage.

Huff, C. R. (Ed.). (2002). *Gangs in America*. (3rd ed.). Thousand Oaks, CA: Sage.

Hunter, R. D., & Dantzker, M. L. (2002). *Crime and criminality: Causes and consequences*. Upper Saddle River, NJ: Prentice Hall.

Lanier, M. M., & Henry, S. (2004). *Essential criminology*. (2nd ed.). Boulder, CO: Westview Press.

Latessa, E. J., & Holsinger, A. M. (Eds.). (2006). *Correctional contexts: Contemporary and classical readings*. (3rd ed.). Los Angeles, CA: Roxbury.

Lilly, J. R., Cullen, F. T., & Ball, R. A. (2007). *Criminological theory: Context and consequences* (4th ed.). Thousand Oaks, CA: Sage.

Lofquist, W. S., Cohen, M. A., & Rabe, G. A. (Eds.). (1997). *Debating corporate crime*. Cincinnati, OH: Anderson.

Lynch, M. J., & Michalowski, R. (2006). *Primer in radical criminology: Critical perspectives on crime, power, and identity* (4th ed.). Monsey, NY: Criminal Justice Press.

MacLean, B., & Milovanovic, D. (Eds.). (1991) *New directions in critical criminology*. Vancouver, Canada: The Collective Press.

Martin, R., Mutchnick, R. J., & Austin, W. Timothy (Eds.). (1990). *Criminological thought: Pioneers past and present*. New York: Macmillan.

McCarthy, C. (2002). *I'd rather teach peace*. Maryknoll, NY: Orbis Books.

Miller, J. M., Schreck, C., & Tewksbury, R. (2006). *Criminological theory: A brief introduction*. Boston, MA: Allyn and Bacon.

Monk, R. C. (Ed.). (2001). *Taking sides: Clashing views on controversial issues in crime and criminology*. (6th ed.). Guilford, CT: Dushkin/McGraw Hill.

Moriarty, L. J. (Ed.). (2003). *Controversies in victimology*. Cincinnati, OH: Anderson.

Morris, R. (2000). *Stories of transformative justice*. Toronto, ON: Canadian Scholars' Press.

Paternoster, R., & Bachman, R. (Eds.). (2001). *Explaining criminals and crime: Essays in contemporary criminological theory*. Los Angeles, CA; Roxbury.

Pearce, F., & Snider, L. (Eds.). (1995). *Corporate crime: Contemporary debates*. Toronto, ON: University of Toronto Press.

Pepinsky, H. E. (1989). Peacemaking in criminology. *Critical Criminologist 1* (Summer): 6-10.

Pepinsky, H. E. (1991). Peacemaking in criminology and criminal justice. In H. E. Pepinsky & R. Quinney (Eds.), *Criminology as peacemaking* (p. 299-327). Bloomington, IN: Indiana University Press.

Pepinsky, H.E. (2000). Educating for peace. *Annals of the American Academy of Political and Social Science* 567 (January): 158-170.

Pepinsky, H. (2006). *Peacemaking: Reflections of a radical criminologist*. Ottawa, ON: University Press of Ottawa.

Pepinsky, H. E., & Quinney, R. (Eds.). (1991). *Criminology as peacemaking*. Bloomington, IN: Indiana University Press.

Petersilia, J. (Ed.). (1998). *Community corrections: Probation, parole, and intermediate sanctions*. New York: Oxford University Press.

Potter, G. W. (Ed.). (2002). *Controversies in white-collar crime*. Cincinnati, OH: Anderson.

Quinney, R. (1970). *The social reality of crime*. Boston: Little, Brown.

Quinney, R. (1977). *Class, state, and crime*. New York: Longman.

Quinney, R. (1979). *Criminology*. (2nd ed.). Boston, MA: Little, Brown.

Quinney, R. (1991). The way of peace: On crime, suffering, and service. In H. E. Pepinsky & R. Quinney (Eds.), *Criminology as peacemaking* (pp. 3-13). Bloomington, IN: Indiana University Press.

Quinney, R. (2000a). *Bearing witness to crime and social justice*. Albany: State University of New York Press.

Quinney, R. (2000b). Socialist humanism and the problem of crime: Thinking about Erich Fromm in the development of critical/peacemaking criminology. In K. Anderson & R. Quinney, *Erich Fromm and critical criminology: Beyond the punitive society* (pp. 21-30). Urbana, IL: University of Illinois Press.

Quinney, R., & Wildeman, J. (1991). *The problem of crime: A peace and social justice perspective*. Mountain View, CA: Mayfield.

Renzetti, C. M., Curran, D. J., & Carr, P. (Eds.). (2003). *Theories of crime: A reader*. Boston: Allyn and Bacon.

Renzetti, C. M., & Goodstein, L. (Eds.). (2001). *Women, crime, and criminal justice: Original feminist readings*. Los Angeles, CA: Roxbury.

Renzetti, C. M., Goodstein, L., & Miller, S. L. (Eds.). (2006). *Rethinking gender, crime, and justice: Feminist readings*. Los Angeles, CA: Roxbury.

Sanzen, P. (1991). The role of education in peacemaking. In H. E. Pepinsky & R. Quinney (Eds.), *Criminology as peacemaking* (pp. 239-244). Bloomington, IN: Indiana University Press.

Schmalleger, F. (2006). *Criminology today: An integrative introduction* (4th ed.). Upper Saddle River, NJ: Pearson Prentice Hall.

Schram, P. J., & Koons-Witt, B. (Eds.). (2004). *Gendered (in)justice: Theory and practice in feminist criminology*. Long Grove, IL: Waveland Press.

Schwartz, M. D., & Hatty, S. (Eds.). (2003). *Controversies in critical criminology*. Cincinnati, OH: Anderson.

Schwarz, M. D., & Travis, III, L. F. (Eds.). (1997). *Corrections: An issues approach*. (4th ed.). Cincinnati, OH: Anderson.

Shichor, D., Gaines, L., & Ball, R. (Eds.). (2002). *Readings in white-collar crime*. Prospect Heights, IL: Waveland Press.

Siegel, L. (2007). *Criminology: Theories, patterns, and typologies* (9th ed.). Belmont, CA: Thomson/Wadsworth.

Shover, N., & Wright, J. P. (Eds.). (2001). *Crimes of privilege: Readings in white-collar crime*. New York: Oxford University Press.

Sullivan, D., & Tifft, L. (2005). *Restorative justice: Healing the foundations of our everyday lives*. (2nd ed.). Monsey, NY: Willow Tress Press.

Weis, J. G., Crutchfield, R. D., & Bridges, G. S. (Eds.). (2001). *Juvenile delinquency readings*. (2nd ed.). Thousand Oaks, CA: Pine Forge Press.

Welch, M. (2004). *Corrections: A critical approach* (2nd ed.). New York: McGraw Hill.

Williams, III., F. P., & McShane, M. D. (Eds.). (1998). *Criminology theory: Selected classic readings*. (2nd ed.). Cincinnati, OH: Anderson.

Wozniak, J. F. (2000). The voices of peacemaking criminology: Insights into a perspective with an eye toward teaching. *Contemporary Justice Review* 3(3): 267-289.

Wozniak, J. F. (2006). Teaching to shift people's thinking toward peace: The relevance of Colman McCarthy's work for peacemaking criminology. Paper presented at the Annual meeting of the Justice Studies Association, Berkeley, CA.

Part I

Critical Themes

Chapter 2

Richard Quinney's Journey: The Marxist Dimension

Kevin B. Anderson

The relationship of Richard Quinney's critical criminology to Marxism is explored in this article. The originality of his version of critical criminology is discussed, from its origins in social constructionism, to his engagement with Marxism in the 1970s, to the importance in his later work of issues such as existentialism, Eastern thought, and Erich Fromm's socialist humanism. It is argued that Quinney's writings, despite several shifts of perspective, nonetheless exhibit some basic continuities and that an engagement with various forms of unorthodox, humanistic Marxism is one of these.

What is one to make of Richard Quinney's journey to, through, and beyond Marxism? Of his move from social constructionism to neo-Marxism and, most recently, to an orientation characterized in large part by an uneasy coexistence between Eastern thought and existentialism?[1] Despite these at times wrenching shifts of perspective, often accompanied by personal crisis and change as well, I believe that one can discern some important continuities within these discontinuities. Among those continuities are first, a sense of empathy with the suffering and the oppressed; and second, a philosophically grounded social critique that is unseparated from a closely honed and reflexive sensitivity to the subjectivity of individual lived experience.

Richard Quinney was born to a farm family in southern Wisconsin in 1934, in the middle of the Great Depression. In such a situation, it was impossible not to develop a sense of the class realities of American society. His father Floyd, who journeyed to California in the 1920s, wrote home of his first impressions of Los Angeles: "Fine homes with pretty flowers and big palm trees. Surely a rich man's city" (cited in Quinney, 1998, p. 99). That was five years before the Depression hit.

Three decades later, in 1953, Richard Quinney, not yet involved in radical or even liberal politics, had reached young adulthood during the height of McCarthyism. Still using his given name, Earl Quinney, he was working at a local grocery store, having returned home after his first year of college. Suddenly, he felt the full consequences of McCarthyism:

> One summer evening in June, following a day of work at the grocery store, Earl sat in a chair in front of the Colonial Hotel waiting for his mother to pick him up. The setting sun cast a golden light down the brick-paved street. Bold headlines on the evening paper announced the execution of Julius and Ethel Rosenberg. Still proclaiming their innocence of the charge of espionage, and after the final refusal of the judge to consider their appeals, they were turned into smoldering flesh in the electric chair. The *Milwaukee Journal* graphically detailed the final moments of their lives as the electric current passed through their bodies. Earl began to cry as he read about the Rosenbergs and what had been done to them that day. Senator Joseph McCarthy, dressed in a bombardier suit, had sent a postcard several years earlier to the farm, asking his parents for a vote. The era of the witch hunt had followed. Now, through a newspaper report of an execution, Earl was becoming politically aware. (Quinney, 1991, p. 43)

These feelings seemed to lay dormant—perhaps silenced by intimidation—until they were unlocked by the Civil Rights Movement.

As a young professor in Kentucky in 1963, Quinney joined demonstrations against racial segregation. He recounted how this affected his emerging view of crime and criminology:

> My thoughts in sociology are being shaped by what is going on around me and by my participation in daily events. Why, I ask, does the law make some behaviors criminal and others legal? My main development in criminology during this period is learning to see crime as a political phenomenon. Future consideration of crime clearly must be within a framework that places it in the struggle for control of the social order. (Quinney, 1991, p. 52)

By the early 1970s, when he had adopted Marxist and revolutionary perspectives, Quinney evidently felt that this also involved making a personal stand.

This now took the form of resigning from a rather economically comfortable full professorship at New York University. Years later, he wrote,

> I have decided not to return to my tenured professorship at New York University. I am doing things in Chapel Hill that are not possible in New York while holding a full-time teaching job. I am helping to write and distribute a socialist monthly newsletter that we call *Bread and Roses*. (Quinney, 1991, p. 76)

This leave-taking was probably not unconnected to the constant sniping that a radical in academia had to withstand. For example, the vituperative ex-Marxist Sidney Hook had once tried to get New York University's faculty senate to censure Quinney for having announced that he was giving A's to all of his students as a challenge to the hierarchy of the academic system.

The incidents that I have cited from Quinney's autobiographical reflections suggest that his turn toward Marxism had deeply experiential, even existential roots. Thus, his embrace of Marxism not only flowed out of but also shaped a certain type of lived experience.[2] I believe that these kinds of issues are crucial to an understanding of Quinney's well-known theoretical writings.

A Social Constructionist Marxism

How does one connect Marxism to criminology? The answer to this question was by no means obvious in the 1960s and early 1970s, when little work had yet been done along these lines. One possibility might have been to follow out earlier work by the economistically oriented Frankfurt School scholars Georg Rusche and Otto Kirchheimer (1939). In an examination of centuries of European history, they had connected the severity of punishment as well as the crime rate itself to the economic structure of capitalism, especially to changes in the labor market. Using contemporary data, one could also have used Marxian class analysis to explain variations in the crime rate or in sentencing rates across different sectors of the population, for example. In short, one could have continued to discuss crime as a problem rooted in the social and economic oppression of the working classes.[3]

Quinney, however, moved in quite a different direction, building not on Rusche and Kirchheimer but on perspectives that had emerged from within liberal criminology and sociology in the United States. These perspectives led one to focus on the process by which something was defined to be a crime, on how crime was socially constructed. But who was actually constructing this particular form of social reality? To the liberals, it was usually seen as society as a whole, operating in some type of consensus. To Quinney and the new radical criminologists, that very process of definition and social construction came to be seen as a most contested one.

It is here that Marxian class analysis, broadly speaking, was linked to American social constructionism, producing the theoretical grounding for a new radical criminology. In his well-known but at the time very distinctive formulation in *The Social Reality of Crime* (1970), here still writing as a radical social constructionist. Quinney wrote:

> PROPOSITION 1 (DEFINITION OF CRIME): Crime is a definition of human conduct that is created by authorized agents in a politically organized society. . . . PROPOSITION 2 (FORMULATION OF CRIMINAL DEFINITIONS): Criminal definitions describe behaviors that conflict with the interests of the segments of society that have the power to shape public policy. . . . PROPOSITION 3 (APPLICATION OF CRIMINAL DEFINITIONS): Criminal definitions are applied by the segments of society that have the power to shape the enforcement and administration of criminal law. . . . PROPOSITION 4 (DEVELOPMENT OF BEHAVIOR PATTERNS IN RELATION TO CRIMINAL DEFINITIONS): Behavior patterns are structured in segmentally organized society in relation to criminal definitions, and within this context persons engage in actions that have relative probabilities of being defined as criminal. . . . PROPOSITION 5 CONSTRUCTION OF CRIMINAL CONCEPTIONS): Conceptions of crime are constructed and diffused in the segments of society by various means of communication. . . . PROPOSITION 6

> (THE SOCIAL REALITY OF CRIME): The social reality of crime is constructed by the formulation and application of criminal definitions, the development of behavior patterns related to criminal definitions, and the construction of criminal conceptions. (pp. 15–22)

As against the liberal consensus model, here those with power are the ones who socially construct crime and the criminal rather than society as a whole.

The more orthodox British Marxists Ian Taylor, Paul Walton, and Jock Young caught immediately the distinctiveness of this position in their book *The New Criminology* (1973), which ended with a lengthy critique—not of mainstream liberal thought but of Quinney's radical but not yet explicitly Marxist position. Writing from a more objectivist standpoint that bore traces of positivism, they took particular umbrage at Quinney's more phenomenological, subjective version of radical criminology. In a single page, Taylor et al. wrote that "Quinney's statements about the social reality of crime seem to be the products more of the author's own existential *Angst* than they are the result of clear-headed theoretical analysis," referring also to "Quinney's solipsistic disbelief in the objective existence of anything" and his "relativistic confusion" and "uncritical subjectivism" (p. 253). As Taylor et al. saw it, the crux of Quinney's error, however, is that his position "leads him away from a structural analysis of the forces conducive to crime and disorder," resulting in "nothing more than a sociology of civil liberties" (p. 262). In short, Quinney's theory is undersocialized and too individualistic. Their critique anticipated some of the fault lines that would soon develop within radical and Marxist criminology between more humanist, phenomenological, and subject-centered approaches, on one hand, and more hard-nosed structuralist and critical realist ones, on the other hand (Anderson, 1992).

At the stage of *The Social Reality of Crime* (1970) Quinney had not yet embraced Marxism, but in his *Critique of Legal Order* (1974) he did so. Interestingly, his most explicit critique of the limitations of social constructionism in that 1974 work centered not on its lack class analysis, but on the subjective factor, on the notion of social alternatives. Although Quinney wrote that "the social constructionist perspective . . . has given new vitality to the study of crime and the law" (p. 7), he also faulted constructionism (here including his own 1970 book cited above) for failing to develop an alternative vision of the future:

> The legal order, accordingly, is . . . created for political purposes, to assure the hegemony of the ruling class. However, social constructionist thought stops at this point. To be sure, there are critical implications. There is the libertarian ideal that individuals should not be controlled by others, that people must be free to pursue their human potential. But there is, nevertheless, a failure to provide an image of what a new world should look like. Without such an image of what could be, an understanding of the current reality lacks a critical perspective. (pp. 7–8)

In addition, he wrote that even the phenomenological perspective "lacks the critical edge that would allow us to truly transcend the present, in life as in mind" (p. 10). For the philosophical foundation of his Marxian perspective in

Critique of Legal Order (1974), he relied most often on critiques by the Frankfurt School philosophers Herbert Marcuse and Jürgen Habermas of positivism and other dominant perspectives in the social sciences.

However, some of Quinney's statements about the legal system itself in this book lend themselves to the subsequent criticism that he had lapsed into an instrumentalist view of the state and law. This is true, for example, when Quinney (1974) wrote without qualification that "criminal law is an instrument of the state and ruling class to maintain and perpetuate the existing social and economic order" (p. 16). There are many similar statements here and in Quinney's other Marxist writings in the next few years.[4] As a whole, *Critique of Legal Order* (1974) manifests a somewhat uneasy synthesis of critical, phenomenological Marxism and more instrumentalist versions.

More important, however, Quinney's social constructionist Marxism opened new vistas for American criminology. It enabled a host of previously existing perspectives that had critiqued prisons and reformatories, police repression, or the labeling of delinquents to be seen in a newer, broader context. For example, rather than seeing juveniles as being labeled as delinquent by the community or school officials, the role of the dominant classes in shaping the definitions that led to the criteria for labeling could be brought to the fore. Equally important, the sketching out of a vision of a new human society free of alienation and domination formed a vantage point from which to mount a more radical critique than before of existing society as a whole, here challenging the cynical liberalism that is the predominant attitude in so much social analysis, even on the critical side.

Quinney's development of a radical Marxist criminology came in the context of Richard Nixon's repressive policies toward radical protest movements from 1969 to 1974. This was before Nixon's resignation over Watergate, a crisis spawned by his attempt to use methods similar to those he had used against the left to undermine the Democratic Party, itself a wing of the dominant classes. During the same period, even as uprisings at Attica and elsewhere allowed prisoners to show themselves to the world as creative, thinking, human subjects, the court-mandated gains in prisoner rights that followed were offset in other areas. America began to embark on an orgy, continuing unabated today, of massive prison-building and dramatically increased rates of incarceration.

Quinney's second major study in Marxist criminology, *Class, State, and Crime* (1980), first published in 1977, took this somber situation as its point of departure. Once again, he connected Marxian class analysis to phenomenological and social constructionist perspectives, citing the phenomenological Marxist Karel Kosík to the effect that "the world of reality is not . . . a ready-made and timeless state, but is a process in which mankind and the individual *realize* their truth, i.e., humanize man" (p. 5). Here, one has the phenomenological notion of the world as a humanly created one but now connected to the Marxian notion of a drive toward universal humanism.[5]

At a more empirical level, as Quinney (1980) outlined a typology of crime in this work, he began in the opposite direction from that taken in the usual approach: He dealt first with corporate crime and its link to the capitalist state. In second place were "crimes of government," here including not only Watergate but also "the crimes of warfare and the political assassination of foreign and domestic leaders" (p. 58). Third, there was everyday police repression and harassment of citizens: "Violence and brutality have become a recognized part of police work" (p. 58). Fourth, he listed the state's "denial of basic human rights (resulting in sexism, racism, and economic exploitation)" (p. 59). It is only after listing all of these that he finally came to a fifth category, "criminality among the oppressed classes" (p. 60), involving predatory and personal crime and, in some cases, resistance to the system. As to the prison system, he noted, this already more than two decades ago, that "it is apparent that the U.S. has the highest rate of incarceration in the world" (p. 150). On a depressing but prescient note, he also suggested that a likely possibility for the future is "the construction of roughly 1,000 new prisons, at an estimated cost of $20 billion" (p. 151).

On one hand, *Class, State, and Crime* (1980) summed up and brought to a conclusion themes from the Marxist criminology that Quinney had been developing throughout the 1970s. On the other hand, the book's 1980 second edition showed the beginnings of the move toward a new spirituality, religious mysticism, and existentialism that was to characterize Quinney's thinking during the 1980s and since. In a discussion of "prophetic criticism," Quinney identified with the Old Testament prophet whom he characterized as "the radical critic of the time and place, witnessing to the divine judgment" (p. 200). It should be noted that the word *witness* has important critical, even revolutionary meanings, as seen in contemporary groups like Witness for Peace. Thus, in the concluding paragraph to the new edition, he added, "The socialist struggle in our age is a search for God at the same time that it is a struggle for justice in human society" (p. 204).

Eastern Thought, Existentialism, and Socialist Humanism

As is well known, since 1980, Quinney's thought has become more concerned with ontological and existential issues than with social critique. At no time, though, has he renounced the basic premises of his earlier radical Marxian critique of capitalist society.[6] Increasingly, however, he has come to see the struggle against crime and violence as an internal, existential struggle within all of us, as much as it is a social struggle against an oppressive social system.[7] In short, he holds that part of the oppressive system lives within each of us, and until we overcome that internal form of violence or the wish for violence, we will not be able to overcome its more external, social forms. It was with this perspective in mind that Quinney helped to launch the field of peacemaking criminology (Pepinsky & Quinney, 1991).

In "Criminology as Moral Philosophy, Criminologist as Witness" (2000a), an essay first published in 1998, Quinney connected together these newer themes with ones from his earlier work, including his Marxist criminology of the 1970s. In this essay, he continued to view Marxism as a major foundation of critical/peacemaking criminology, in large part because it allows us to "move out of the classical dichotomy between value and fact" (p. 201). This helps us to avoid what he believed to be the trap of a "value neutral" position, one that in reality excludes a moral perspective on violence and injustice.

During the same period, Quinney became increasingly interested in the work of the humanist psychologist Erich Fromm. In a certain sense, Fromm, who coincidentally was born the same year as Quinney's father, had traveled an intellectual path that anticipated that of Quinney. Although Fromm has faded from public view to an extent, most today are aware of his humanist revision of Freud in works such as *The Art of Loving* (1956), as well as his earlier Freudian Marxist analysis of fascism (Fromm, 1941). Many also remember his writings on Marx and socialist humanism (Fromm, 1961, 1965). Fewer, however, are aware of Fromm's lifelong concern with Zen and other forms of Eastern thought, which he sometimes attempted to synthesize with Marx and Freud (Fromm, 1976; Fromm & Suzuki, 1960). Evidently, it was all three of these strands within Fromm, but especially the last two, with which Quinney now felt an affinity.

In one of his most recent writings, Quinney took up the implications of Fromm for criminology in an essay titled "Socialist Humanism and the Problem of Crime: Thinking about Erich Fromm in the Development of Critical/Peacemaking Criminology" (2000b). After discussing Fromm directly, especially his notion of being rather than having, itself derived from the young Marx, Quinney wrote that he considered the "having" mode to be a major source of violence and crime. After taking up other thinkers as well, most notably Mahatma Gandhi, Quinney concluded on a broader note that

> responses to crime that are fueled by hate, rather than generated by love, are necessarily punitive. Such responses are a form of violence, a violence that can only beget further violence. Much of what is called "criminal justice" is a violent reaction to, or anticipation of, crime. The criminal justice system, with all of its procedures, is a form of *negative peace*, its purpose being to deter or process acts of crime through the threat and application of force. *Positive peace*, on the other hand, is something other than the deterrence or punishment of crime. Positive peace is more than merely the absence of crime and violence—and of war. . . . Thus our socialist humanism attends to everyday existence, love and compassion, and social justice. . . . The way is simply that of peace in everyday life. (pp. 28–29)

To the orthodox Marxist, this might seem a long distance from any form of Marxism. However, it is not so far away from the version of Marxism espoused by Fromm.

To some, it might sound like an exaggeration to describe Fromm's thought as a version of Marxism, because he acknowledged many influences. Here it could be recalled that Fromm himself, as much as he admired Freud or Eastern thought, nonetheless kept drawing on Marx, whether in his earliest work on crime and capitalist society (Anderson & Quinney, 2000) or in his last book (Fromm, 1976). For example, whereas Fromm is most often linked to Freud, it was in fact Marx whom he most admired, as seen in the following statement, drawn from an autobiographical text from the 1960s:

> That Marx is a figure of world historical significance with whom Freud cannot even be compared in this respect hardly needs to be said. Even if one, as I do, deeply regrets the fact that a distorted and degraded "Marxism" is preached in almost one-third of the world, this fact does not diminish the unique historical significance of Marx. But quite aside from this historical fact, I consider Marx, the thinker, as being of much greater depth and scope than Freud. (Fromm, 1962, p. 12)

I do not know if Quinney would make Marx quite as central to his own perspectives today, as did Fromm in the above statement. But it is quite evident that despite Quinney's many intellectual shifts during the past two decades, he still felt some strong ties to Marx.

Let me then end this article by quoting Quinney's recent appreciation of Marx as a thinker who offered us a vision of a new world, one radically different from the violent, repressive, exploitative one of today's globalized capitalism:

> If any body of thought has a notion of truth and beauty, of how things could be, it is that of Marxism. In fact, Marxism is the philosophy of our time that takes as its primary focus the oppression inherent in capitalist society. Marxist analysis is historically specific and locates contemporary problems in the existing political economy. Marxist theory provides, most importantly, a form of thought that allows us to transcend in theory and in practice the oppression of the capitalist order. (Quinney, 2000a, p. 200)

Notes

1. In a recent book, Quinney (1998) referred to a "contradiction" in the thinking of "the professor" (himself): "I am referring, on the one hand, to his faith in the unity of life, a oneness in the universe that can be sensed in a sublime state of mind. On the other hand, in an existentialist mode, the professor holds to an indifference in the universe" (p. 154). See also his more recent reflections in Quinney (2001).

2. It could be noted that, as an ever-active and deeply humanist thinker, Karl Marx himself also rooted his thought in lived experience. This is seen, for example, in a letter he wrote in 1844 at age 26 to his fellow philosopher Ludwig Feuerbach from Paris. Marx, who had just come into contact with workers for the first time, wrote, "You would have to attend one of the meetings of the French workers to appreciate the pure freshness, the nobility which burst forth from these work-worn men" (Marx & Engels, 1975, p. 355). Feuerbach, unmoved by these accounts, was to remain an abstract philosopher without links to the emerging labor movement.

3. Rusche and Kirchheimer's fairly orthodox Marxism was not typical of the Frankfurt School. American criminologists of the 1960s and 1970s were almost certainly unaware of the work on crime of another Frankfurt School member, Erich Fromm, who did not share such economistic orientations in his approach to criminology. In 1930 and 1931, in two long-forgotten articles that were among his first publications, Fromm had come closer than Rusche and Kirchheimer to the fusion of social constructionist perspectives and Marxism that Quinney and others eventually developed. Using Freud as well as

Marx, Fromm had written of the ideological role played by the issue of crime and criminal justice in a class society. He concluded that the debate over crime and criminal justice influenced the masses in ways that bound them more closely to the capitalist state, thus diverting mass anger that might otherwise have been aimed at the system itself toward the criminal. Fromm (2000) wrote that this function of criminal justice under capitalism operated in "the same direction" as did war, which diverted mass anger against capitalism in "a manner that is harmless to the state" (p. 126).

4. However, it should be noted that here Quinney limited himself to criminal law. Thus, some forms of law may not fit this instrumentalist model.

5. Obviously, such perspectives are at variance with another major form of Marxian sociology, that rooted in structuralism, particularly the versions developed by Louis Althusser and his followers.

6. It could be added here that the period of the 1980s and early 1990s was a time when many intellectuals were publicly renouncing Marxism, something that Quinney himself could have done and which would have won him accolades in certain quarters, not least in American criminology.

7. For a somewhat similar perspective, see Pepinsky (1991).

References

Anderson, K. (1992). Humanism and anti-humanism in radical criminological theory. *Perspectives on Social Problems*, *3*, 19-38.

Anderson, K., & Quinney, R. (Eds.). (2000). *Erich Fromm and critical criminology: Beyond the punitive society*. Urbana: University of Illinois Press.

Fromm, E. (1941). *Escape from freedom*. New York: Farrar and Rinehart.

Fromm, E. (1956). *The art of loving: An inquiry into the nature of love*. New York: Harper & Row.

Fromm, E. (1961). *Marx's concept of man*. New York: Frederick Ungar.

Fromm, E. (1962). *Beyond the chains of illusion: My encounter with Marx and Freud*. New York: Simon and Schuster.

Fromm, E. (Ed.). (1965). *Socialist humanism*. New York: Doubleday.

Fromm, E. (1976). *To have or to be?* New York: Harper & Row.

Fromm, E. (2000). The state as educator: On the psychology of criminal justice. In K. Anderson & R. Quinney (Eds.), *Erich Fromm and critical criminology: Beyond the punitive society* (pp. 123-128). Urbana: University of Illinois Press.

Fromm, E., & Suzuki, D. T. (1960). *Zen Buddhism and psychoanalysis*. New York: Harper & Row.

Marx, K., & Engels, F. (1975). *Collected works* (Vol. 3). New York: International.

Pepinsky, H. E. (1991). *The geometry of violence and democracy*. Bloomington: Indiana University Press

Pepinsky, H. E., & Quinney, R. (Eds.). (1991). *Criminology as peacemaking*. Bloomington: Indiana University Press.

Quinney, R. (1970). *The social reality of crime*. Boston: Little, Brown.

Quinney, R. (1974). *Critique of legal order: Crime control in a capitalist society*. Boston: Little, Brown.

Quinney, R. (1980). *Class, state, and crime* (2nd ed.). New York: Longman.

Quinney, R. (1991). *Journey to a far place: Autobiographical reflections*. Philadelphia: Temple University Press.

Quinney, R. (1998). *For the time being: Ethnography of everyday life*. Albany: State University of New York Press.

Quinney, R. (2000a). Criminology as moral philosophy, criminologist as witness. In R. Quinney, *Bearing witness to crime and social justice* (pp. 193-213). Albany: State University of New York Press.

Quinney, R. (2000b). Socialist humanism and the problem of crime: Thinking about Erich Fromm in the development of critical/peacemaking criminology. In K. Anderson & R. Quinney (Eds.), *Erich Fromm and critical criminology: Beyond the punitive society* (pp. 21-30). Urbana: University of Illinois Press.

Quinney, R. (2001). *Borderland: A Midwest journal*. Madison: University of Wisconsin Press.

Rusche, G., & Kirchheimer, O. (1939). *Punishment and social structure*. New York: Columbia University Press.

Taylor, I., Walton, P., & Young, J. (1973). *The new criminology: For a social theory of deviance*. New York: Harper & Row.

Chapter 3

Crime and Peace: A Walk with Richard Quinney

Larry L. Tifft

Two paths are inspired by Richard Quinney's deep insights into self and society: a path that stimulates sociological imagination and helps us analyze the political economy of crime, and a path of personal and collective transformation. Following the first path, we discover that the problem of crime is a problem with social arrangements that thwart individual and collective potential; foster economic inequality; generate physical, emotional, and spiritual suffering; and necessitate participatory injustice. Following the second path, we recognize that personal and collective well-being is dependant on the understanding that the more we become conscious of being bound to others' well-being, the more the true self emerges and peace becomes our way.

More than twenty-five years ago, while exploring the political economy of crime, Richard Quinney (1975) wrote,

> Never before has our understanding of [the political economy of crime] been so crucial. Never before has our understanding been so closely related to the way in which we must live our lives. To think critically and radically today is to be revolutionary. To do otherwise is to concede to oppression. . . . As we develop a critical imagination, we [begin to think] about things that have never appeared to us [before]. [Our critical imagination takes] us to places where no one has been. In thought and in action, we [enter] new realms of life, imagination, and human possibility. (p. 291)

Today, Richard writes bearing witness to suffering, injustice, and the prospect of social justice. His witnessing is to the kinds of suffering and violence that are a systematic and structured part of our contemporary existence (Quinney, 1998a, p. 361; 2001, p. ix). His witnessing informs us that the largest portion of violence in our society is structural violence (Gil, 1999) generated or committed by agents of the state and corporate economic organizations. Much of this structural violence is directed against the poor. It is a war to maintain inequalities. Whole populations are being held hostage in poverty, sickness, addiction, and brutality against one another (Quinney, 2001, p. ix). In our own nonviolent actions and protests founded on witnessing, we take our stand (Quinney, 2001, p. x). Everything we do as people and criminologists is grounded in a moral philosophy. Whatever we think and do—our actions, our criminology—is the advancement of one moral philosophy or another. And each moral philosophy

> generates its own kind of witnessing—in the events to be witnessed and in the form of the witnessing. . . . As witnesses, we are on the side of life; a reverence for all life. Such is the way of peace. (Quinney, 2001, p. x)

Richard's way of peace, life, and witnessing—his moral philosophy and criminology—is based on human transformation in the processes of creating peace and justice. Without peace within us and in our actions, there can be no peace in the manner in which society is organized (Quinney, 1991, pp. 11–12).

When peace is the way, it emerges in our relationships and in the social organization of society, but only when we develop a sense of "self in all"— only when we act on a peace that we know and practice within ourselves (Quinney, 1998b, p. 46). Only out of a peace that is spiritually grounded in our very being can we bring to an end the construction and perpetuation of an existence that makes crime possible. This requires a transformation of our human being: "We as human beings must *be* peace if we are to live in a world free of crime" (Quinney, 1991, p. 11).

Such a set of thoughts is moving and instructive, but no short set of quotes could possibly communicate Richard's deep insight into self and society or begin to characterize his criminologies (Quinney, 2000). His witnessing has greatly inspired many of us and I am pleased to share his paths. In these next few pages, let us walk with Richard on two analytically separable yet inseparable paths: a path of critical analysis, sociological imagination; and a path of transformative being and social change.

A Path of Critical Analysis: The Political Economy of Crime

Path Markers

Along the path of critical analysis concerning the political economy of crime, we come across a number of markers. The first path marker tells us that the core social, political, and economic arrangements in any society fundamentally shape the choices and behavior opportunities of individuals. Consequently, we can better understand the behavior of individuals when we first understand how a society is organized and what ideas and choices the basic system-defining arrangements embody and offer (Gordon, 1973, p. 173). When real participation in collective decision making, in decisions as to how we are to live with one another and develop our potentialities, is limited to a few, then relations of power, dominance, and inequitable well-being are well-developed and lead to considerable suffering for many.

The second path marker tells us that in a society wherein economic relationships are the most important relationships, and wherein relations of production and reproduction create inequitable access to life's necessities (e.g., create a class structure that obstructs development), one cannot understand the behavior of individuals and their choices unless one examines the opportunities to which differently located individuals (members of each economic class) are more or less availed or confined.

The third path marker tells us that in an advanced capitalist society such as our current U.S. society, the activities of the state serve to preserve and solidify the structure of class and power inequities. Hence, one primary function of law and other arrangements of state is to legitimate the core economic arrangements. Subsequently, the primary function of the criminal justice process is to restore and preserve these specific economic arrangements when there is a breach of these relations—criminal law and criminal justice processes preserve an order. The substantive question is, then, What is the nature of the social order—the arrangements, rights and entitlements, and distributions—that is legitimated when agents of state respond to actions that violate these arrangements?

In highly nondemocratic capitalist social orders, the state acts to restore arrangements that secure a highly inequitable opportunity for meaningful participation in collective decision making, a highly inequitable distribution of rights and privileges, and a highly inequitable distribution of access to resources, personal development, food and health, and spiritual well-being. Crime, as most commonly understood (as a violation of state criminal law), results when, for example, someone acts so as to violate the property rights of another. Those who own property rights possess by law the right to deny access to their property. If I own a shirt or car, I have a legally guaranteed right to deny you access to that shirt or car. You might respond by saying that this is as it should be, and further assert that it is also acceptable and just that individuals have the legal right to deny others access to one's body, to one's self. But what if a few individuals or corporate organizations hold the right to own and control and therefore distribute a substantial portion of the food in the society and therefore hold the right to determine how much and what types of food will be produced, how this food shall be produced, who shall eat this food, who shall be healthy, who shall suffer from hunger or malnutrition, who will steal food in order to eat, and who will be prosecuted for the crime of violating the institutionally guaranteed right to deny access to this food? Law restores an order. But the order might be disorderly and unjust. In fact, it might be structurally violent (Gil, 1996, 1999).

When rights are violated and crimes occur, most persons in our society, including criminologists, present a set of varying justifications for differing collective responses to these violations of rights to deny. Some common justifications presented are: vengeance, social defense, incapacitation, deterrence, rehabilitation, and recently, restorative justice (Bazemore & Schiff, 2001; Braithwaite, 2002; Daly & Immarigeon, 1998; Galaway & Hudson, 1996; Hudson, Morris, & Galaway, 1998; Johnstone, 2002; Johnstone & Van Ness, 2007; McCold, 2000;

Strang & Braithwaite, 2000; Sullivan & Tifft, 1998b, 2005, 2006; Von Hirsch, et al., 2003; Zehr, 1990; Zehr & Mika, 1998; Zehr & Toews, 2004). But the most commonly presented justification is retribution.

Retributive collective responses are responses that are believed necessary and justified simply because the legitimated arrangements/rights have been violated. This is easily understood, for if we do not collectively respond when a harm or crime occurs, then the order/arrangements/distributions will not be restored. In reference to the illustrations above, if there is no collective response when a person's property or body is violated, the right to deny others access to one's personal property or body/self will no longer be upheld or held to be sacred. Or, if there is no collective response to the theft of food, then the rights of the few to own/control/distribute and make investment decisions regarding food—to deny others food—will not be upheld.

Recognizing this, we can more easily understand that the essence of retributive collective responses such as incarceration or punishment, as we generally speak of it, is to restore the order—the distribution of rights, privileges, and distributions in the society. Unfortunately, most folks, including criminologists, shift their gaze away from this essential understanding. The shift of focus away from the arrangements or distributions, away from how our society is organized, occurs, for to focus directly on these arrangements raises a question about the acceptability and justness of these arrangements and distributions. If these arrangements are to be maintained, and the current distributions secured and believed to be right and just, then some sort of process that morally condemns actions that violate these arrangements must be initiated to secure these specific arrangements—no matter their degree of justness, no matter if they are structurally violent, and no matter if these power arrangements lead to great suffering, human indignity, and death.

The fourth path marker tells us even more pointedly that the social problems, miseries, assaults on human dignity, and sufferings that people individually and collectively endure and struggle against are substantially produced by the arrangements preserved. Social problems such as public or private tyranny and poverty cannot be ameliorated or alleviated if hierarchical, nondemocratic decision making, and economic arrangements are upheld. Solutions to participatory injustice and poverty require these institutional and legitimized relations to be changed (Albee, 1982, 1986; Reiman, 2007; Waller, 1936). The problem of poverty, the presence and degree of poverty, is integral to the ways in which decisions concerning the ownership and control of the means of production and distribution are organized. If poverty exists from other than natural environmental conditions, it is a result of how wealth is produced and distributed. Similarly, homelessness is a result of how housing is produced and distributed. Hunger and malnutrition result from how food is produced and distributed in the society, and so forth. No matter the social organization of society, social problems emanate from the substantive nature of this social organization. To realistically address the social problems of our society, the specific decision making and economic arrangements of our society must be changed, and they can be. Social change is constantly occurring, life is process. Democracy, a real opportunity for those who wish to participate in the decision-making processes, especially investment decisions that affect everyone, can only be increased by altering the hierarchical power and participatory relations that currently restrict real consciousness and participation. If this were to occur, the state (if these arrangements were to be retained) would be forced to serve interests other than those of the persons who currently make public and private investment decisions in our society (Gordon, 1973).

In our current world, democratic arrangements are in their infancy. Very few of us are actively involved in major societal investment decisions: What is produced and in what quantity? What methods and conditions of production are selected? How to distribute that which is produced? And so forth. In our society, these decisions are primarily made within private tyrannies, within arrangements that are only very weakly influenced by either official public decision-making arrangements (such as the federal government), or by us as individuals. And as we all know, the regulatory power of the federal government is being effectively weakened by the acceptance and adoption of policies of deregulation and devolution—strategies that at this time make great sense if you believe in extending private corporate power (Chomsky, 1996).

Strategies attempting to convince us to advocate devolution are a clever set of maneuvers executed by those who hold positions of power and decision making in the globalizing private corporate world. Devolution is the thesis that those who are most directly affected by investment decisions ought to be those who most fully participate in these decisions. Spokespersons who propagandize for these arrangement changes advocate decentralizing, defederalizing, and localizing public sector collective decision making. One can not very well argue against these organizational changes in theory, for they are an advocacy for democracy and decentralization. But advocacy for these organizational changes applied only to public sector decision-making arrangements is leading to a legitimacy crisis for the federal government, and the federal government has been quite successfully demonized and diminished in its credibility. Subsequently, an enhancement of the power of those who make decisions in private sector globalizing economic institutions has taken place. The result is that decisions that most affect us are increasingly being made in the world's private board rooms where the federal government and we as individuals have little power to either regulate or influence these decisions. Increasingly, we are subjected to the tyranny of private power. Therefore, as we have in the past turned our collective attention to dismantling public, political tyrannical arrangements (e.g., Bolshevism, Fascism), we must now very quickly and diligently turn our attention to dismantling private, economic tyrannies (Chomsky, 1996, pp. 18–19).

This exhortation brings us to the final path marker. The fifth path marker states that only with the collapse of capitalist society will there be a solution to the crime problem (Quinney, 1975, p. 291).

Leaving all the path markers behind, we are struck by this straightforward assertion that the problem of crime is primarily a problem of the arrangements for the production and distribution of wealth and for making investment decisions in the society. We are here directly faced with the stark truth that stratification and social control arrangements are inextricably related; that social justice and criminal justice arrangements are inextricably related. We are left with the realization that any disconnecting of these truths is a maneuver initiated to divert attentive focus on how we live with one another—how our society is organized. Finally, we are left with the understanding that the problem of crime in our society is a problem with the core social arrangements that thwart individual and collective potential; foster economic inequality; contribute to physical, emotional, and spiritual suffering; and ensure participatory injustice and environmental destruction.

Radical Analysis: Definitions of Crime

Let us briefly explore Richard's assertion that only with the collapse of capitalist society will there be a solution to the crime problem. The validity of this assertion turns on the meaning of the crime problem and the related definitional question, What is crime? It also turns on the nature of the decision making and economic arrangements that might replace these arrangements following the collapse of our capitalist society.

How crime is defined is a major controversy in criminological inquiry (Henry & Lanier, 2001a, 2001b; Henry & Milovanovic, 1993, 1996; Lanier & Henry, 1998; Pepinsky, 1991; Schwendinger & Schwendinger, 1970). For analytic simplicity, let us briefly explore just two of the many differing definitions of crime: the traditional legal definition and the needs-based, social harms definition.

The traditional legal definition of crime defines crime as an act intended to harm, which is proscribed by the state's criminal law. The social harms definition of crime extends this definition to include social conditions, social arrangements, or actions of intent or indifference that interfere with the fulfillment of fundamental needs and obstruct the spontaneous unfolding of human potential (Gil, 1996, 1999; Sullivan & Tifft, 2001, 2005; Tifft, 1993; Tifft & Sullivan, 2001, 2005). The extent of social structural harm or structural violence in a society reflects the degree to which its members can neither meet their fundamental needs nor realize their potentialities in the context of the normal workings of the arrangements of the society (Tifft, 2000; Tifft & Sullivan, 2005). Interpersonal harms such as theft, rape, robbery, wife battery, and child abuse are significant social harms. They are also crimes as defined by the traditional legal definition. However, this set of harms comprises only one set of the countless actions, arrangements, and social conditions that embody power-based relations and result in undeniable social injury, harm, and suffering (Elias, 1986; Henry & Milovanovic, 1993, 1996; Michalowski, 1985; Pepinsky, 1991; Tifft, 2000; Tifft & Sullivan, 2001, 2005).

Historically, social injuries, harms, and institutional power relations (e.g., slavery, marital rape, crimes of state, crimes of economy, state-corporate crimes) have been legitimized by those able to successfully undertake legal maneuvering in support of power and privilege (Foucault, 1977). Many of the most serious social harms and threats to human safety, health, and life have been committed by those who have been successful in having their harms either embodied in the legal social arrangements of society or excluded from the processes of penal social control (Kennedy, 1970). From a needs-based, social harms definition of crime, the twentieth century poignantly demonstrated that we cannot accept the notion that a legal order is either a moral order or a just one.

Law in the United States has historically guaranteed the right to deny access to one's person to only some members of society. Those bound into slavery had no guaranteed right to deny owners or masters access to their person until emancipation was legally enacted and rigorously enforced. Similarly, until the late 1980s, women in most states in the U.S. were not guaranteed the right to deny access to their bodies (sexual access) to their husbands. Physical slavery and marital rape were not acts that violated criminal law. They were religiously, culturally, and legally accepted appropriations of the dignity, human rights, and potentialities of African Americans and married women, respectively. The legality of physical slavery and marital rape reflected the rights, privileges, and distributions—the institutionalized positions—of these persons in the legal economic and power relations of society at a particular time in U.S. history.

Table 3.1. Political Economy, Crime, and Social Harms

Arrangement	*Crime*	*Social Harm*
Capitalism and state	Yes	Yes
Capitalism and no state	No	Yes
No capitalism and state	Yes	Yes
No capitalism, no state, and hierarchies	No	Yes
No capitalism, no state, and no hierarchies	No	Yes

Numerous legal orders have justified the institutionalization of unimaginable harms, for example, Hitler's Germany; Stalin's USSR; South Africa's apartheid; U.S. slavery, internment of Japanese Americans (Brimmer, 1994; Chang, 1999); and policies of invasion, genocide, and dictatorship. Today, actions that are for reasons of state legal but assuredly grave social harms are highly prevalent. State terrorism, administrative torture, low-intensity warfare, death squad killings and disappearances, covert and counterintelligence, political assassinations, ethnic cleansings, capital punishment, and participatory exclusion are prime examples. But there is no short list of crimes for reasons of state (Clark, 1999; Huggins, 1998; Tifft, 1994–1995).

The needs-based, social harms definition of crime also defines many twentieth century legal modes of production and distribution as crimes, for they not only institutionalize the systematic appropriation/theft of surplus value produced by labor, but also create poverty, malnutrition, and death due to preventable starvation, disease, and injury (Elias, 1986). Significant crimes for reasons of capital (Michalowski, 1985) arise from patterns of interaction associated with the processes of capital accumulation, concentration, and centralization. Crimes for reasons of profit and market share are not limited to actions prohibited by criminal, regulatory, or civil law. They include acts not presently under the control of either nation-state or international law (Friedrichs & Friedrichs, 2002; Michalowski & Kramer, 1987, 1998, 2006; Wonders & Danner, 2002).

Radical Analysis: Questions of Structural Possibilities

With these two contrasting definitions of crime outlined, we can more fully assess Richard's assertion by looking at differing sets of social arrangements or structural possibilities that produce differing prevalences of crime and social harm. Table 3.1 presents variations of social structural arrangements and whether or not legal crimes and social harms would be stimulated by these arrangements. One structural variant presented in Table 3.1 indicates the presence of state and capitalist arrangements—capitalist society today. Under these structural conditions, our first analytic task is to assess the validity of the inference that underlies Richard's assertion that capitalist society produces unacceptable levels of crime, social harm, suffering, and human indignity: How do these arrangements foster crimes and social harms, and what is the extent of human suffering and indignity produced by these arrangements?

In our current society, the crime problem is generally projected and propagandized as the problem of the crimes of the poor or those of the dangerous class (Michalowski, 1985; Platt, 1974; Quinney, 1975, 2001; Reiman, 2007; Sheldon, 2001). If we focus on the ideological function of law and the retributive processing of criminals, we are repeatedly told that the problem of crime is the threat that those who commit street crimes, ghetto crimes, or interpersonally violent crimes pose to us. The ideological messages delivered by today's corporate media graphically show us what these persons who most threaten our safety and security look like (young African American men) and what their offenses are (robbery, drugs, and homicide). They also tell us that the crime problem is one of individual choice, personal responsibility, and personal troubles or pathology (Tifft, 1982). Societal distributions and arrangements are out of focus—out of sight—and not pictured in the photo opportunity. The central discourse is that of tertiary prevention and after the fact moral, public condemnation of criminal act and actor. Subsequent public wisdom is that those who commit these crimes deserve their punishments. But we must wonder if those who choose to act in ways that are legally proscribed deserve to live in the contexts of power and privilege that offer them sharply constrained choices for the development of their potentialities. Capitalist societies, David Gordon (1973) argued,

> depend . . . on . . . competitive forms of social and economic interaction and upon substantial inequalities in the allocations of social resources. Without inequalities, it would be much more difficult to induce workers to work in alienating [and dangerous] environments. Without competition and a competitive ideology, workers might not be inclined to struggle to improve their relative

> income and status in society by working harder. Finally, although rights of property are protected, capitalist societies do not guarantee economic security to most of [their] individual members. Individuals must fend for themselves, finding the best available opportunities to provide for themselves and their families. . . . Inevitably, . . . many of the best opportunities for economic survival open to different citizens will violate some of the historically [created] laws. Driven by the fear of economic insecurity and by a competitive desire to gain some of the goods unequally distributed throughout the society, many individuals will eventually become "criminals." (p. 174)

Economic crimes, which are the vast majority of legally defined crimes in capitalist society, represent rational responses to the structure of the institutions and culture upon which capitalist societies are based. Crimes of many different varieties constitute functionally similar responses to the organization of capitalist institutions. Let us focus on ghetto crimes. According to Gordon (1973, p. 174), it is especially clear that ghetto crimes are committed by people responding quite reasonably to the structure of economic opportunities available to them. "Only rarely," he argued,

> can [persons who commit ghetto crimes] be regarded as raving, irrational, antisocial, lunatics. The "legitimate" jobs open to many ghetto residents, especially to young black males, typically pay low wages, offer relatively demeaning assignments, and carry the constant risk of layoff. [They are as well, often dangerous and violate our commonly held definition of human dignity]. In contrast, many kinds of crime available in the ghetto often bring higher monetary return, offer higher social status, and—at least in some cases . . . carry relatively low risk of arrest and punishment. (pp. 174–175)

When "the problem of crime" is defined as "street crime" committed by members of "the dangerous class or race," we are blinded to the egregious legal social harms of those who act for the benefit of institutionalized arrangements of power and privilege. Again, actions for reasons of state or for reasons of organizational profit and market share lead to enormous social injury, even though they are not legally defined as crimes. These corporate harms also represent a quite rational response to life in capitalist society.

Corporations are organized to protect and augment the capital of their investors/owners. Specifically, corporate crimes as actions or arrangements seek to facilitate capital accumulation through profit maximization in socially injurious ways by either (a) reducing the costs of production, or (b) increasing the price and/or the volume of goods or services marketed (Michalowski, 1985, pp. 318–325). Production costs can be reduced by failing to make costly changes in known hazardous products (e.g., Ford Pinto, Dalkon Shield, Firestone-Bridgestone tires) by avoiding the expenses associated with protecting worker safety or meeting environmental protection expectations and requirements and by repressing the organization of labor. Price and volume maximization can be facilitated through such actions as securing a monopolistic position in the marketplace, issuing false advertising, bribing or giving kickbacks for favorable contracts or policies, or by fixing prices or creating administered pricing structures.

When stratification arrangements are reinforced and reconstituted through our collective responses to crime, the need to implement public policies or alter the distributions so as to reduce social harms, crimes, or the arrangements or social conditions that produce these crimes is generally lost from sight. The facts are that if the stratification arrangements are to be upheld, then there is a systemic need to continue the practices of class-based substantive law and differential criminal justice processing. Law, the criminal justice process, and the retributive industry—the penal harm industry (Clear, 1994)—then become successful in producing a politically, economically, and environmentally less dangerous criminality (Foucault, 1977). Our safety, security, well-being, health, freedoms, and potentialities are far more seriously damaged by the institutional behavior and decisions of those in positions of decision making in state and capitalist organizations—by class-based, institutionalized crimes/harms—than by the choices of persons at the bottom of our hierarchies that violate the law (Foucault, 1977; Reiman, 2007). There is substantial evidence, then, that a solid argument can be made that the social arrangements of capitalist society produce and stimulate, in fact, constitute, a criminogenic set of social relations.

Returning to Table 3.1, there are other structural possibilities that might develop if capitalist society collapsed. A society with state arrangements but without private capitalist relations is one of these. Under these structural conditions, in the possible future, would there be a decrease in the prevalence of crimes and social harms? What types of crimes and social harms with what prevalences would be produced? Or would these statist arrangements themselves constitute crimes? Here, crime, as the power to deny others a presence, is the ultimate form of reification in which those subject to the power of others suffer the pain of being denied their own humanity—the human need to create, interact, make a difference, and participate (Henry & Milovanovic, 1993; Pepinsky, 1991; Tifft & Sullivan, 1980, 2001).

Another structural possibility, presented in Table 3.1, would be a global society with capitalist arrangements, perhaps a set of interlocking private global tyrannies, but without the state. Under these conditions there would be no crime as there is no state to define actions as crimes, but there would assuredly be social harms, perhaps of a much greater magnitude than produced within our current state and capitalist political economy. Unfettered by any state-based counter power (nation-state or a world state), I imagine that these arrangements would constitute and generate far more extensive social harm and injury. A society or world of private corporate power arrangements would produce a massive criminogenic tyranny of environmental destruction and human indignity and suffering.

Another structural possibility presented in Table 3.1 that might occur if there were a collapse of capitalist society is living in a society without capitalist relations and without the state. The effect that this social organization might have on the solution to the crime problem—on the prevalence of crimes and social harms—would clearly depend on the nature of the social organization of such a society or world. In this social order we might suffer decision-making arrangements and production/distribution relations that would be far worse than those of the combinations of arrangements assessed above. We might live in a highly repressive patriarchy or a chaotic hell-hole of power exercise with massive violence, suffering, and environmental deconstruction.

On the other hand, without either state or capitalist arrangements, we might quite creatively organize a society or world constructed on "socialist principles" (Quinney, 1975, p. 291), a needs-based societal projection—a federation of human-scale societies that would be without legally defined crime and without institutionally imposed and generated social harms—a global society that might structurally negate or prevent relations of power, greatly diminish the sources of all types of violence, and reduce to a minimum structural and reflective/reactive interpersonal harm (Gil, 1999; Kropotkin, 1924; Le Guin, 1974; Piercy, 1976; Sullivan & Tifft, 2001, 2005; Tifft, 1979; Tifft & Sullivan, 2001, 2005). This is a structural possibility that needs to be discussed, for its diverse patterns of interaction might encourage us to take a path of personal and collective transformation.

A Path of Peace: Personal and Collective Transformation

The Political Economy of No-Self

The possibility of creating social arrangements and relationships that meet our needs and foster personal and collective well-being is dampened and thwarted in the political economies of power, hierarchy, and inequality. In fact, many of the arrangements in our society, based on power and privilege, negate human presence. They demand of those subjected to the vicissitudes of power a sacrifice of voice, energy, talent, and desired self to produce power-wielders' satisfactions and support the social arrangements for which power-wielding is undertaken. When we live and force others to live in accord with the specifications of power-based existence, we fix our identities and those of others; we set boundaries around the kinds of persons we can imagine ourselves becoming (Sullivan & Tifft, 2005). We imagine ourselves to be a certain way rather than actively creating the self we desire. We force ourselves and others to accept conceptualizations of self, of personhood, and what it means to be human that are radically different from the selves we would create for ourselves under quite different social conditions and consciousnesses—under needs-based social arrangements (Piercy, 1976; Sullivan & Tifft, 2005; Tifft & Sullivan, 2005).

To survive economically, emotionally, and even physically in person dismissing and person-diminishing power arrangements, many of us currently engage in a process of self-editing and self-falsification. We forge an alien or alienated self. It is understandable, then, that under hierarchical conditions many people have to talk themselves into going to work or school or into spending time at home. The possibility of living, of being one's authentic self in such environments, is virtually nonexistent. In these arrangements there is little hope of expressing the core of self and creating a self with a strong and clear sense of our true being. In these conditions we are unable to connect with others in truly enjoyable ways—to be ourselves. And we know all too well that to feel that we cannot be ourselves in a situation drains us of energy and creates for us a loss. In denying light to those dimensions of ourselves that we see as, for example, interfering with our market- or power-based selves, true enjoyment in life is vitiated (Brown, 1959). We become structure-bound selves, disabled in communicating our real self experiences to others (Rogers, 1961, p. 133).

But when we commit ourselves to the processes of confronting power relationships, we experience a dissolution of self, a surrender of self, a stripping away of self, and an emptying of self. We begin to live the way of peace, the way of helping others meet their needs. Such processes of self transformation and transcendence of self involve an examination of and a dislodging of the justifications for treating others' needs as less important than one's own, of treating others as less than one's self, and of inflicting loss on others to satisfy one's own needs (Sullivan & Tifft, 2005).

For most of us it is difficult to put a needs-based conception of justice or the way of peace into practice, as doing so requires us to abandon all notions of power. In social arrangements organized for the satisfaction of the needs of each (a needs-based political economy), a great premium is placed on the participation of everyone, on the voice of each. The feelings, thoughts, sentiments, and needs of everyone involved are primary. Each person should feel that his or her needs have been acknowledged, respected, and met, and therefore feel justly present (Kropotkin, 1924).When differences in need exist, for whatever reason, they can be neither dismissed or homogenized through categoric placement nor sacrificed for the interests of others for relations of power. The intention of needs-based justice is to respond to the uniquely different and special needs of each person and thereby collaboratively create equality of well-being for all (Miller, 1976; Kropotkin, 1924; Sullivan & Tifft, 1998a, 1998b, 2001, 2005, 2006; Tifft & Sullivan, 2005).

Transformational Contexts for No-Self

The tensions between self and other and between individual and community are present in our personal and collective relations with the natural environment (Amster, 1998, 2001; Bookchin, 1971; Vitek & Jackson, 1996). To move in the direction of a needs-based relationship with the natural environment, we need to recognize the true cost of things (Sullivan, 1986–1987) and restore and preserve harmonious conditions that ensure sustainable agricultures and biospheres.

In our most personal interactions, the processes of creating needs-based patterns of interaction begins with our intimates, our partners, and the children and elderly parents who live with us. It is in these relationships that we most stake our hopes, for the quality and nature of these relationship patterns and the values they embody spill over into our relationships and the social organization of our preschools or learning centers, daycare and schooling arrangements, work experiences, and throughout society (Forsey, 1995; Sullivan & Tifft, 1998a, 2005; Tifft, 1993).

As we develop needs-based relations in our most intimate and personal relationships, we come to recognize that hierarchies and power relations are neither universal nor necessary components of social life (Barclay, 1982; Kropotkin, 1924). Here we learn that we can structure into any sphere of our daily lives a sense of justice that takes into account the needs of others as well as our own (Sullivan, 1980).

In our intimate relationships we know it is possible to relate to a partner as an equal, without power, and without seeking to achieve and enforce a favored status for one's self. We can be encouraged and inspired to develop our potentialities, strengths, skills, talents, and gifts. We can create and enjoy relationships wherein there is no overt or hidden hierarchy or power maneuvering. We can give up the roots of relational distance with our partners that have led to separate spheres and parallel lives, and the accompanying power- and privilege-based feelings of resentment and existential separateness–non-oneness (Bernard, 1986).

Those of us who begin to create relations of equal well-being share in a collaboration of love and labor that produces profound intimacy, friendship, and mutual respect (Blumstein & Schwartz, 1985; Schwartz, 1994, p. 56). When we are deep mates, we know each other and love each other; each of us can think and feel for the other. We can complete one another's sentences. We can become one; existentially and physically separate, yet inseparable. We think and behave in terms of the other. And if we were asked to give a narrative about ourselves, to describe ourselves, we would tell you about the other, our closest friends, and the children whom we love and spend time with.

In relationships bound by such affection, we can freely share in our family work (laundry, food preparation, etc.) and in the key decisions that affect our family life together. We can arrange equal needs-based access to the family's resources and equal weight in developing and pursuing our individual and family life plans (Kinkade, 1994; Schwartz, 1994). When it comes to family life and family work, young and old alike can encourage one another to participate in the creation of decisions and rules or guidances that affect everyone (Piercy, 1976). Children especially need to know that they are appreciated as co-creators of the family dynamic and not subjects of a parental dynasty that reinforces stratification. This means not only that all need to be participants, but also that all need to understand that everyone has needs.

Of course, such relationships do not emerge in a vacuum or spontaneously. They require creativity, attentiveness, and "conscious and sustained effort" (Conze, 1967, p. 81). They require each of us to be available to the other and take responsibility for generating real conversation and warmth, for listening, and for developing an awareness of one's own needs and the desire and effort to articulate these to one another (Macmurray, 1961, pp. 157–158; Mounier, 1971, p. 19).

Creating such patterns of interaction requires constant attentiveness to each person's needs and realities and to the root of his or her personal concerns or troubles when they arise (Schumacher, 1998).Only then can the genesis of these concerns or troubles be addressed, the incidence of troubled behaviors decreased, and more supportive and responsive processes developed for meeting the needs of the child, parent, or grandparent (Brazelton, 1992). When a parent or parents become open to the observations, insights, and criticisms of children, trust and mutual understanding and the unique needs of each person are fostered (Berry, 1996).

Yet families that strive to take into account the needs of all their members require external support themselves. It is essential, for example, that the work arrangements that family members are a part of outside the home be organized in ways that differ from those prevalent in many large-scale corporate operations. Work arrangements that defy human scale deny us our basic need for enjoyable contact with others and lead to the demise of our initiative and creativity, all of which has implications for what we carry back home with us (Kimbrell, 1992; Sale, 1980; Tifft, 1993).When parents must care for a sick child or an older family member, they should not be treated in a begrudging manner by workplace managers. Fortunately, an increasing number of those who manage or coordinate workplaces, if only for reasons of organizational cost-effectiveness and increased production, have come to acknowledge how important it is for the organization to respond to the entire life of the worker. They also see that those of us who live peaceful, joyous, and healthy family lives (with living wages, healthcare, flextime, and transferable retirement benefits) are able to contribute far more to our coworkers on the job and ultimately to the productivity of the company or the quality of the services given by the agency (Freudenheim, 1988; Leary, 1988).

Not surprisingly, therefore, on some fronts we are witnessing an increased sensitivity to the effect that the atmosphere, policies, and arrangements of the workplace have on the personal well-being, productivity of and quality of service given by those of us who work outside the home. Those of us who have worked to develop collaborative work arrangements know that truly creative and productive work occurs far more frequently when we fully share in all workplace decisions and processes and when we are valued as whole people and can be ourselves at work (Marshall, 1995, pp. 127–139). Under work conditions that foster collaboration and personal well-being, we experience a bevy of positive experiences and relations to carry home and share with family members (Hart, 1992; Krimerman & Lindenfeld, 1992; Tifft, 1993).

Similarly in school settings, in an effort to address the structural harm done to children in demeaning school environments, some administrators, principals, and teachers have begun to move away from arrangements that concentrate on comparing, differentiating, homogenizing, hierarchically ordering, and excluding students (Foucault, 1977, p. 183; Sullivan, 2001; Sullivan, 1998). Many are now attempting to develop and implement work/learning environments in which all collaborate (Nevin, Thousand, Paolucci-Whitcomb, & Villa, 1990). Indeed, some educators increasingly speak of the school and learning in terms of community (Kohn, 1993, 1996; Power, Higgins, & Kohlberg, 1989). Instead of spending effort and resources classifying and segregating children according to special need categories or teaching children as if they each learned in the same manner, many educators now involve all students in learning processes whereby they learn from each other's ways of learning. In such environments, children are given a chance to interact with and learn from one another, help select what they learn, and learn in ways that each learns best; in short, they learn how to be in charge of themselves (Armstrong, 1987). The expert teacher, like the collaborative principal, understands people's essential needs, such as the need to control one's destiny, and involves students in making decisions affecting their presence in their workplace, the school (Sullivan, 2001; Sullivan, 1998).

As we seek to create the kinds of arrangements that I have illustrated here, to create needs-based relationships, each of us can be moved not only to take the risk to experience and create the self one desires or has constructed down deep, but also to become a presence to others that serves as a foundation for social life without power that takes the other unto one's self so as to become a seamless All.

As we have taken our walk with Richard, we have discovered that the more conscious we are of being bound to others and nature, the more free each of us is to be unique, different, and autonomous. As we commit ourselves to risk and vulnerability, to person and idea, we are more free to experience spiritual transformation, to realize that the true self is no-self (Sullivan & Tifft, 2005). Living in harmony with this truth, life is an act of service, a gift. When our hearts are filled with loving concern and our minds with willingness to serve, we know what is to be done and how it is to be done (Quinney, 1991). It is to be done everywhere and every time we interact with others. Peace is the path.

References

Albee, G.W. (1982). Preventing psychotherapy and promoting human potential. *American Psychologist*, *37*, 1043-1050.

Albee, G.W. (1986). Toward a just society: Lessons from observations on the primary prevention of psychotherapy. *American Psychologist*, *41*, 891-898.

Amster, R. (1998). Anarchism as moral theory: Praxis, property, and the postmodern. *Anarchist Studies*, *6*, 97-112.

Amster, R. (2001). Changing rainbows: Utopian pragmatics and the search for anarchist communities. *Anarchist Studies*, *9*, 29-52.

Armstrong, T. (1987). *In their own way: Discovering your child's personal learning style*. Los Angeles: Tarcher.

Barclay, H. (1982). *People without government: An anthropology of anarchism*. London: Kahn and Averril with Cienguegos Press.

Bazemore, G., & Schiff, M. (Eds.). (2001). *Restorative community justice: Repairing harm and transforming communities*. Cincinnati, OH: Anderson.

Bernard, J. (1986). The good provider role: Its rise and fall. In A. S. Skolnick & J. H. Skolnick (Eds.), *Family in transition* (5th ed., pp. 125-144). Boston: Little, Brown.

Berry, W. (1996). Conserving communities. In W. Vitek & W. Jackson (Eds.), *Rooted in the land: Essays on community and place* (pp. 76-4). New Haven, CT: Yale University Press.

Blumstein, P., & Schwartz, P. (1985). *American couples: Money, work, sex*. New York: Pocket Books.

Bookchin, M. (1971). *Post scarcity anarchism*. Palo Alto, CA: Ramparts Press.

Braithwaite, J. (2002). *Restorative justice and responsive regulation*. New York: Oxford University Press.

Brazelton, T. B. (1992). *To listen to a child: Understanding the normal problems of growing up*. Redding, MA: Addison-Wesley.

Brimmer, L.D. (1994). *Voices from the camps: Internment of Japanese Americans during World War II*. Danbury, CT: Franklin Watts.

Brown, N. O. (1959). *Life against death: The psychoanalytical meaning of history*. Hanover, NH: Wesleyan University Press.

Chang, G. H. (1999). *Morning glory, evening shadow: Yamato Ichihashi and his internment writings, 1942-1945*. Stanford, CA: Stanford University Press.

Chomsky, N. (1996, March). You say you want a devolution? *Progressive*, pp. 18-19.

Clark, R. (1999). The "celling" of America, the political economy of force, and the violence of economic sanctions in international relations. *Contemporary Justice Review*, *2*, 5-22.

Clear, T. (1994). Harm in American penology: Offenders, victims, and their communities. Albany: State University of New York Press.

Coles, R. (1997). *The moral intelligence of children*. New York: Random House.

Conze, E. (1967). *Buddhist thought in India: Three phases of Buddhist philosophy*. Ann Arbor: University of Michigan Press.

Daly, K., & Immarigeon, R. (1998). The past, present, and future of restorative justice: Some critical reflections. *Contemporary Justice Review*, *1*, 21-45.

Elias, R. (1986). *The politics of victimization: Victims, victimology and human rights*. New York: Oxford University Press.

Forsey, H. (1995). Community as crucible. In *Communities directory: A guide to cooperative living* (pp. 27-30). Langley, WA: Fellowship for International Community.

Foucault, M. (1977). *Discipline and punish: The birth of the prison*. New York: Pantheon.

Friedrichs, D. O., & Friedrichs J. (2002). The World Bank and crimes of globalization: A case study. *Social Justice* 29, 1-2: 13-36.

Freudenheim, M. (1988, August 23). Employees act to stop family violence. *The New York Times*, p. A1.

Galaway, B., & Hudson, J. (Eds.). (1996). *Restorative justice: International perspectives*. Monsey, NY: Criminal Justice Press.

Gil, D. G. (1996). Preventing violence in a structurally violent society: Mission impossible. *American Journal of Orthopsychiatry*, *66*, 77-84.

Gil, D.G. (1999).Understanding and overcoming social-structural violence. *Contemporary Justice Review*, *2*, 23-35.

Gordon, D. M. (1973). Capitalism, class, and crime in America. *Crime & Delinquency*, *19*, 136-186.

Hart, E. (1992). Salsedo Press: Community roots, quality printing. In L. Krimerman & F. Lindenfeld (Eds.), *When workers decide: Workplace democracy takes root in North America* (pp. 13-20). Philadelphia: New Society.

Henry, S., & Lanier, M. M. (2001a). The prism of crime: Toward an integrated definition of crime. In S. Henry & M.M. Lanier (Eds.), *What is crime? Controversies over the nature of crime and what to do about it* (pp. 227-243). Lanham, MD: Rowman and Littlefield.

Henry, S., & Lanier, M. M. (Eds.). (2001b). *What is crime? Controversies over the nature of crime and what to do about it*. Lanham, MD: Rowman and Littlefield.

Henry, S., & Milovanovic, D. (1993). Back to basics: A postmodern redefinition of crime. *Critical Criminologist*, *5*, 1-2, 6, 12.

Henry, S., & Milovanovic, D. (1996). *Constitutive criminology: Beyond postmodernism*. London: Sage.

Hudson, J., Morris, A., & Galaway, B. (Eds.). (1998). *Family group conferences: Perspectives in policy in practice*. Monsey, NY: Crime Justice Press.

Huggins, M. K. (1998). *Political policing: The United States and Latin America*. Durham, NC: Duke University Press.

Johnstone, G. (2002). *Restorative justice: Ideas, values, debates*. Cullompton, Devon, UK: Willan Publishing.

Johnstone, G., & Van Ness, D. (Eds.). (2007). *Handbook of restorative justice*. Cullompton, Devon, UK: Willan Publishing.

Kennedy, M. (1970). Beyond incrimination: Some neglected facts of the history of punishment. *Catalyst*, *5*, 1-16.

Kimbrell, A. (1992, May/June). Time for men to pull together. *Utne Reader*, pp. 66-74.

Kinkade, K. (1994). *Is it utopia yet? An insider's view of Twin Oaks community in its 26th year*. Louisa, VA: Twin Oaks.

Kohn, A. (1993). *Punished by rewards: The trouble with gold stars, incentive plans, A's, praise, and other bribes*. Boston: Houghton Mifflin.

Kohn, A. (1996). *Beyond discipline: From compliance to community*. Alexandria, VA: Association for Supervision and Curriculum Development.

Krimerman, L., & Lindenfeld, F. (1992). Drawing in and reaching out: Strategies to strengthen the workplace democracy movement. In L. Krimerman & F. Lindenfeld (Eds.), *When workers decide: Workplace democracy takes root in America* (pp. 239-246). Philadelphia: New Society.

Kropotkin, P. (1924). *Ethics: Origin and development*. New York: Mother Earth.

Lanier, M., & Henry, S. (1998). *Essential criminology*. Boulder, CO: Westview.

Leary,W.E. (1988, August 5). U.S. urged to fight infant mortality. *The New York Times*, p. D17.

Le Guin, U. K. (1974). *The dispossessed*. New York: Avon.

Macmurray, J. (1961). *Persons in relation*. New York: Harper and Brothers.

Marshall, E. M. (1995). *Transforming the way we work: The power of the collaborative workplace*. New York: AMA Co.

McCold, P. (2000). Toward a holistic vision of restorative juvenile justice: A reply to the maximalist model. *Contemporary Justice Review*, *3*, 357-414.

Michalowski, R. J. (1985). *Order, law, and crime: An introduction to criminology*. New York: Random House.

Michalowski, R. J., & Kramer, R. C. (1987). The space between the laws: The problem of corporate crime in the transnational context. *Social Problems*, *34*, 34-53.

Michalowski, R. J., & Kramer, R. C. (1998).*Globalization and shifting legal spaces: An inquiry into transnational corporate crime under the newworld order*. Paper presented at the Annual Society of Criminology, Annual Meeting, Washington, DC.

Michalowski, R. J., & Kramer, R. C. (2006). *State-corporate crime: Wrongdoing at the intersection of business & government*. New Brunswick, NJ: Rutgers University Press.

Miller, D. (1976). *Social justice*. Oxford, UK: Oxford University Press.

Mounier, E. (1971). *Personalism*. South Bend, IN: University of Notre Dame Press.

Nevin, A., Thousand, J., Paolucci-Whitcomb, P.,& Villa, R. (1990). Collaborative consultation: Empowering public school personnel to provide heterogeneous schools for all. *Journal of Educational and Psychological Consultation*, *1*, 41-67.

Pepinsky, H. E. (1991). *The geometry of violence and democracy*. Bloomington: Indiana University Press.

Piercy, M. (1976). *Woman on the edge of time*. New York: Fawcett Crest.

Platt, A. M. (1974). The triumph of benevolence: Origins of juvenile justice in the U.S. In R. Quinney (Ed.), *Criminal justice in America: A critical understanding* (pp. 356-389).Boston: Little, Brown.

Power, F.C., Higgins, A., & Kohlberg, L. (1989). The habit of the common life: Building character through democratic community schools. In L. Nucci (Ed.), *Moral development and character education: A dialogue* (pp. 125-143). Berkeley, CA: McCutchan.

Quinney, R. (1975). *Criminology: Analysis and critique of crime in America*. Boston: Little, Brown.

Quinney, R. (1991). The way of peace: On crime, suffering and service. In H. E. Pepinsky & R. Quinney (Eds.), *Criminology as peacemaking* (pp. 3-13). Bloomington: Indiana University Press.

Quinney, R. (1998a). Criminology as moral philosophy, criminologist as witness. *Contemporary Justice Review*, *1*, 347-364.

Quinney, R. (1998b). The question of crime: Enlightenment in the ten ox herding pictures. *Justice Professional*, *11*, 35-46.

Quinney, R. (2000). *Bearing witness to crime and social justice*. Albany: State University of New York Press.

Quinney, R. (2001). Foreword. In R. Sheldon (Ed.), *Controlling the dangerous classes: A critical introduction to the history of criminal justice* (pp. ix-x). Boston: Allyn & Bacon.

Reiman, J. (2007). *The rich get richer and the poor get prison: Ideology, class, and criminal justice* (8th ed.). Boston: Allyn & Bacon.

Rogers, C. R. (1961). *On becoming a person*. Boston: Houghton Mifflin.

Sale, K. (1980). *Human scale*. New York: Coward, McCann, & Geoghegan.

Schwartz, P. (1994, September/October). Modernizing marriage. *Psychology Today*, pp. 54, 56, 58-59, 86.

Schumacher, J. (1998). Questions for students of justice. *Contemporary Justice Review*, *1*, 213-241.

Schwendinger, H., & Schwendinger, J. (1970). Defenders of order or guardians of human rights? *Issues in Criminology*, *5*, 123-157.

Sheldon, R. G. (2001). *Controlling the dangerous classes: A critical introduction to the history of criminal justice*. Boston: Allyn & Bacon.

Strang, H., & Braithwaite, J. (Eds.). (2000). *Restorative justice: Philosophy to practice*. Burlington, VT: Ashgate Publishing.

Sullivan, D. (1980). *The mask of love: Corrections in America; toward a mutual aid alternative*. Port Washington, NY: Kennikat Press.

Sullivan, D. (1986-1987). The true cost of things: The loss of the commons and radical change. *Social Anarchism*, *6*, 20-26.

Sullivan, D. (2001). The school as a community of learners: Meeting the needs of all in the inclusion classroom; an interview with John Sullivan. *Contemporary Justice Review*, *4*, 219-231.

Sullivan, D., & Tifft, L. (1998a). Criminology as peacemaking: A peace-oriented perspective on crime, punishment, and justice that takes into account the needs of all. *Justice Professional*, *11*, 5-34.

Sullivan, D., & Tifft, L. (1998b). The transformative and economic dimensions of restorative justice. *Humanity and Society*, *22*, 38-54.

Sullivan, D., & Tifft, L. (2001). The requirements of just community: An introduction that takes into account the political economy of relationship. *Contemporary Justice Review*, *3*, 121-152.

Sullivan, D., & Tifft, L. (2005). *Restorative justice: Healing the foundations of our everyday lives*. (2nd. Edition). Monsey, NY: Willow Tree Press.

Sullivan, D., & Tifft, L., (Eds.). (2006). *Handbook of restorative justice: A global perspective*. London: Routledge International.

Sullivan, J. (1998). Meeting the individual needs of all learners in the inclusion classroom. *Justice Professional*, *11*, 175-187.

Tifft, L. (1979). The coming definitions of crime: An anarchist perspective. *Social Problems*, 26, 392-402.

Tifft, L. (1982). Capital punishment research, policy, and ethics: Defining murder and placing murderers. *Crime and Social Justice*, *17*, 61-68.

Tifft, L. (1993). *The battering of women: The failure of intervention and the case for prevention*. Boulder, CO: Westview.

Tifft, L. (1994-1995). A social harms definition of crime. *Critical Criminologist*, *6*, 9-13.

Tifft, L. (2000). Social justice and criminologies: A commentary. *Contemporary Justice Review*, *3*, 43-52.

Tifft, L., & Sullivan, D. (1980). *The struggle to be human: Crime, criminology, and anarchism*. Over the Water, Sanday, Orkney, Scotland: Cienfuegos Press.

Tifft, L., & Sullivan, D. (2001). A needs-based social harms approach to defining crime. In S. Henry & M. Lanier (Eds.), *What is crime? Controversies over the nature of crime and what we should do about it* (pp. 179-203). Lanham, MD: Rowan and Littlefield.

Tifft, L., & Sullivan, D. (2005). Needs-based anarchist criminology. In S. Henry & M. Lanier (Eds.) *The Essential Criminology Reader* (pp. 259-277). Boulder, CO: Westview Press.

Van Ness, D., & Strong, K. H. (1997). *Restoring justice*. Cincinnati, OH: Anderson.

Vitek, W., & Jackson, W. (1996). *Rooted in the land: Essays on community and place*. New Haven, CT: Yale University Press.

Von Hirsch, A., Roberts, J., Bottoms, A. E., Roach, K., & Schiff, M. (Eds.). (2003). *Restorative justice and criminal justice: Competing or reconcilable paradigms*. Oxford: Hart Publishing.

Waller, W. (1936). Social problems and the mores. *American Sociological Review, 1*, 924-930.

Wonders, N. A., & Danner M., (2002). Globalization, State-corporate crime, and women: The strategic role of women's NGOs in the new world order. In G. Potter (Ed.) *Controversies in white-collar crime* (pp. 165-184). Cincinnati, OH: Anderson.

Zehr, H. (1990). *Changing lenses.* Scottsdale, PA: Herald Press.

Zehr, H., & Mika, H. (1998). Fundamental concepts of restorative justice. *Contemporary Justice Review, 1*, 47-55.

Zehr, H., & Toews, B. (Eds.) (2004). *Critical issues in restorative justice.* Monsey, NY: Criminal Justice Press.

Chapter 4

The Origins and Development of the Concept and Theory of State-Corporate Crime

Ronald C. Kramer
Raymond J. Michalowski
David Kauzlarich

The important contributions made by Richard Quinney to the study of corporate crime and the sociology of law, crime, and justice have influenced the development of the concept of state-corporate crime. This concept has been advanced to examine how corporations and governments intersect to produce social harm. State-corporate crime is defined as criminal acts that occur when one or more institutions of political governance pursue a goal in direct cooperation with one or more institutions of economic production and distribution. The creation of this concept has directed attention to a neglected form of organizational crime and inspired numerous empirical studies and theoretical refinements.

Knowing when an idea first appeared is far different than knowing where it began. Whereas the concept of state-corporate crime made its first public appearance in 1990 in a series of articles presented by Kramer (1990a, 1990b, 1990c) and Kramer and Michalowski (1990), explaining where the framework for examining how corporations and governments intersect to produce social harm is a much longer story. The term itself began as a spontaneous comment during an informal discussion of a research project in a Berkeley, California, restaurant during the Society for the Study of Social Problems meeting in 1989. The research project was an outgrowth of an earlier investigation of the power of corporations to shape state laws in the context of emergent globalization (Michalowski & Kramer, 1987). Although we can locate the initial development of this idea in the late 1980s, if we continue unraveling the intellectual origins of this idea, much like one might unwind a ball of yarn, our search will lead back to many of the contributions made by Richard Quinney to the study of corporate crime and the sociology of law, crime, and justice.

Background: The Contributions of Richard Quinney

Calling Attention to White-Collar and Corporate Crime

Early in his career, Quinney made several important contributions to the study of white-collar and corporate crime. His dissertation, completed in 1962, was a study of prescription violations by retail pharmacists. This study of occupational crime led to Quinney's first publication in 1963 in the journal *Social Problems.* One year later, Quinney (1964) suggested that Sutherland's definition of the concept of white-collar crime be expanded to include all violations that occur in the course of occupational activity regardless of the social status of the offender. Having helped to establish occupational crime as one important form of white-collar crime, Quinney, with his dissertation advisor Marshall Clinard (a former student of Sutherland), then decided that the concept of white-collar crime was in need of further reformulation. In the second edition of their book, *Criminal Behavior Systems: A Typology* (1973), Clinard and Quinney divided white-collar crime into two distinct types: occupational crime and corporate crime.

According to Clinard and Quinney (1973),

> occupational crime consists of offenses committed by individuals for themselves in the course of their occupations and the offenses of employees against their employers. Corporate crime consists of the offenses committed by corporate officials for their corporation and the offenses of the corporation itself. (p. 188)

The significance of Clinard and Quinney's distinction between occupational crime and corporate crime is that it helped to rescue the more radical component of Sutherland's work on white-collar crime. After Sutherland's death in 1950, research on white-collar crime, what little there was, tended to drift away from Sutherland's original concern with the harmful acts of large corporations and their upper status executives. Clinard and Quinney helped to bring the focus of criminological work back on the corporate organization itself, paving the way for the development of a sociology of organizational crime in the late 1970s (Clinard & Yeager, 1980; Ermann & Lundman, 1978; Gross, 1978; Schrager & Short, 1978) and eventually the creation of the concept of state-corporate crime in the late 1980s. Foreshadowing the development of a theory of state-corporate crime in the 1990s, Clinard and Quinney (1973) also drew attention to the role of corporations in the larger political economy and their power to shape criminal law and government regulations to their benefit:

> Criminal law alone does not assure compliance as long as those corporations that are controlled exercise political control and influence over regulatory agencies and courts. What is needed is greater political control by the public

over the corporations and their power and influence in the political economy. And only with basic changes in the culture and structure of American society will there be a solution to corporate crime. (p. 221)

Toward a Radical Criminology

In addition to calling attention to the topic of corporate crime, Richard Quinney made even more important contributions to the sociology of law, crime, and justice in the 1970s. The 1970s was a period of both national political turmoil and intellectual ferment within sociology. On the political front the United States was convulsed by the Vietnam War and its aftermath, the continuing battle for minority rights, and the emergence of a second-wave feminist movement. On the intellectual front, the structural-functionalist and positivist vision that had dominated sociology since the 1930s faced increasing challenges from insurgent intellectual movements searching for more critical, politicized, and dynamic models for understanding human society generally, and America's internal conflicts specifically (Bannister, 1987). These intellectual changes were manifest in criminology and the sociology of law through the emergence of a movement first known as radical criminology and later as critical criminology (Michalowski, 1998). And in the front ranks of that movement stood Richard Quinney who, in perfect dialectical fashion, proved to be both a cause and effect of new ways of thinking about the relationship between social life, law, and criminal behavior.

Although it emerged almost two decades after the initial challenges to correctional criminology posed by Quinney and his contemporaries, the concept of state-corporate crime is nevertheless a reflection of those early years of radical intellectual ferment in criminology, particularly as these are represented in the phenomenology of Richard Quinney's *The Social Reality of Crime* (1970) and political economy of his *Critique of Legal Order* (1974b), *Criminal Justice in America* (1974a), and *Class, State and Crime* (1977). The concept and theory of state-corporate crime blends the phenomenology of lawmaking with the political economy of crime into a single framework for studying wrongdoing in the upper reaches of industrial/postindustrial society. In doing so, it links the two intellectual streams that shaped the creation of a critical criminology—social constructionism and Marxism (Taylor, Walton, & Young, 1973)—and that were so well represented in Richard Quinney's early radical thought.

As a phenomenology of lawmaking, the concept of state-corporate crime rests on the proposition that the designation and control of some behaviors as criminal and the selection of others as acceptable are the consequences of socially imbedded processes of naming, not qualities resident in the behaviors so named. As a political economy of crime, it recognizes that the social process of naming *crime* is significantly shaped by those who enjoyed the economic and political power to ensure that the naming of crime in most instances will reflect, or at least not seriously threaten, their worldview and interests.

Reimaging the Social Reality of Crime

The concept of state-corporate crime is, in many ways, the null version of Quinney's phenomenology of crime. In *The Social Reality of Crime* (1970), Quinney proposed that "crime is a definition of human conduct that is created by authorized agents in a politically organized state" (p. 15). Quinney's analysis in *Social Reality* focused specifically on how some behaviors come to be defined as crime. The theory of state-corporate crime focuses on the opposite: how certain behaviors, committed at the intersection of corporate and state goals, come to be understood as not-crime, either because they are not named as such by law or are not treated as such by those who administer and enforce the law, regardless of the social harm these behaviors cause. The concept of state-corporate crime proposes that the sociological study of upper world wrongdoing must look beyond behaviors formally designated and treated as crime to equally injurious activities that are registered as acceptable by the law or handled only lightly by the justice system, for it is in the differences between crime and not-crime that the underlying dynamics of making law and practicing "justice" are revealed (Michalowski, 1985, p. 315). Although the attention the concept of state-corporate crime gives to harms that are rarely criminalized may be the inverse of studying how certain behaviors are criminalized, it is a question that grows out of Quinney's insistence that we recognize crime as a social reality rather than an ontological one.

Keeping Classes In

The theory of state-corporate crime is deeply concerned with the political and economic processes that enable state and corporate managers to pursue plans and policies—often in concert with one another—that result in death, injury, ill health, financial loss, and increasingly in the globalized capitalist economy, cultural destruction, all the while being insulated from the full weight of criminalization for these actions. Although the theory of state-corporate crime offers a new perspective on the intersection of the interests of capital and the interests of the state (and renders the state an equal rather than subsidiary player in the process), it is nevertheless grounded in fundamentals of Marxian political economy as applied to law and justice—and herein lies another of our intellectual debts to Richard Quinney.

Although a number of radical criminologists of the 1970s worked to index criminology to Marxian political economy, some of the clearest and most developed early statements of this project were Quinney's *Critique of Legal Order* (1974b), his introduction to the edited volume *Criminal Justice in America* (1974a), and the later *Class, State and Crime* (1977). Quinney's version of a Marxist criminology was courageous in its willingness to speak the truth about the reality of power, and unapologetic in its demands that we recognize that the primary function of the political state in the United States is to secure and reproduce the process of capital accumulation, the legal/justice system on which the state rests and reflects the will of economic and political elites in ways that will ensure that the bulk of the society's wealth and political power will continue to be delivered into their hands, and that the continued maintenance of this state requires the application of the coercion and ideological manipulation to non elite sectors of the society (Quinney, 1977).

Although sometimes criticized in later years for being overly instrumentalist, Quinney's work remains relevant in its willingness to admit what much of criminology continually tries to forget: law and justice in the United States (and elsewhere) are not the products of participatory democracies in which all voices take part in what Habermas (1973) termed "undistorted communication," but rather are the products of institutional arrangements through which the interests and worldview of the investor class and their political allies continue to exert a disproportionate influence over the content and application of law. In recent years, much of critical criminology has moved away from examining the institutional expressions of economic and political power toward a greater emphasis on postmodern sites of power such as discourse, identity construction, and gender relations (Lanier & Henry, 1998). Although these developments have significantly expanded the horizon and wisdom of critical criminology, Quinney's early insistence that the institutional arrangement of economy and power resulting from the division of society into unequal classes mattered remains relevant. The evolution of a globalized capitalist order in the post-Soviet era has (or should have) made it abundantly clear that a great deal of how daily life is being lived around the world is currently being shaped by decisions in pursuit of profit made by relatively few individuals operating from institutional control centers situated in a small number of global cities (Sassen, 1998). It is toward these decision makers and the political-economic arrangements in which they operate that the concept and theory of state-corporate crime is directed.

The concept and theory of state-corporate crime owes much to Quinney's examination of the construction of political power in a capitalist state. It accepts that there is a class of powerful elites composed of investors and state and corporate managers, that these elites are more able than others to have law and law enforcement reflect their interests and worldview, and that the intersection of corporate and governmental interests does simultaneously increase the likelihood of social harm while decreasing the likelihood that these harms will be criminalized or aggressively controlled in some other way.

The Creation of the Concept of State-Corporate Crime

Whereas Quinney's radical criminology stimulated a general interest in the critical issues that the concept and theory of state-corporate crime are concerned with, the specific source of the development of the concept was a case study of the space shuttle Challenger disaster. Several months after the explosion of the Challenger in January 1986, Ron Kramer made a presentation to the Center for the Study of Ethics in Society at Western Michigan University on the topic of organizational crime. The presentation defined the concept of organizational crime, described the two major forms of this type of criminality (corporate crime and government crime), and reviewed the theory and research related to the topic. After the presentation, one of Kramer's colleagues at Western Michigan University remarked to him that much of what he had said about his theoretical approach to organizational crime seemed to apply to the Challenger tragedy and suggested that it would make an interesting case study. Unaware of many of the specific details concerning the Challenger case, Kramer gave no further thought to the remark at that time. Several months later, when he read the report of the President's Commission on the Space Shuttle Challenger Accident (1986), Kramer remembered his colleague's remark and decided that the Challenger disaster might indeed make for a good case study of organizational crime. He then proceeded to start work on the project.

As Kramer worked on the Challenger study, it became apparent that the disaster was the collective product of the interaction between two separate organizations: The National Aeronautics and Space Administration (NASA), a government agency, and Morton Thiokol, Inc., a private business corporation. The fact that these two organizations had acted together in this case to produce a serious social harm suggested that a more general conceptualization of deviant interorganizational relationships between business corporations and government agencies was needed. At the 1989 Society for the Study of Social Problems (SSSP) meeting in Berkeley, Kramer discussed the issue with Ray Michalowski. It was Michalowski's suggestion to label the phenomena *state-corporate crime*. Kramer liked the concept and began using it in his work on the Challenger case and in his writings more generally on organizational crime.

In March 1990, Kramer made a presentation at the joint meeting of the North Central Sociological Association and the Southern Sociological Society in Louisville, where the concept of state-corporate crime was used publicly for the first time. In May of that year he presented the paper, "State-Corporate Crime: A Case Study of the Space Shuttle Challenger Explosion" at the Edwin Sutherland Conference on White Collar Crime: 50 Years of Research and Beyond held at Indiana University. This was the first time he had used the concept of state-corporate crime in connection with the Challenger study. In August 1990, Kramer presented a paper titled, "The Concept of State-Corporate Crime" at the Annual Meeting of the Society for the Study of Social Problems in Washington, D.C. In all of these presentations (Kramer, 1990a, 1990b, 1990c), he pointed out that although a considerable amount of work had been done on both corporate and state crime, no mention had been made in the literature to that point of the fact that corporations and government agencies can act together to produce serious criminality. The concept of state-corporate crime was advanced to draw attention to this neglected form of organizational misconduct. In the first of these early papers, Kramer defined state-corporate crime in the following way:

> State-corporate crime is defined as an illegal or socially injurious social action that is the collective product of the interaction between a business corporation and a state agency engaged in a joint endeavor. These crimes involve the active participation of two or more organizations, at least one of which is private and

> one of which is public. They are the harmful result of an interorganizational relationship between business and government. (p. 1)

In the Fall of 1990, Kramer and Michalowski began working together to flesh out the concept of state-corporate crime and to develop a theoretical approach to the topic. In November of that year they presented their work at the annual meeting of the American Society of Criminology in Baltimore. This presentation, titled "Toward an Integrated Theory of State-Corporate Crime," has become the most widely cited paper concerning the phenomenon of state-corporate crime. The paper (which has since been published in Michalowski and Kramer, 2006) presented a significant refinement of the definition of the concept and offered an integrated theoretical model for the analysis of state-corporate crime and other organizational offenses.

Kramer and Michalowski (1990) started the paper by noting that the study of corporate crime to that point had resulted in an important insight and an important oversight. The insight, due in part to the earlier distinction between occupational and corporate crime drawn by Clinard and Quinney (1973), was that corporate crime is actually a form of organizational deviance. Insofar as corporations are formal organizations, the study of corporate crime can and should incorporate the theoretical and substantive insights of organizational research (Vaughan, 1982, 1983). The oversight was the failure to recognize that since the modern corporation emerged as the basic unit of economic activity within private production systems in the late nineteenth century, corporations and governments have been functionally interdependent. The modern corporation in the United States could not have developed, nor could it currently function, without the legal, economic, and political infrastructure provided by government (Sklar, 1988). Governments in private production systems, in turn, depend on corporations to supply necessary goods and services and to provide the economic base in the form of individual salaries and/or corporate profits on which governments must depend for their revenues (Offe & Ronge, 1982). The general influence of Quinney, among many others, is readily apparent in this political economy approach to the interdependence of corporations and government under capitalism.

In their American Society of Criminology paper, Kramer and Michalowski (1990) went on to note that despite its ubiquity, the structural relations between corporate and governmental organizations had been relatively peripheral to the study of corporate crime. Instead, two nearly independent bodies of research had developed. Theory and research in the area of corporate crime had concentrated primarily on organizational deviance within private business corporations. Paralleling that work but seldom intersecting with it, others had examined crimes and malfeasance by governments, what Chambliss (1989) had called "state-organized crime." Kramer and Michalowski suggested that many forms of organizational deviance are generated at the interstices of corporations and government. They used the term *state-corporate crime* to denote these forms of organizational deviance, and offered this revised definition of the concept (p. 4):

> State-corporate crimes are illegal or socially injurious actions that occur when one or more institutions of political governance pursue a goal in direct cooperation with one or more institutions of economic production and distribution.

Kramer and Michalowski (1990) pointed out that this definition can be applied to illegal or socially injurious actions in societies ranging from private production systems to centrally planned political economies. Their focus in this paper, however, was on state-corporate crimes within the private production system of U.S. capitalism. State-corporate crimes within a capitalist economy involve the active participation of two or more organizations, at least one of which is in the civil sector and one of which is in the state sector. Thus, within a capitalist economy, state-corporate crimes are the harmful consequences of deviant interorganizational relationships between business and government.

State-Initiated and State-Facilitated Corporate Crime

The deviant interorganizational relationships that serve as the basis for state-corporate crime can take several forms. Kramer's (1992) analysis of the space shuttle Challenger explosion and Kauzlarich and Kramer's (1993) study of the relationship between the U.S. government and weapons manufacturers in the nuclear weapons production process both emphasize the central and direct role of the state in initiating a cooperative activity involving both government and business that led to a deviant outcome. Aulette and Michalowski's (1993) examination of the fire at the Imperial Food Products chicken processing plant in Hamlet, North Carolina, suggested a different kind of relationship, one where government omissions permit corporations to pursue illegal and potentially harmful courses of action that, in a general way, facilitate the fulfillment of certain state policies. Thus, Aulette and Michalowski (1993) suggested the following modification of the definition of state-corporate crime:

> State-corporate crimes are illegal or socially injurious actions that result from a mutually reinforcing interaction between (1) policies and/or practices in pursuit of the goals of one or more institutions of political governance and (2) policies and/or practices in pursuit of the goals of one or more institutions of economic production and distribution. (p. 175)

Building on Aulette and Michalowski's (1993) work, Kramer and Michalowski (1993) asserted that state-corporate crime can take two distinct forms. One is state-initiated corporate crime and the other is state-facilitated corporate crime. State-initiated corporate crime (such as the Challenger explosion) occurs when corporations, employed by the government, engage in organizational deviance at the direction of, or with the tacit approval of, the government. State-facilitated corporate crime (such as the Imperial Food Products fire in Hamlet) occurs when government regulatory institutions fail to restrain deviant business activities, either because of direct collusion between business and government or because they adhere to shared goals whose attainment would be hampered by aggressive regulation.

As a sensitizing concept, the term *state-corporate crime* has three useful characteristics. First, it directs attention toward the way in which deviant organizational outcomes are not discreet acts but rather the product of the relationships between different social institutions. Second, by focusing on the relational character of the state (Wonders & Solop, 1993), the concept of state-corporate crime foregrounds the ways in which horizontal relationships between economic and political institutions contain powerful potentials for the production of socially injurious actions. This relational approach provides a more nuanced understanding of the processes leading to deviant organizational outcomes than approaches that treat either businesses or governments as closed systems. Third, the relational character of state-corporate crime also directs us to consider the vertical relationships between different levels of organizational action: the individual, the institutional, and the political-economic. This point leads toward the development of a theory of state-corporate crime.

Toward the Development of a Theory of State-Corporate Crime

In addition to presenting an important revision of the concept of state corporate crime, the Kramer and Michalowski (1990) American Society of Criminology paper also introduced an integrated theoretical framework that can be used to analyze organizational offenses like state-corporate crimes. They noted that at that time there were three major theoretical approaches to the study of corporate crime, and each corresponded to a different level of social action. The first was differential association theory, as developed by Sutherland (1940, 1949/1961). The second was based on organizational theory, which argued that organizations could be criminogenic either due to the performance emphasis on goals (Finney & Lesieur, 1982; Gross, 1978; Kramer, 1982) or as a result of defective standard operating procedures (Hopkins, 1978). This organizational approach would eventually be merged with an anomie perspective (Passas, 1990; Vaughan, 1982, 1983, 1997) on corporate crime. The third approach located the criminogenic forces in the wider political economic structure of capitalism (Barnett, 1981; Michalowski, 1985; Quinney, 1977; Young, 1981). Differential association addressed the individual level of action; organizational theory focused on specific institutional factors promoting or retarding corporate crime; and political-economic or radical approaches examined the way broad, preexisting societal characteristics interact with the individual and organizational levels of action.

Although the differential association, organizational, and political economic perspectives represented divergent approaches to explaining corporate and government crime, Kramer and Michalowski (1990) argued that they can be brought together into an integrated theoretical framework. The structure, dynamics, and cultural meanings associated with the political economic arrangements of any particular society will shape the goals and means of economic and political organizations, as well as the constraints they face. The organizational level of analysis links the internal structure of specific economic or political units with the external political-economic environment on one hand, and with the way in which the work-related thoughts and actions of the individuals who occupy positions in those units are conditioned by the requirements of the positions they hold and the procedures of the organization on the other hand. Differential association, by focusing on the social relations that give meaning to individual experience, directs us to examine the symbolic reality derived from social interaction within bounded organizational niches.

Table 4.1, created by Kramer and Michalowski (1990) and revised by Kauzlarich and Kramer (1998), presents an analytic framework for this integrated theory of organizational deviance. This framework links the three levels of analysis discussed above with three catalysts for action. These catalysts are (a) motivation or performance pressure, (b) opportunity structure, and (c) the operationality of control. This framework is designed to indicate the key factors that will contribute to or restrain organizational deviance at each intersection of a catalyst for action and a level of analysis.

This theoretical framework is based on the proposition that criminal or deviant behavior at the organizational level results from a coincidence of pressure for goal attainment, availability and perceived attractiveness of illegitimate means, and an absence of effective social control. The first catalyst for action is the emphasis on goal attainment. Political and economic structures, organizations, and individuals may place greater or lesser emphasis on the attainment of rationalized goals as the engine for social action. Thus, a highly goal-oriented individual, working in an organization that evaluates performance strictly on goal attainment by its workers in a society whose cultural and institutional framework emphasizes goal attainment above all else, will be more susceptible to pursuing deviant organizational strategies than if one or more of these conditions is absent.

The second catalyst for action suggests that organizational deviance is more likely in a society where legitimate means are scarce relative to goals. The likelihood of deviance increases for those organizations or organizational subunits where the allocation of means by the internal structure is inadequate relative to the organization's goals, increasing the likelihood that individuals will perceive themselves to be blocked from access to legitimate means and will subsequently seek deviant alternative routes.

Finally, the operationality of social control at all three levels will serve as both an important restraint on organizational deviance and a critical element in constructing symbolic frameworks that will operate at the societal, organizational, and personal levels as time passes. Thus, societies with high operationality of social control are more likely to produce organizations with strong corporate cultures favoring compliance with laws and regulations. Individuals who function in these organizations in such a society will be more likely to develop forms of personal morality that would mitigate against engaging in organizational deviance.

Table 4.1 An Integrated Theoretical Model of State-Corporate Crime

	Catalyst for Action		
Level of Analysis	*Motivation*	*Opportunity Structure*	*Operationality of Control*
Institutional environment (history, political economy, culture)	Culture of competition Economic pressure Organizational goals Performance emphasis	Availability of legal means Obstacles & constraints Blocked goals/strain Availability of illegal means Access to resources	International reactions Political pressure Legal sanctions Media scrutiny Public opinion Social movements
Organizational (structure and process)	Corporate culture Operative goals Subunit goals Managerial pressure	Instrumental rationality Internal constraints Defective SOPs Creation of illegal means Role specialization Task segregation Computer, telecommunication and networking technologies Normalization of deviance	Culture of compliance Subcultures of resistance Codes of conduct Reward structure Safety & quality control procedures Communication processes
Interaction (face-to-face interaction, individual action)	Socialization Social meaning Individual goals Competitive individualism Material success emphasis	Definitions of situation Perceptions of availability & attractiveness of illegal means	Personal morality Rationalizations & techniques of neutralization Separation from consequences Obedience to authority Group think Diffusion of responsibility

Source: From *Crimes of the American Nuclear State: At Home and Abroad*, by David Kauzlarich and Ronald C. Kramer. Copyright 1998 by David Kauzlarich and Ronald C. Kramer. Reprinted with the permission of Northeastern University Press.
NOTE: SOPs = standard operating procedures.

By its very nature, state-corporate crime directs us to examine the linkages-between levels of analysis and catalysts for action. When the topic is profit-oriented violations of law by some business, it is possible, although not necessarily sufficient, to treat the crime as organizationally self-contained. Injurious social actions that result from concerted actions by organizations operating in different social spheres (e.g., production vs. governance), however, require that we must expand the frame of analysis, and that is what this theoretical framework attempts to do.

Since the concept and theory of state-corporate crime has been created, it has had a fair amount of influence in the field of criminology and the subfield of organizational deviance. The concept is discussed in a number of popular criminology textbooks (Barkan, 2006; Barlow & Kauzlarich, 2002; Siegel, 2001) and in several textbooks on white-collar, government, and corporate crime (Friedrichs, 2007; Simon, 1999). Published articles on the topic have been reprinted in a number of anthologies on white-collar, government, and corporate crime (Friedrichs, 1998; Geis, Meier, & Salinger, 1995; Potter, 2002; Shover & Wright, 2001;Tunnell, 1993). Several new handbooks and encyclopedias on white-collar and corporate crime contain entries on state-corporate crime (Pontell and Geis, 2007; Gerber and Jensen, 2007). But most important, the origin and development of the concept and theory of state-corporate crime has resulted in the publication of a number of important case studies. Some of the original research on the topic will be briefly reviewed in the following section.

Research on State-Corporate Crime

Kramer published the first case study of state-corporate crime in Kip Schlegel and David Weisburd's 1992 anthology *White-Collar Crime Reconsidered* (a book that grew out of the 1990 Sutherland Conference on White Collar Crime at Indiana University). At the time, most people viewed the Challenger disaster simply as an accident. In his paper, however, Kramer explained how state and corporate actors (NASA and Morton Thiokol) interacted with one another to produce risky decision-making processes and unsafe actions that resulted in the death of six astronauts and school teacher Christa McAuliffe.

Although the technical cause of the explosion was the failure of the O-ring seal in a field joint of a solid rocket booster, larger structural and organizational factors shaped the decision making in such a way as to make the disaster more probable (for a later and more comprehensive analysis of the Challenger disaster, see Vaughan, 1996). Kramer's case study illustrated the usefulness of a multidimensional empirical analysis, as the case is best understood at points where institutional and organizational forces conjoin with cultural and definitional processes to produce conditions favorable to organizational crime. This interest in the interaction effects of historical, political, and contextual factors is also found in the second published case study of state-corporate crime, authored by Kauzlarich and Kramer (1993).

The Department of Energy (DOE) and the Atomic Energy Commission produced nuclear and atomic weapons for fifty years by contracting with private firms, mostly large, multinational corporations like Westinghouse, DuPont, General Electric, and Martin Marietta. These corporations were charged with the day-to-day manufacture and production of the weapons. The DOE owned the production equipment, but its real activities involved consulting and supervisory roles over various technical aspects of the weapons building process. The DOE also made sure that production quotas were being met.

Kauzlarich and Kramer (1993) showed how this institutional arrangement, guided by cold war cultural beliefs and structural forces both propelled and sustained by the desire for continued American capitalist expansion, resulted in massive environmental injury. For example, in 1986 the Savannah facility generated more than 200,000 gallons of waste each day, and the Hanford plant in Washington state has dumped more than 200 billion gallons of radioactive and hazardous wastes since its inception in 1942 (Steele, 1989). The contamination wrought by nuclear weapons production over the decades is so severe that in the 1990s, estimates of getting the complex into compliance with applicable environmental laws have approached $400 billion (Congressional Budget Office, 1994).

Both the Kramer, and Kauzlarich and Kramer papers examined instances of state-initiated, state-corporate crime, as the state in both cases was consciously and explicitly involved in acts of crime commission. The next two published case studies of state-corporate crime focused on state-facilitated crimes.

Like the previously reviewed case studies, Aulette and Michalowski (1993) examined another disastrous conjoining of state and corporate interests. On September 3, 1991, an explosion and fire at the Imperial Food Products chicken processing plant in Hamlet, North Carolina, killed 25 workers and injured another 56. The technical cause of the fire was the rupture of a hydraulic line near a deep fryer that resulted in a fireball that quickly swept through the chicken processing plant. Why did so many people die and become injured by the fire? Most immediate, it was because the company routinely locked several of its fire doors, effectively sealing off many potential exits from the flames and smoke. The company later said that it had locked the fire doors to prevent employee theft of chicken and to keep flies out of the factory. But much more than these physically proximate causes and the larger drive for capital accumulation, the deaths and injuries were a product of a series of local, state, and federal crimes of omission that can be directly tied to the fate of the workers at the plant. For example, the state of North Carolina refused to support the Occupational Safety and Health Administration (OSHA) endeavors that would have made places like Imperial Foods safer for workers, even doing so little that it actually returned nearly a half a million dollars in unspent OSHA money to the federal government just prior to the fire. Also, a U.S. Department of Agriculture (USDA) inspector admitted that he knew of the company's practice of locking doors (potential fire escapes) but thought that he had no authority to do anything about it. Furthering the tragic irony, another USDA inspector actually approved of the locking of doors because he thought that it would prevent flies from contaminating the chicken inside the plant. In these ways and others (e.g., the failure of local, regional, and federal polity and assorted regulatory bodies), the worker deaths were facilitated by state inaction and negligence.

State-facilitated, state-corporate crimes like those in Hamlet involve elements of both crime commission and omission, and as such are likely to be one of the least recognizable forms of state involvement in crime. Yet injury that is tacitly allowed or mildly encouraged by the state fills the world with as much injury and suffering as those that are explicitly triggered by conspiring corporate and governmental elites. This observation inspired Matthews and Kauzlarich (2000) to analyze another catastrophic event as a state-facilitated, state-corporate crime.

On May 11, 1996, ValuJet Flight 592 crashed in the Florida Everglades, killing all 105 passengers and 5 crew members. The technical cause of the crash was a fire that erupted after one or more oxygen generators exploded in a cargo compartment. Governmental investigations have indicated that ValuJet and Sabre Tech (an airline maintenance company) failed to comply with a host of regulations concerning the presentation, storage, and transportation of hazardous materials by air. More generally, however, the Federal Aviation Administration (FAA) has been found to be negligent in its oversight of airlines by not adequately monitoring the general safety of commercial aircrafts as well as its refusal to institute safeguards and guidelines that would have protected passengers and crews from crashes like that of Flight 592.

Following the lead of the earlier studies reviewed, Matthews and Kauzlarich's (2000) case study of the disaster highlighted the broader structural policies that contributed to the crash (deregulation and unbridled capital accumulation) but also addressed the very specific items marginalized or overlooked by the FAA that can be directly linked to the deaths of those on ValuJet Flight 592. These include ignoring two clear recommendations by the National Transportation Safety Board (NTSB) to (a) place smoke detectors in cargo holds exactly like the area in which the fire started on Flight 592, and (b) reclassify cargo holds so that they would contain a fire and not spread to the rest of the plane. Had the FAA followed these recommendations, the probability that Flight 592 would have landed safely would have been tremendously increased. Additionally, officials in the FAA also ignored several damning reports about the low quality and maintenance of ValuJet planes not only from other agencies such as the U.S. Department of Defense but also by FAA field inspectors.

In sum, the four published case studies of state-corporate crime show how state and corporate interests can join to produce profound social and personal injury and death. Sometimes, as with state-initiated, state-corporate crime, the state is actively and explicitly involved in crime commission. Other times, the state is complicit because it or one of its agencies has failed to protect people vulnerable to potentially harmful organizational practices. More research has been carried out on the topic of state-corporate crime since this article first appeared in *Crime & Delinquency* in 2002. This additional research, along with the 1990 Kramer and Michalowski ASC paper and the four case studies described above, have been gathered together and published in an anthology edited by

Michalowski and Kramer (2006). The new case studies focus on topics such as: globalization, state-corporate crime and women; corporate facilitated state crime in Nazi Germany; Bridgestone-Firestone tires, Ford Explorers and the National Highway Traffic Administration; the Exxon Valdez oil spill; the violation of American Indian treaty rights; Enron and economic democracy; the 2003 U.S. invasion of Iraq; and Halliburton's role in Iraq. And more research continues to be done on state-corporate crime.

Conclusion

The concept and theory of state-corporate owes a heavy intellectual debt to the kind of theorizing and research conducted by Richard Quinney. To conclude this article, we shall revisit three major themes associated with his work that are found in the original case studies and theory of state-corporate crime.

First, work on state-corporate crime has been largely inspired by Quinney's vision of a criminology that not only takes the crimes of powerful individuals seriously but also harmful organizational and institutional practices that result from economic and political stratification in advanced capitalist societies. Institutional and organizational arrangements reflecting economic inequality can and do produce criminogenic patterns and practices, even when they are tacit or latent results of normative economic and political processes. In the cases reviewed here, it is also noteworthy that the major regulatory/social control bodies were inadequate because they were either guided by elites or working directly or indirectly for elite interests. The theory of state-corporate crime suggests that formal social control is but one, and perhaps the least effective, way to control organizational crime and deviance. Real control must grow from social movements, grass-root activities, a truly aggressive and inquisitive media, and most important, open and democratic participation in the political process. Furthermore, the tragedies reviewed here were made more likely by the lethal mix of apathy, disinformation, secrecy, and a reliance on elite regulation of elites.

Second, the case studies and theory reflect the precept that the intersection of history and political economy is a starting point for the scholarly investigation of crime, not simply an intervening, mediating, or exogenous factor or variable. Indeed, the various goals of the offending organizations are nested in particular historical contexts and have their roots in the drive for capital accumulation, capital facilitation, political legitimacy, and/or hegemony. Cultural definitions favorable to capitalism along with a conspicuous ambivalence displayed by elites for the safety of workers, consumers, and the natural environment also provided fertile grounds for the crimes. To wit: deregulation in the ValuJet case, political expediency in the Challenger disaster, imperialism in the nuclear weapons production case, and incredibly high levels of anti-worker and pro-business interests in the Imperial Food case. Of course, other levels of analysis and catalysts for action must also be examined as proximate causes of organizational misconduct, but always within the nexus of a multidimensional analytical framework.

Finally, whereas each of the original papers on state-corporate crime made an academic contribution to the study of elite crime and deviance, the empirical, theoretical, and substantive advances were rooted in and imbued with the spirit of humanism, a quality found throughout Quinney's work during the years. This humanist spirit prompts fundamental questions such as, How and why are peace and harmony compromised by the interests of state legitimacy and the drive for corporate profit? and, How and why are the human rights of others disrespected and marginalized because of political expediency and the banality of bureaucratic organization? These kinds of questions will continue to drive further research and theorizing on state-corporate crime. And state-corporate crime researchers will always be able to look, as we have, to the body of work produced by Richard Quinney for guidance and inspiration.

References

Aulette, J.R., & Michalowski, R. (1993). Fire in Hamlet: A case study of a state-corporate crime. In K. D. Tunnell (Ed.), *Political crime in contemporary America: A critical approach* (pp. 171-206). New York: Garland.

Bannister, R. C. (1987). *Sociology and scientism: The American quest for objectivity, 1880-1940.* Chapel Hill: University of North Carolina Press.

Barkan, S. (2006). *Criminology: A sociological understanding* (Third ed.). Upper Saddle River, NJ: Prentice Hall.

Barlow, H. D., & Kauzlarich, D. (2002). *Introduction to criminology* (8th ed.). Upper Saddle River, NJ: Prentice Hall.

Barnett, H. (1981). Corporate capitalism, corporate crime. *Crime & Delinquency*, *27*, 4-23.

Chambliss, W. (1989). State-organized crime. *Criminology*, *27*, 183-208.

Clinard, M., & Quinney, R. (1973). *Criminal behavior systems: A typology* (2nd ed.). New York: Holt, Rinehart and Winston.

Clinard, M., & Yeager, P. (1980). *Corporate crime.* New York: Free Press.

Congressional Budget Office. (1994). *Cleaning up the DOE's nuclear weapons complex.* Washington, DC: Author.

Ermann, M. D., & Lundman, R. J. (1978). *Corporate and governmental deviance: Problems of organizational behavior in contemporary society.* New York: Oxford University Press.

Finney, H. C., & Lesieur, H. R. (1982). A contingency theory of organizational crime. *Research in the Sociology of Organizations*, *1*, 255-299.

Friedrichs, D. O. (2007). *Trusted criminals: White collar crime in contemporary society.* Third edition. Belmont, CA: Wadsworth.

Friedrichs, D. O. (Ed.). (1998). *State crime. Volume I: Defining, delineating and explaining state crime.* Aldershot, UK: Ashgate.

Geis, G., Meier, R. F., & Salinger, L. M. (Eds.). (1995). *White-collar crime: Classic and contemporary views* (3rd ed.). New York: Free Press.

Gerber, J. & Jensen, E.L. (Eds.) (2007). Encyclopedia of white-collar crime. Westport, CT: Greenwood Press.

Gross, E. (1978).Organizational crime: A theoretical perspective. In N. Denzin (Ed.), *Studies in symbolic interaction* (pp. 55-85). Greenwich, CT: JAI.

Habermas, J. (1973). *Legitimation crisis.* Boston: Beacon.

Hopkins, A. (1978). The anatomy of corporate crime. In P. R. Wilson & J. Braithwaite (Eds.), *Two faces of deviance: Crimes of the powerless and powerful* (pp. 214-229). Brisbane, Australia: University of Queensland Press.

Kauzlarich, D., & Kramer, R. C. (1993). State-corporate crime in the US nuclear weapons production complex. *Journal of Human Justice*, *5*(1), 4-28.

Kauzlarich, D., & Kramer, R. C. (1998). *Crimes of the American nuclear state: At home and abroad.* Boston: Northeastern University Press.

Kramer, R. C. (1982). Corporate crime: An organizational perspective. In P. Wickman & T. Daily (Eds.), *White collar and economic crime* (pp. 75-94). Lexington, KY: Lexington Books.

Kramer, R. C. (1990a, March). *State-corporate crime.* Paper presented at the North Central Sociological Association and the Southern Sociological Association, Louisville, KY.

Kramer, R. C. (1990b, May). *State-corporate crime: A case study of the space shuttle Challenger explosion.* Paper presented at the Edwin Sutherland Conference on White Collar Crime: 50 Years of Research and Beyond, Indiana University.

Kramer, R. C. (1990c, August). *The concept of state-corporate crime.* Paper presented at the Society for the Study of Social Problems, Washington, DC.

Kramer, R. C. (1992). The space shuttle Challenger explosion: A case study of state-corporate crime. In K. Schlegel & D. Weisburd (Eds.), *White collar crime reconsidered* (pp. 212-241). Boston: Northeastern University Press.

Kramer, R. ,& Michalowski, R. (1990, November). *Toward an integrated theory of state-corporate crime.* Paper presented at the American Society of Criminology, Baltimore, MD.

Kramer, R. C., & Michalowski, R. J. (1993). *State-corporate crime: Case studies in organizational deviance.* Unpublished manuscript.

Lanier, M. M., & Henry, S. (1998). *Essential criminology.* Boulder, CO: Westview.

Matthews, R. A., & Kauzlarich, D. (2000). The crash of ValuJet Flight 592: A case study in state-corporate crime. *Sociological Focus, 3*(3), 281-298.

Michalowski, R. J. (1985). *Order, law and crime.* New York: Random House.

Michalowski, R. J. (1998). Radical criminology: The history of an intellectual movement. *Critical Criminology, 1*(1), 1-15.

Michalowski, R. J., & Kramer, R. C. (1987). The space between laws: The problem of corporate crime in a transnational context. *Social Problems, 34,* 34-53.

Michalowski, R. J., & Kramer, R.C. (2006). State-Corporate crime: Wrongdoing at the intersection of business and government. New Brunswick, N.J: Rutgers University Press.

Offe, C., & Ronge, V. (1982). Theses on the theory of the state. In A. Giddens & D. Held (Eds.), *Classes, power and conflict* (pp. 249-256). Berkeley: University of California Press.

Passas, N. (1990). Anomie and corporate deviance. *Contemporary Crises, 14,* 157-178.

Pontell, H. and Geis, G. (Eds.). (2007). International handbook of white-collar and corporate crime. New York: Springer.

Potter, G. (Ed.). (2002). Controversies in white-collar crime. Cincinnati: Anderson Publishing.

President's Commission on the Space Shuttle Challenger Accident. (1986). *Report of the Presidential Commission on the space shuttle Challenger accident* (Vols. 1-4).Washington, DC: U.S. Government Printing Office.

Quinney, R. (1963). Occupational structure and criminal behavior: Prescription violation by retail pharmacists. *Social Problems, 11,* 179-185.

Quinney, R. (1964). The study of white collar crime: Toward a reorientation in theory and research. *Journal of Criminal Law, Criminology and Police Science, 55,* 208-214.

Quinney, R. (1970). *The social reality of crime.* Boston: Little, Brown.

Quinney, R. (1974a). *Criminal justice in America: A critical understanding.* Boston: Little, Brown.

Quinney, R. (1974b). *Critique of legal order: Crime control in capitalist society.* Boston: Little, Brown.

Quinney, R. (1977). *Class, state and crime: On the theory and practice of criminal justice.* New York: Longman.

Sassen, S. (1998). *Globalization and its discontents: Essays on the new mobility of people and money.* New York: New Press.

Schlegel, K., & Weisburd, D. (Eds.). (1992). *White collar crime reconsidered.* Boston: Northeastern University Press.

Schrager, L. S., & Short, J. F. (1978). Toward a sociology of organizational crime. *Social Problems, 25,* 407-419.

Shover, N., & Wright, J. P. (Eds.). (2001). *Crimes of privilege: Readings in white-collar crime.* New York: Oxford.

Siegel, L.J. (2001). *Criminology: Theories, patterns, and typologies* (7th ed.). Belmont, CA: Wadsworth.

Simon, D. R. (1999). *Elite deviance* (6th ed.). Boston: Allyn & Bacon.

Sklar, M. J. (1988). *The corporate reconstruction of American capitalism: 1890-1916*. New York: Cambridge University Press.

Steele, K. D. (1989, October). Hanford: America's nuclear graveyard. *Bulletin of Atomic Scientists, 45*, 15-23.

Sutherland, E. H. (1940, February).White-collar criminality. *American Sociological Review, 5*, 1-12.

Sutherland, E. H. (1961). *White collar crime*. New York: Holt, Rinehart and Winston. (Original work published 1949).

Taylor, I. R., Walton, P., & Young, J. (1973). *The new criminology: For a social theory of deviance*. London: Routledge and Kegan Paul.

Tunnell, K. (Ed.). (1993). Political crime in contemporary America. New York: Garland.

Vaughan, D. (1982). Toward understanding unlawful organizational behavior. *Michigan Law Review, 80*, 1377-1402.

Vaughan, D. (1983). *Controlling unlawful organizational behavior: Social structure and corporate misconduct*. Chicago: University of Chicago Press.

Vaughan, D. (1996). *The Challenger launch decision: Risky technology, culture, and deviance at NASA*. Chicago: University of Chicago Press.

Vaughan, D. (1997). Anomie theory and organizations: Culture and the normalization of deviance at NASA. In N. Passas & R. Agnew (Eds.), *The future of anomie theory* (pp. 95-123). Boston: Northeastern University Press.

Wonders, N., & Solop, F. (1993).Understanding the emergence of law and public policy: Toward a relational model of the state. In W. Chambliss & M. Zatz (Eds.), *Making law* (pp. 204-225). Bloomington: Indiana University Press.

Young, T. R. (1981). Corporate crime: A critique of the Clinard report. *Contemporary Crisis, 5*, 323-336.

Chapter 5

On Moral Enterprises, Pragmatism, and Feminist Criminology

M. Joan McDermott

This article affirms Richard Quinney's claim that criminology is a moral enterprise. The author examines the intersection of pragmatism and feminism and its links to feminist criminology (undoing thc past and looking to the future, goal of liberation, epistemology and methods, and social responsibility). The article links these pragmatist-feminist themes to Richard Quinney's criminology.

Contributors to this volume were invited to write about how Richard Quinney's life work had influenced their own thoughts and then to write on a particular topic "in the spirit of Richard." What a remarkably thrilling, humbling, and easy but difficult assignment this turned out to be. Although my specific focus is feminist criminology, this article's goal is to affirm Richard Quinney's (2000) claim that "whatever else we do as criminologists, we are engaged in a moral enterprise" (p. 194).

In the first part of this article, I write about how Richard Quinney's thought has influenced my own thinking about crime and justice. Second, I will discuss the intersection of pragmatism and feminism and its links to feminist criminology. (It is "in the spirit of Richard" to venture beyond the boundaries of conventional criminology.) Feminist philosophers have engaged in a project "to join the resources of feminism and pragmatism, to think about contemporary issues" (Seigfried, 1993a, p. 1). A pragmatist-feminist analysis, which might seem oddly out of place, is most appropriate for this issue—forward looking yet backward looking, hopeful, and reflective of criminology as a moral enterprise. Throughout the article but mostly in the concluding section, I comment on the conceptual linkages between pragmatist-feminism and Richard Quinney's criminology.

Criminology as a Moral Enterprise

My own thinking about crime and justice is, like life, an ongoing project. My thoughts do not resemble a finely embroidered tapestry; rather, they are much like a patchwork quilt—bright new patches replace worn old ones, and the design itself always evolving. In *Bearing Witness to Crime and Social Justice* (2000), Richard Quinney returns to his home, a farm in the Midwest. During the span of his life's work thinking and writing about crime and justice, Quinney's writings become personal and autobiographical, and giving testament becomes a means of personal and social change. My own autobiographical reflections (and I agree with him that they take me back to who I am becoming) include growing up in a middle-class, traditional Roman Catholic household in western Pennsylvania. I was safe. I was good. The sisters at St. Malachy's grade school were highly effective at teaching lessons (wielding weapons) like "save the pagan babies," "ex-communication," and the "Legion of Decency." I experienced Catholic high school as well, and attended a Jesuit college and a Jesuit university for my BA and MA in sociology. (The distinction between Jesuit and Catholic is meaningful.) Add to the mix experiences with wonderfully exciting, wild, compassionate, intelligent, and funny feminists[1] in the early 1970s, and this fairly sums up my life prior to my Ph.D. work at SUNY Albany in the second half of the 1970s.

It was at Albany that I read *The Social Reality of Crime* (Quinney, 1970). In retrospect, this was a "wow" experience for me, just as reading Berger and Luckmann's (1966) *The Social Construction of Reality* had been a few years earlier. I have been greatly influenced by writings in the sociology of knowledge, particularly in understanding changing constructions of domestic violence and sexual assault, and have been guided also by conflict theory. Still, I confess that as a graduate student I was quintessentially a conformer, and although impressed by Quinney's work on the social construction of crime, I was more invested in completing my degree than in thinking about anything meaningful.

For most of the 1980s I worked in criminal justice policy analysis, program development, and data systems in a New York State agency. Here I developed a healthy respect for the many public servants who work hard to shape a better world (this was the Cuomo administration), and an equally healthy skepticism about criminal justice politics and the quality of official criminal justice data. During this decade I was almost completely out of touch with developments in theoretical criminology, although I continued to read feminist scholarship. It was not until 1991, when I came to Southern Illinois University at Carbondale, that I returned to theoretical criminology. *Criminology as Peacemaking* (Pepinsky & Quinney, 1991) affected me profoundly. I was then at a time and place to reflect on those larger issues in life, and this criminology touched my soul. Certainly Quinney's opening article in that volume was (and is still) amazingly on target for me: We cannot transform the world unless we are open to transforming ourselves, and this entails compassion and kindness. The many other articles in the collection impressed me, each in their own way. The feminist vision of justice described by M. Kay Harris (1991) struck a responsive chord in my thinking about justice, peacemaking, and feminism (McDermott, 1994).

These are prominent patches in my crime and justice quilt—social constructionism, conflict theory, and peacemaking. I hope this is clear in the discussion that follows. Criminology as a moral enterprise is not a patch; it is the quilt. Like Quinney, I believe that we are social beings, that the meaning in our lives is all about connections and sensitivities to others, that it is possible to change the world for the better, and that even small steps in personal transformation will help transform the world. These ideas have naturally influenced both what I teach and how I teach my criminology students.

Pragmatist-Feminism and Feminist Criminology

This article draws on contemporary examinations of John Dewey's classical pragmatism. My emphasis is on current, secondary sources, both pragmatist and feminist philosophers, because these scholars are developing new insights and interpretations. First I will provide a brief introduction to pragmatism and Dewey's place in North American philosophy. Then I will outline the shared conceptual foundations of feminists-pragmatists and feminist criminology.

Pragmatism

Pragmatism emerged in the United States in the late nineteenth century and was influential during the first quarter of the twentieth century. The most well-known classical pragmatists are Charles Sanders Peirce, William James, and John Dewey. Recent feminist analyses of classical pragmatism examine the works of Peirce, James, and Dewey, as well as other prominent Chicago School figures, such as George Herbert Mead. Also included are the writings of Charlotte Perkins Gilman and Jane Addams.[2] By the end of World War II, pragmatism had been supplanted by logical positivism and other analytical philosophy. The past two decades have shown a rebirth in philosophy of interest in pragmatism.

Fundamental to pragmatism is the tenet that, in general, the meaning of concepts lies in determining what consequences flow from them, and in particular, all knowledge consists of working hypotheses to be tested through experience (Dewey, 1981b). The contention that knowledge is experience based separated the classical pragmatists in the United States from traditions that contended that knowledge (truth) could be arrived at through interpretive processes of human reasoning apart from human action. For the pragmatists, no abstract, binding axioms existed. Knowledge is fallible and approximate. The classical pragmatists looked to the richness of human experience, including human interaction with others and with the environment, as the path toward knowledge and meaningful social change.[3]

The core tenets of pragmatism are found in the work of pragmatist philosopher, educator, and psychologist John Dewey (1859–1952). Early in his academic career, Dewey was influenced by the work of Charles Sanders Peirce and William James, as well as the psychology of G. Stanley Hall. After teaching philosophy in Michigan, Dewey moved to Chicago in 1894 and during the next decade worked in the same social and intellectual climate as George Herbert Mead and others at the University of Chicago, as well as Jane Addams of Hull House. The Progressive reform movement was a shared framework for pragmatists and early feminists. Later Dewey taught philosophy and was professor emeritus at Columbia University from 1904 to 1939 (Westbrook, 1991).

Dewey shared with Charles Sanders Peirce and William James the view that thought occurs because of disturbances of habits or problematic conditions or conflict and is directed to resolving the conflict (therefore instrumental in producing truths). For Dewey, as explained by K. Wallace (1993),

> All knowledge is contextual, historically and culturally located and motivated. The knower is the whole self, not a disembodied mind; she is a transactional self, an organism engaged in and with a world. Dewey developed the category of "intelligence" (rather than "reason") as the human capacity to think, infer, and solve problems. All thinking is experimental, and even logic has its origins in bodily experience. . . . Emotion is a mode of intelligence. (p. 68)

Dewey was critical of the centrality in philosophy of both epistemology as conceived by British philosophers and traditional, formal logic as the tool of philosophy. His insistence on the role of emotion and experience in knowledge, coupled with the view that knowledge is historically and culturally situated, makes Dewey's pragmatism attractive to feminist philosophers who have been likewise critical of "disembodied minds" and absolutism. In addition to his critique of epistemology, elements of Dewey's philosophy that are mirrored in contemporary feminist philosophy are his political and social theory, his aesthetics, and his philosophy of science.

Pragmatism and Feminist Criminology

Current analyses of classical pragmatism and feminist philosophy suggest numerous shared conceptual foundations, which in turn have direct links to feminist criminology. The following analysis outlines elements of the shared conceptual terrain and demonstrates the connections to feminist criminology. These elements, also found in Richard Quinney's work, include: a future orientation in scholarship, the goal of liberation, a critique of dominant epistemology and methods, and an emphasis on social responsibility and the integration of theory and practice.

Undoing the past and looking toward the future. Perhaps most directly relevant to feminist criminology is the view that both "feminists and pragmatists are curiously perched between the past and the future" (Rooney, 1993, p. 18). Pragmatism developed in the United States largely in response to social and scientific developments and to a perceived failure of the then dominant Western philosophy to deal with new possibilities. Dewey sought to reconstruct philosophy by undoing sharp dualisms. Seigfried (1993b) pointed to four such dualisms, which "turn out to be the same ones that feminists have also identified as oppressive":

> (a) the depreciation of doing and making and the over-evaluation of pure thinking and reflection, (b) the contempt for bodies and matter and praise of spirit and immateriality, (c) the sharp division of practice and theory, and (d) the inferiority of changing things and events and the superiority of a fixed reality. (pp. 112–113)

The parallel to the emergence and development of feminist philosophy (and criminology) is clear: "This effort to deal with various inherited dichotomies, dualisms, and disjunctions" (Rooney, 1993, p. 17).

Critical of past philosophies, pragmatism and feminism are open to new possibilities and the creative potential of individuals. Rooney's (1993) analysis concluded that feminists and pragmatists are

> essentially futurists in philosophy. Both believe that humanly motivated change matters. . . . Theories must be held to account for our historical and political locations in the world and must answer to the demands for constructive change. (p. 18)

By analogy, feminist criminology is located between the past and the future. During the past two decades, feminist criminology in the United States has matured into a recognized body of thought, as evidenced, for example, by introductory criminology textbooks that include feminist criminology among contemporary theoretical developments. There is no "one" feminist perspective in criminology, thus leading at times to wide differences among feminists in terms of what "ought to be done." Diverse feminist perspectives in criminology (i.e., liberal, Marxist, radical, socialist, psychoanalytic, existential, and postmodern) do have common threads, such as "accepting the view that women experience subordination on the basis of their sex and working toward the elimination of that subordination" (Gelsthorpe & Morris, 1990b, p. 2). The emphasis on change, on doing something to eliminate inequality is deserving of emphasis—it is the moral enterprise of which Quinney wrote. Daly (1995) provided a succinct summary of the stages of development in the feminist production of knowledge and pointed to directions for the future, including some of the themes raised in the discussion that follows.

Mainstream criminology unabashedly identifies scientific with the positivist theory of what science ought to be like. Dewey and feminist theorists offer an alternative. Feminist criminology is a contemporary outgrowth of a rich tradition and long history of humanist/critical criminology that includes labeling, conflict and radical, and peacemaking criminology. The humanist tradition emphasizes the study of human behavior within its historical and cultural contexts. Like pragmatists, feminists view knowledge in its context. Criminological knowledge (including concepts, theories, and methods) is a product of social processes and social structures, including hierarchical gender relations. Feminists view science in the Deweyan sense of developing knowledge through lived experiences, with a critical eye toward questions such as whose science, whose methods, and whose experiences. Uncovering and examining the gendered nature of knowledge has been a central activity of feminist criminology.

Feminists have made significant contributions to criminology in three ways. First, they have critiqued and evaluated traditional criminology's concepts, theories, and methods. Scholarship has identified ways in which women in crime and criminal justice have been overlooked, stereotyped, and misunderstood, and research on women as victims, offenders, and criminal justice practitioners has corrected many of these deficiencies. Second, feminists in criminology have contributed new concepts and unique methodological insights. Particularly in areas such as the definition of victimization, women's voices have drawn attention to wife battering, marital and date rape, sexual harassment, and a variety of other harms. Third, feminist theory emerged as an interdisciplinary effort (R.A. Wallace, 1989). Studies in criminology and criminal justice, which already reflect a tradition of multiple disciplinary perspectives, can benefit from the struggles and lessons learned by feminists engaged in interdisciplinary scholarship.

Current feminist criminology identifies numerous theoretical and methodological questions: Should feminists abandon criminology or hope to reform it? What will feminist theories look like? Is a paradigm shift in the offing? and Are there uniquely feminist methods of inquiry (Daly, 1995; Fonow & Cook, 1991; Gelsthorpe & Morris, 1990a; Harding, 1987; Reinharz, 1992; R. A. Wallace, 1989)?

This shared theme in feminist-pragmatism and feminist criminology—undoing the past and looking to the future—runs as well through Richard Quinney's lifetime of scholarship. In *The Social Reality of Crime* (1970), Quinney expressed his intention to provide a theoretical reorientation to criminology. Through his thoughtful applications of conflict theory, radical and peacemaking criminology, prophetic criticism, and Buddhism, Quinney continued to challenge existing systems of knowledge and social arrangements.

Sources of oppression and the goal of liberation. Dewey's concept of democracy was not a democratic government ruled by an elite of aristocrats or experts. Ordinary people in society have the intelligence to direct affairs of the government. This democracy depended on the success of education in teaching people to inquire, communicate, and cooperate. "For the democrat, the realization of the ethical ideal must be entrusted to the self-conscious, freely willed actions of every individual in society" (Westbrook, 1991, p. 42). While emphasizing the community, Dewey sought to preserve the diversity of cultures and values.

The diversity of women's experiences and life chances is more and more often the focus of feminist scholarship, although not all varieties of feminist thought are equal in the theoretical significance that they attach to sources of oppression other than sex/gender (i.e., race, class, religion, sexual orientation, disability, and age). The recognition among feminists that not all women are alike (White, middle class, heterosexual, etc.) directs attention to multiple sources of oppression and unites feminism with other struggles for equality and social justice, placing feminist thought (e.g., in criminology) in a broader humanist and critical context. On the other hand, admitting multiple realities can lead to a postmodern feminist rejection of positivism. In feminist criminology, this view is expressed by Carol Smart (1990), who suggested that feminist scholars abandon criminology.

The increasing popularity of pragmatism among feminists may be attributed, in part, to pragmatism's reaction against contemporary theories of deconstruction at the same time it offers a project of reconstruction. Alexander (1987) wrote that "between naive optimism and cynical despair are courage and commitment" (p. xxi). Charlene Haddock Seigfried (1993a), in a special issue of the *Hypatia* devoted to pragmatism and feminism, observed that "the more feminism continues revising its theories and practices to include those of other disadvantaged groups, the more it can rely on the principled pluralism of pragmatist theory, which does not advocate an artificial balancing of competing interest groups" (p. 2).

For the feminist-pragmatist, as feminist criminologists have shown (again, see Daly, 1995), "adding on" studies about particular groups—be they lesbians, women of color, or welfare mothers—is not enough. Nor is feminist criminology a search for experiences universal to women. The question for the pragmatist is how to create social unity from diversity and at the same time preserve diversity in unity. By analogy, the theoretical problems for feminists lie in capturing the multiple standpoints and developing an objective, coherent framework that will preserve and elucidate them. Because the knower, the researcher, is always situated by gender, race, and class, the challenge is objectivity. Gatens-Robinson (1991) showed how feminist epistemology can "reopen the question of how a genuinely pluralistic science can become a possibility" (p. 417). And so the feminist recognition of multiple standpoints draws us into ever-widening questions of validity as it underscores the fallibilism of science. This view is completely consistent with the Deweyan view of objectivity and knowledge.

Contemporary feminist criminologists are addressing the intersections of class, race, and gender and their meanings for social life and social action. Daly (1995) offered insight into the application of class-race-gender analysis in the social sciences and the difficulties that arise. Daly (1995) contended that a class-race-gender analysis may transform sociological theories of inequality, and added that "it is difficult to imagine today what new theories of inequality will be like, since our inherited ways of thinking can act to stymie the imagination" (p. 450). Class-race-gender analysis is found increasingly in feminist and other critical criminology, with the argument that for a critical criminology to advance, race, class, and gender can no longer be seen as presenting competing models (see Lynch, 1996; Messerschmidt, 1997). Class-race-gender analysis is entirely congruent with pragmatist-feminist thought, that is, the democratic ideal is more than the liberation of women.

Attention to the multiple sources of oppression and suffering and the goal of liberation are most evident in the scholarship of Richard Quinney but particularly in his writings on peacemaking. We cannot achieve peace unless we eliminate social inequalities. Quinney (2000) wrote,

> Positive peace demands that attention be given to all those things, most of them structured in society, that cause crime, that happen before crime occurs. Posi-

> tive peace exists when the sources of crime—including poverty, inequality, racism, and alienation—are not present. There can be no peace—no positive peace—without social justice. (p. 205)

For the purposes of the point here it does not matter that Quinney fails to specifically mention sexism as a source of inequality and suffering. He is clear in multiple points that all sources of social inequality must be eliminated and this is entirely consistent with current directions in feminist criminology and other critical theory.

Epistemology and methods. Dewey's philosophy of knowledge, science, and art, as revealed in current interpretations of his work, provides historical context for contemporary feminists (philosophers and criminologists) who have been critical of both gendered knowledge and gendered methods of inquiry. Most important are Dewey's views that: knowledge is historically and culturally situated, knowledge is created through human interaction with and experience of the world, science is art, and emotion has a role in the production of knowledge.

Pragmatism rejected the notion of universal, a priori principles derived solely through processes of pure human reasoning. Rather, all knowledge existed in the form of hypotheses subject to test. Ratner (1939) described Dewey's critique of epistemology:

> Philosophic pretensions to superhuman universality inevitably generate theories that degrade human life and experience to subhuman estate. While pretending jurisdiction over all time and existence, such theories actually function to support and justify the practices of intolerance and the barbarities of fanaticism. To *rid philosophy of pretentiousness* [italics added]—the prolific mother of evil—is the all-controlling, all-permeating purpose of Dewey's lifework. (p. 8)

Therefore, for Dewey, the method of science—testing hypotheses through experience in the world—becomes the tool of philosophy. Objectivity depends on a community of inquirers, extending creatively and assessing critically their methods in an ongoing process. This view of knowledge is different from the view espoused in most contemporary social science research texts and courses where it is argued that even scientists with different subjective views will achieve the same results (and approximate objectivity) if they use accepted techniques.

Dewey contended that both knowledge and the processes for producing knowledge are social constructs, products of social relations and social structures. For Dewey, because knowledge evolves with human experience and is shaped by historical and social processes, knowledge reflects existing arrangements. Dewey and other pragmatists directly attacked the supposed neutrality of science (Seigfried, 1993a). In feminist epistemology this is mirrored in the view that as a social construct, knowledge reflects power arrangements, who is involved in the shaping of ideas and under what conditions (Anderson, 1988). Feminist criminology has similarly evolved in part as a critique of "malestream" theories and methods. Thus, feminist criminologists have demonstrated that the vast bulk of twentieth century criminology is male-centered (can only explain male crime) but not gender-conscious (does not consider gender a critical variable) (Chesney-Lind & Shelden, 1992; Messerschmidt, 1993).

Dewey's view of the self in society and the social creation of knowledge is similar to that of George Herbert Mead. The problem for Dewey "was to come up with a model which could explain meaning as the development of symbolically mediated social interaction growing out of the conditional structures of biological activity" (Alexander, 1987, p. 122). Meaning is established through symbolic communication. Dewey also contended that learning a culture involves learning the roles we can take, which then defines who we are (Alexander, 1987). Likewise, discussions of the social self, particularly as mediated by social structures and actions, have been central to discussions of women in crime and criminal justice.

Closer to feminist scholarship in research methodology are Dewey's arguments that science is art (Dewey, 1925/1981a) and that emotion has a role in the creation of knowledge (Gatens-Robinson, 1991). According to Westbrook (1991), Dewey was "anxious to establish the claim that 'thinking is preeminently an art' and thereby to call into question rigid distinctions between art and science" (p. 339). Dewey was opposed to a method that required "passionless imperturbability, absolute detachment, complete subjection to a ready-made and finished reality" and that eliminated "the reality of affection, and the gallantry of adventure, the genuineness of the incomplete, the tentative" (quoted in Upin, 1993, p. 45).

For Dewey, emotion arose naturally in human experience. Alexander (1987) wrote that

> emotion is properly considered a phase of the ongoing situation, and to the extent that experience is dramatic, intelligent, and informed, it will also have a depth of emotion to it and be expressive. . . . The integrated experience, which Dewey sees exemplified in the aesthetic, will be alive with mind and feeling thoroughly interwoven. (p. 139)

Likewise, feminist scholars have argued that to understand experience of the social world it is necessary to abandon the artificial dichotomy between thinking and feeling, reason and emotion (Anderson, 1988). Science, as art, is the human enterprise that draws on the full range of (interwoven) human capacities to solve problems.

Considerations of science as art and of emotion as a source of knowledge in the Deweyan sense may enable criminologists to go beyond debates over qualitative versus quantitative methods and beyond passionless inquiry. This is radical empiricism. Similar to Dewey's concept of intelligence (rather than reason), feminist criminology's concern is with the development of theory that arises out of experience. "Experience, then, is more than anecdote; it constitutes a starting point for scholarly analysis and critique" (Hudson, 1990, p. 121).

The focus on understanding derived from experience need not exclude quantitative research on gender. In an introduction to a special issue of the *Journal of Quantitative Criminology* dedicated to gender, crime, and justice, Candace Kruttschnitt and Rosemary Gartner (1993) argued forcefully for the use of quantitative methods. "All good researchers," they observed, "must grapple with the difficult question of how their methodology influences their findings" (p. 324). Thus, feminist criminologists use a wide array of data and data collection strategies. The emphasis on a multiplicity of methods has meant renewed interest in less frequently used methods of social research, such as oral histories and case studies (Reinharz, 1992). A distinguishing factor is feminist criminology's insistence that researchers do not view or collect data uncritically. Official crime data are products of a complex milieu that reflects differences by gender, race, class, and so forth. Original data collection efforts by feminist criminologists frequently reveal a commitment to letting research participants give voice to their experiences—without predetermining what those experiences might be and how they might be categorized for analysis. A related theme in feminist methodology is the attention given to establishing nonhierarchical relations between the researcher and the research participant (Fonow & Cook, 1991), and the practical moral and political issues that these relationships raise.

Although the multiple method approach should continue to characterize feminist research, there will still be profound differences among feminists in forms of inquiry. The feminist-pragmatist challenge is: (a) to develop methods that capture the full range of motivators of human behavior, including the rational, emotional, social, and biological; and (b) to develop methods that allow the researcher to use the full range of ways of "knowing," including emotions such as wonder, curiosity, and personal passion.

Acknowledgment of the power-knowledge link and criticism of dominant epistemology and method are clearly evident in the work of Richard Quinney, although he is perhaps more broadly concerned with how systems of power effect the social construction of the crime problem. In a 1984 address delivered on receiving the Edwin H. Sutherland Award from the American Society of Criminology, Quinney (2000) went beyond a critique of positivism in his discussion of criminology and the making of the crime problem:

> First "crime" is one of the predominant myths of our contemporary culture. . . . And, we as criminologists are an integral part of the myth. There are those who are the subjects of the myth: the public and the large part of the public that is defined as criminal at any time. There is the apparatus—the reifying structure—of the myth: the police, the courts, the prisons, and all the functionaries of these institutions. And, not least, are the storytellers: the newspaper reporters, the social critics, the preachers, and the criminologists. As high priests of the myth, we criminologists tell the story in detail and make it appropriate for the time and place. We all are part of the myth, whether we are conservative criminologists, liberal or radical criminologists, sociobiological criminologists or Marxist criminologists. . . . Second, thought of such kind necessarily leads us beyond the traditional boundaries of criminology. . . . What I am doing at the moment is asking other questions, but the asking is still about what it is to be human and how we can live a decent life in the world. (pp. 175–176)

Quinney's (2000) epistemology becomes the path of spiritual awareness to "envision a time and place when and where we could live by some other means and thereby have a different life" (p. 176).

Social responsibility and the integration of theory and practice. Two additional themes emerge from feminist analyses of John Dewey's pragmatism, an emphasis on social ethics and an integration of theory and practice. These themes are related. The commitment to improving society by empowering individuals—the democratic ideal—can only be achieved in the context of uniting knowledge of the social world with the way we live our lives. Seigfried (1993a) wrote,

> The first-generation pragmatists, like contemporary feminists, refused the false neutrality of the epistemological turn and argued that theory be joined to practice and that practice be held accountable to the values that make up life work living for all members of the varied communities that make up the larger social order. (p. 13)

Alexander (1987) explained that for Dewey, the term *democracy* referred not to a political institution but rather to a "creative-critical culture" (p. 272).

This means

> that culture must recognize itself as a creative project in which the need for critical self-reflection, reevaluation, and exploration of the possibilities of life are of utmost importance. *Such a culture must see itself problematically rather than ideologically, and yet it will be consciously dedicated to the ultimate of enriching life with its full aesthetic potential for meaning and value* [italics added]. (Alexander, 1987, p. 272)

To view culture critically and maintain a dedication to the improvement of the social world is central to feminism. As Dewey viewed knowledge in light of progressive liberation, feminist criminologists exhibit an orientation of social ethics, action, and empowerment. The function of science in feminist thought, as it was for Dewey, is "deeply moral and social, not merely cognitive" (Gatens-Robinson, 1991, p. 418). Like early pragmatism, feminist scholarship has committed itself to an action orientation in seeking to eliminate the subordination of women (and other powerless groups). Central to the action orientation is a belief that research can and should facilitate political and social change (Daly, 1995; Fonow & Cook, 1991; McDermott, 1992).

Feminist criminology implies a radical connection to other human beings, including research participants and audiences. The consequences of this connection have been discussed in detail elsewhere (Fonow & Cook, 1991; Gelsthorpe & Morris, 1990a; McDermott, 1992). Practical and ethical issues arise in nonhierarchical research. Where do I draw the line in terms of the participants' participation in defining the research question? Is empathy another form of manipulation?

For feminists, commitment to action is driven by ethical priorities: We are not autonomous; rather, we are radically connected to each other and obligated to sustain human relationships. In criminology and criminal justice, these feminist ethical priorities are shared by humanist and peacemaking criminologists. Pragmatism provides a theoretical foundation for an ethic of care that will include "not only ourselves and our intimate circle of family and friends but also those human beings who would appear to be unconnected to us" (Leffers, 1993, p. 65).

Commitment to social action raises exceedingly difficult questions, questions that are only now being documented in the works of feminist criminologists. Empowerment can be a messy goal. Largely poor, minority, and undereducated women in prison may be lining up for cosmetology classes at the same time their educated, middle-class sisters are arguing for courses in computers and data processing in women's prisons. In my own research locally, a domestic violence counselor says that she struggles with how counseling can "empower" women who choose to stay with their abusers. To say that these are issues of false consciousness is to gloss over the feminist goal of letting women give voice to their own experiences.

Connections

I see numerous connections among pragmatist-feminist philosophy, feminist criminology, and the criminology of Richard Quinney, particularly in reflections on the social self, the social construction of reality, thought as problem solving, experience as the basis of knowledge, the goal of knowledge as liberation, and a deep and abiding concern with social ethics and social responsibility. It is this latter theme—social ethics and social responsibility—that I have chosen to emphasize in the title of this article, and I return to this below.

Because I simply do not know enough about Zen Buddhism, what is not clear to me are the ways in which the pragmatist-feminist criminology I have outlined here depart from Richard Quinney's most recent (1990s and beyond) journey into theology and Buddhism. This is particularly the case with respect to the role of science in knowing. Pragmatist-feminists do not have a blind faith in science but in fact are skeptical of disembodied minds and traditional Western modes of thinking, and this is in keeping with Quinney's writing. Certainly a pragmatist-feminist criminology has the same starting point as Quinney (2000):

> It is not natural—it is unhealthy—for the academic intellectual (sociologist, criminologist) to continue strictly in the rational mode of speculative and dualistic thought as he or she matures, although this is the approved and rewarded form for the modern academic. To continue solely in the rational mode of thought is retrogressive for the maturing person, and for a discipline as well. (p. 182)

Additionally, pragmatist-feminist criminology is grounded in the experiential, in narrative, in knowledge as participatory and liberating.

Will feminism have a lasting influence in criminology? I think so. The issue will be whether, in addition to expanding our knowledge, feminist and other critical criminology will have an effect in transforming the larger discipline. Although the answer may lie in class-race-gender analyses and the increasing application of qualitative methods and sensitive quantification, transformation is difficult. And although elements of feminist criminology are entirely compatible with other strands of critical thought, as illustrated by the consistency with Richard Quinney's writings, feminists continue to have unique concerns and special emphases. To return to my autobiographical musings on Jesuits, it is always amazing to me when individuals can work zealously for social justice and yet remain uncritical of patriarchy.

A unique contribution of feminist criminology has been theory and research/social action in domestic and sexual violence. Violence against women is the one area in which I personally have difficulty thinking in terms of peacemaking criminology. This challenge is brought to the foreground as I listen to victims, victim advocates, offender treatment professionals, police, and prosecutors in a local project evaluating a coordinated community response to domestic violence. But as a matter of criminal justice policy, is there a nonviolent response to men who batter women? Does it matter to what we "do" with or for batterers that we think of them as victims? Does it matter that therapeutic models based on educating abusers about sexism do not appear to be effective?

I recently read an interview with Nancy Baker, a Buddhist-feminist philosopher (Rubenstein, Greeenstein, & Dzialo, 2001), and she showed me a different perspective on feminist issues. As I write this, I am still not sure what I think, but it is worthwhile to consider what she had to say on Buddhism and feminist issues and to ask if this has relevance for the problem of violence against women. In the interview, Baker was asked about anger over racism and sexism, and asked about how resistance happens when you are bearing witness. I think her answer is worth quoting at some length:

> What we need is . . . "bearing witness," or what in my sitting group, we call "compassionate allowing." In both there is a slowing down and a taking in of what's happening. Unless you can see clearly what's happening you can't really do anything about it. Any transformation of a situation requires this. . . . Bearing witness, like compassionate allowing, is a necessary step, but it is only a first step. It might sound like doing nothing, but again, that is not at all what is meant. Look at nonviolent resistance. It's a form of bearing witness. When I react, attention goes to me and is taken away from the perpetrator, whereas *not* reacting reveals the truth of the situation to others, including the perpetrator. If I am going to help other women and not just myself, the truth of oppression has to be seen for what it is by everyone. I need to invite the whole world to bear witness with me. (pp. 59–60)

Bearing witness is an approach to transforming reality. Others are invited to join the struggle against injustices, including all the "isms" and the violence they produce. This does not resolve for me the very practical matter of nonviolent responses to men who batter, but it does open a door: Listening to the multiple and conflicting narratives of victims, victim advocates, offender treatment professionals, police, and prosecutors is a small step in the direction of eliminating violence against women.

All of this takes me back to Quinney's, "Whatever else we do as criminologists, we are engaged in a moral enterprise."

Notes

1. Thank you Mary Ciddio, Mary Moore, and Jeanne Neff.

2. See Charlotte Haddock Seigfried (1996) for an excellent discussion of classical pragmatist feminists, particularly Addams and Gilman, and their contribution to philosophy.

3. Stuhr (1987, pp. 5–11) summarized the major themes of pragmatism: the rejection of modern philosophy, fallibilism, pluralism, radical empiricism, the continuity of science and philosophy, meliorism, and the centrality of community and the social.

References

Alexander, T.M. (1987). *John Dewey's theory of art, experience & nature: The horizons of feeling*. Albany: State University of New York Press.

Anderson, M. L. (1988). *Thinking about women: Sociological perspectives on sex and gender* (2nd ed.). New York: Macmillan.

Berger, P. L., & Luckmann, T. (1966). *The social construction of reality*. New York: Doubleday.

Chesney-Lind, M., & Shelden, R. G. (1992). *Girls, delinquency and juvenile justice*. Pacific Grove, CA: Brooks/Cole.

Daly, K. (1995). Looking back, looking forward: The promise of feminist transformation. In B.R. Price & J. J. Sokoloff (Eds.), *The criminal justice system and women* (2nd ed., pp. 433-457). New York: McGraw-Hill.

Dewey, J. (1981a). Experience, nature and art. In *John Dewey, The latter works*, 1925-1953,Vol. I, (pp. 266-294). Carbondale: Southern Illinois University Press. (Original work published 1925)

Dewey, J. (1981b). The experimental theory of knowledge. In J. J. McDermott (Ed.), *The philosophy of John Dewey* (pp. 175-192). Chicago: University of Chicago Press.

Fonow, M.M., & Cook, J.A. (Eds.). (1991). *Beyond methodology: Feminist scholarship as lived research*. Bloomington: Indiana University Press.

Gatens-Robinson, E. (1991). Dewey and the successor science project. *Transactions of the Charles S. Peirce Society*, *27*(4), 417-434.

Gelsthorpe, L., & Morris, A. (Eds.). (1990a). *Feminist perspectives in criminology*. Philadelphia: Open University Press.

Gelsthorpe, L., & Morris, A. (1990b). Introduction: Transforming and transgressing criminology. In L. Gelsthorpe & A. Morris (Eds.), *Feminist perspectives in criminology* (pp. 1-6). Philadelphia: Open University Press.

Harding, S. (Ed.). (1987). *Feminism & methodology*. Bloomington: Indiana University Press and Open University Press.

Harris, M.K. (1991). Moving into the new millennium: Toward a feminist vision of justice. In H.E. Pepinsky & R. Quinney (Eds.), *Criminology as peacemaking* (pp. 83-97). Bloomington: Indiana University Press.

Hudson, A. (1990). "Elusive subjects": Researching young women in trouble. In L. Gelsthorpe & A. Morris (Eds.), *Feminist perspectives in criminology* (pp. 115-123). Philadelphia: Open University Press.

Kruttschnitt, C., & Gartner, R. (1993). Introduction to the special issue on gender, crime, and criminal justice. *Journal of Quantitative Criminology*, *9*(4), 323-327.

Leffers, M. R. (1993). Pragmatists Jane Addams and John Dewey inform the ethic of care. *Hypatia*, *8*(2), 64-77.

Lynch, M. J. (1996). Assessing the state of radical criminology. In P. Cordella & L. Siegel (Eds.), *Readings in contemporary criminological theory* (pp. 294-304). Boston: Northeastern University Press.

McDermott, M. J. (1992). The personal is empirical: Feminism, research methods and criminal justice education. *Journal of Criminal Justice Education*, *3*(2), 237-250.

McDermott, M. J. (1994). Criminology as peacemaking, feminist ethics, and the victimization of women. *Women and Criminal Justice*, *5*(2), 21-44.

Messerschmidt, J.W. (1993). *Masculinities and crime*. Lanham, MD: Rowman and Littlefield.

Messerschmidt, J. W. (1997). *Crime as structured action*. Thousand Oaks, CA: Sage.

Pepinsky, H. E., & Quinney, R. (Eds.). (1991). *Criminology as peacemaking*. Bloomington: Indiana University Press.

Quinney, R. (1970). *The social reality of crime*. Boston: Little, Brown.

Quinney, R. (2000). *Bearing witness to crime and social justice*. Albany: State University of New York Press.

Ratner, J. (1939). *Intelligence in the modern world: John Dewey's philosophy*. New York: Random House.

Reinharz, S. (1992). *Feminist methods in social research*. New York: Oxford University Press.

Rooney, P. (1993). Feminist-pragmatist revisionings of reason, knowledge, and philosophy. *Hypatia*, *8*(2), 15-37.

Rubenstein, A., Greenstein, T., & Dzialo, C. (2001, Spring). Of samurai and sisterhood: A discussion with Nancy Baker on gender, dharma, and identity. *Tricycle: The Buddhist Review*, *10*(2), 58-63.

Seigfried, C. H. (1993a). Shared communities of interest: Feminism and pragmatism. *Hypatia*, *8*(2), 1-14.

Seigfried, C. H. (1993b). Validating women's experiences pragmatically. In J. J. Stuhr (Ed.), *Philosophy and the reconstruction of culture* (pp. 111-129). Albany: State University of New York Press.

Seigfried, C. H. (1996). *Pragmatism and feminism: Reweaving the social fabric*. Chicago: The University of Chicago Press.

Smart, C. (1990). Feminist approaches to criminology or postmodern woman meets atavistic man. In L. Gelsthorpe & A. Morris (Eds.), *Feminist perspectives in criminology* (pp. 70-84). Philadelphia: Open University Press.

Stuhr, J. J. (1987). *Classical American philosophy*. New York: Oxford University Press.

Upin, J. (1993). Charlotte Perkins Gilman: Instrumentalism beyond Dewey. *Hypatia*, *8*(2), 38-63.

Wallace, K. (1993). Reconstructing judgment: Emotion and moral judgment. *Hypatia*, *8*(3), 61-83.

Wallace, R. A. (1989). Introduction. In R. A. Wallace (Ed.), *Feminism and sociological theory* (pp. 7-22). Newbury Park, CA: Sage.

Westbrook, R. B. (1991). *John Dewey and American democracy*. Ithaca, NY: Cornell University Press.

Chapter 6

Exploring the Paradox of the (Un)reality of Richard Quinney's Criminology

Alan Mobley
Hal Pepinsky
Chuck Terry

A core tenet of Zen Buddhism is that life is full of paradox. This article explores the paradoxical reactions of criminologists to the work of Richard Quinney. Quinney, a renowned criminologist, is known among a majority of his colleagues as "important" yet "unreal." Meanwhile, some people who have undertaken journeys of what might be called self discovery, including the present authors (two of whom are ex-convicts turned criminologists), celebrate his work as the most real criminology around. The article explores this paradox.

Hal

It is a considerable honor to know Richard Quinney, to have used his *Social Reality of Crime* in 1971 (together, for balance, with the *President's Commission on Law Enforcement and Administration of Justice* report of 1967) as a text for the first criminology class I taught, to have grown through his work and through a personal friendship that also began in 1971, and to have occasion to consider what he has contributed to so many criminological and other lives, including mine.

The paradox of how Richard's work is received as real and yet unreal is profound. Some convict criminologists, like Alan and Chuck, who find Richard's work most real, most practical, most enlightening, and most valuable, identify as having belonged to the criminological underclass prisoners. Both have journeyed from the extremely marginalized social world and status of prisoner to the halls of academia. And due to what they discovered about themselves and the world during their years behind bars, they highly value Richard's work.

Meanwhile, it is a truism that criminologists are instruments of the state, a truism, by the way, that Richard was the first prominent post–World War II U.S. criminologist to affirm. The "modern" science of "empirical" criminology in the nineteenth century was founded on explaining differences between prisoners and the rest of us supposedly law-abiding folks. They were poor, and so on. Maybe they were born criminal. Maybe a father was missing from the home. A great teacher of mine, Les Wilkins, once wrote, "Kings and queens have subjects, researchers should not!" It is ironic that Chuck and Alan, who have both been primordial subjects of criminology, most embrace Richard's work as real, whereas among those whose work most accepts state definitions of crime, I daresay Richard is regarded as a well-known kook.

A Note on Method

Hal

Inspired by Richard Quinney's example, Alan, Chuck, and I have joined together to write a rather unorthodox contribution to this volume. We take turns in conversation, each of us writing in the first person. In so doing, we seek to affirm our individuality, even as we join together in celebrating a largely common significance of Richard's writing and friendship to our criminological lives.

In this tribute, Chuck writes about meeting Richard and hearing him present a Chinese Buddhist story of an ox herder at an American Society of Criminology (ASC) meeting. I sat in the front row beside Alan and Chuck at that session. Notwithstanding my longstanding admiration for Richard's work, I was struck by how enraptured Alan and Chuck were by what Richard presented. Before their doctoral study in criminal justice at the University of California at Irvine, Alan and Chuck had each spent long years in prison. They are among those identifying themselves as "convict criminologists." Even then, I found myself reflecting on a seeming paradox, that these two friends with so much real-world experience of crime and criminal justice would find so much meaning in work that others have dismissed as criminologically irrelevant.

I wrote a draft exploration of this paradox on my own. The guest editors of this issue of *Crime & Delinquency* suggested additions. I asked Chuck, who in turn asked Alan, for input.

Chuck and Alan saved me from the danger of speaking for others. That ASC session with them so stood out in my mind that I presumed all convict criminologists to be Quinney fans. That may or may not be true. What Chuck and Alan reminded me is that my inference came from them personally. Within the tradition of peacemaking theory it is entirely appropriate that they intervene in this article to speak for themselves, as I do only for myself. Their participation in this article, now a conversation among us three, is a profound contribution to the exploration I myself undertake here. And so we join together in authorship of this text.

This chapter contains no citations. We focus on Richard's work, which is amply cited in this issue. We ask readers to think through with us the implications of a rather obvious paradox pertaining to how Richard's work is variously received.

Convict Criminology: Act I

Alan

I became interested in Buddhism during my eighth year of incarceration. I was in personal crisis and Eastern thought provided a different way of seeing the world and my place in it. I became aware of the paradox of separation, its myth and reality. Buddhist cosmology holds that part of the nature of being human is for each of us to see the world in a unique way. Subjectivity in perception divides us utterly from one another. Perceiving oneself as a Self, an individual, isolates one from all that in non-Self. This separateness frames our worldview.

It was easy to feel separate in graduate school. I was grateful to be admitted at all, but I felt underutilized. For example, even with all of my practical experience I was never selected to assist for a prisons course. I recognized then that doctoral credentials gave the experts free reign to pursue their agendas. Heady stuff. In my reading I found an academic production process that was prolific in its creation of Others. For solace I turned to African American and postcolonial writers, people who were experts at being on the receiving end of stigma and objectification. I particularly enjoyed titles such as *The West and the Rest* and *The Empire Writes Back.* Within the criminology literature I discovered *Peacemaking Criminology.* It was the perfect antidote to books then current in the field, such as John DiIulio's *Governing Prisons* and *No Way Out: The Future of American Corrections.* Quinney and Pepinsky's *Peacemaking* inspired me to entertain the notion that giving voice to experience could alter the status quo. While working on a class assignment and fueled by frustration, I gave it a try:

> I have a problem. I go to this school where good, well-intentioned people are working to make the criminal justice system an efficient, effective, and more equitable social institution. They work hard, and their efforts are joined to the accumulated sweat and knowledge of many others, past and present. Over the years, scholars such as these have produced a mixed bag of approaches to solving society's crime dilemma. None, however, has yielded better than inconclusive results. The latest trend for cutting edge research is to abandon a measure of scientific detachment and talk right to the horse's mouth: to interact directly and respectfully with criminal justice professionals and learn first-hand of the day-to-day difficulties of operating a conflicted juridic bureaucracy. Relying on the highly vested vantage points of law officers is problematic, but that's not my problem. On principle I have no objection to academics mixing with practitioners. The two camps, in fact, have much to learn from one another. If what they purport to discuss is "organizational management" or "systems behavior" I totally see the point. Many researchers are trained to act as evaluation specialists and operations consultants. They can access the environment, inquire as to

> problems, investigate to determine if perceived problems are indeed real, and, if so, come up with ameliorative solutions. For their part, practitioners are experts at falsification. They know what won't work on the ground.
>
> The interesting thing for me is that when these very well intentioned scholars get together with their technically skilled, professional counterparts, the practitioners, well, the feeling of omnipotence is palpable. There is hardly a single aspect of the criminal justice dilemma that someone in that room doesn't know nearly everything about. Except how to stop people from committing crimes, of course. And that's my problem: If criminologists want to learn how to get people to cease and desist with their criminal activities, why don't they talk to some criminals? Conferring with practitioners, insofar as it gets researchers up and out of their armchairs, is clearly a step in the right direction. The difficult thing for typically insular scholars to recognize, however, is that in restricting their review to officials they are talking to the horse, but they are concentrating on the wrong end of the animal.

Every criminal is a criminologist. Each is a specialist in the manner, means, rationale, cause, and certainly the potential consequences of a certain order of crime/s. The person who is apprehended, sentenced, convicted, and incarcerated acquires an in-depth and extraordinarily vivid view of the criminal justice system. He, and it is usually a he, acquires substantial expertise across many dimensions of criminological discourse. Arguably an amateur, he lacks formal training in the cognate discipline. A possible indication of this amateurishness is his insistence on a positivist orientation. He can tell you where he committed his crime and why, and who talked him into it. If pressed, he can narrate an account of the entire criminal decision-making process. Given time, perhaps behind bars, he may provide a finely grained analysis of when and where he went astray: the family problems, neighborhood pressures, and personal shortcomings that brought him to his present state. Every person who becomes a prison inmate knows that he made mistakes, and that those mistakes finally caught up with him. And more than anyone else, he blames himself for his condition.

"The Logic of Commodities"

Hal

At the 1998 ASC meeting in D.C., former Quinney student Randy Sheldon, at the University of Nevada at Las Vegas, and his former student Bud Brown, at the University of Michigan at Flint, organized a tribute to Richard. Alan and Chuck were there. T-shirts were sold at the event. I wear mine with pride in warm weather when I introduce insights of Richard's into my classes. The back of the shirt lists his books, and the front contains this quote from his 1998 book, *For the Time Being*:

> Although we live in an historical era in which all aspects of everyday life are mediated by the logic of commodities, everyday life is the source of social

> change and transformation. Everyday life is, indeed, of consequence. The lived experience—shared with others—is our social reality. And it is the only reality we can know.

"The logic of commodities" is the key phrase in the first clause of this quote. Are we as criminologists a commodity? Are we forced to solicit state grants and sell our products to survive?

When I met Richard, he directed the graduate sociology program at New York University and had just been awarded a major National Institute of Mental Health (NIMH) grant for developing the doctoral program. Shortly thereafter, he resigned. He lived for several years in a rural commune. Thereafter, he lived off book royalties and had a free office at Brown University. He founded a criminological collective in Boston. Eminent criminologists like Steven Spitzer were nurtured there. Eventually he got a job teaching at Boston College, then returned to near his Wisconsin home, to DeKalb, Illinois, where he and Solveig live today.

To me, as I suppose to Alan and Chuck, Richard lives what he believes. He never believed that he should be a servant of the state. He bowed out.

I entered graduate school in 1968, 1 year after issuance of the crime commission report, 1 year after publication of Richard's first book, refreshing because it was among the few critical volumes around. It was the year of the passage of the Omnibus Crime Control Act, which gave a virtual monopoly on criminal justice research funds to the U.S. Justice Department. The School of Criminal Justice was just becoming the first Ph.D. program of its kind at Albany. I attended my first ASC meeting. Whereas attendance at ASC's annual meetings in the burgeoning crime control industry is now several thousand, that year it was 125. At that time, Richard was already a prominent resister against criminological commodification. His consistent integrity to personal independence is perhaps one of the implicit attractions he offers all of us, including criminologists who have been to prison.

Richard's *Social Reality of Crime* was so refreshing to me and others when it appeared in 1970. In so many ways that Richard carefully reviewed, crime and enforcement were politically arbitrary social constructions. Thanks to Richard, you could be a legitimate criminologist and believe that crime control as we know it is a massive exercise in prejudice and ignorance. He kept pursuing implications of his understanding of crime and his relationship to it. He did not take state definitions of crime at face value. Was he merely, therefore, a nihilist? He noticed one troublesome feature of prevailing definitions of crime and criminality. Those who had the greater power got to vilify subordinate classes hypocritically. Richard's dissertation had been on white-collar crime pharmacists' violations of law. He knew in his heart and experience, as do many of us, that those who define and enforce law are no less violent and exploitative than those they imprison. Although the Berkeley School of Criminology was closed in the early 1970s for being so Marxist, Richard legitimized U.S. reference to Marx and class in his next two volumes, *Critique of Legal Order* and *Class, State, and Crime*. By the early 1980s, I heard a report to a criminological body that Richard had become the most widely cited contemporary criminologist. I did not count citations myself, but I believe it.

Convict Criminology: Act II

Alan

The convict who stumbles onto the formal study of crime and society often gets a surprise. It is called the sociological perspective. In its more radical forms, it implies that he is still responsible for his crimes but that the responsibility is not his alone. Society, through intention or neglect, prepared a criminogenic stage on which he was encouraged, if not compelled, to act. Society abused and discriminated against him, filled his head with materialistic desires, and instilled an urge for power. Society, in its often indiscriminate cruelty, told him in no uncertain terms that he could be whatever he wanted to be. He soon discovered, however, that he could not. If he was going to get what he desired, what he deserved, whether money or power or freedom from worry, he would have to step outside the lines. He knew where the borders of legality lay, and he had a sense of the depths he would have to cross. The popular culture of consumption, that alluring damsel, led him to the water and bade him drink. He drank, but he didn't drink alone.

Chuck

A seldom understood framework for living, one that truly reduces harm in the world, is far removed from mainstream notions of social control, mechanically oriented criminological research, and critical analysis of the social structure. Except for those who have embraced the journey of getting in touch with the core of their being, Richard Quinney's radical solutions that promote peace, love, and compassion must seem unreal because what he is saying is so far removed from their realities.

Roughly three years into my last prison sentence, I inadvertently embarked on a path of self-discovery, one that continues to this day. To break the monotony of prison life, I decided to enroll in the then-available college classes. What resulted was a search for answers, a search for a "way out," a search for the truth about my identity and the meaning of life.

Two years passed, and the foundation of my worldview and self-concept had been shaken by what I had learned in school. I came across a book by Bo Lozoff called *We're All Doing Time: A Guide for Getting Free.* Written for prisoners but applicable to anyone, it teaches about the human spirit, karma (the law of how cause and effect operates in the universe), and how underneath all that we worship—whether it be our looks, our trinkets, our degrees, or our beliefs—we are all fundamentally the same. We are all caught within a cycle of fear and desire. If school rattled my foundation, Bo's book, and the effects of the efforts I made to practice what he suggested, opened windows into worlds I never knew existed.

Bo's teachings motivated me to continue seeking. Before long I was reading books by Stephen Levine, Krishnamurti, Ram Dass, Alan Watts, and other teachers of reality at it deepest levels. I practiced daily meditation that helps quiet the mind. I also became more adept at watching my thoughts and actions as they happened. In short, over time my awareness increased. As these actions became part of my daily life, my view toward others and myself continually changed. Less and less I felt the effects of the hate, rage, and anger that had grown within me since childhood. In their place came love, compassion, and empathy toward others—even those I previously despised.

Believing I was institutionalized, and thinking that school is like prison because both are institutions (and that I might therefore do as well in one as the other), I decided to continue my education after being paroled. Four years later in graduate school, I was exposed to a mostly mainstream overview of criminology. Although I had a great time just being there, the representations of "criminals" and explanations for crime and criminal justice that I was exposed to did not match with my experience. The real lives of the real people who are oppressed by the system were basically missing from the curriculum. And nowhere did I hear anybody talking about the process of self discovery that had not only helped transform my life but also, I believed, could potentially change the world.

Then one day somebody told me about a book called *Peacemaking Criminology*, edited by Hal and Richard. After reading Richard's chapter, "The Way of Peace, on Crime, Suffering, and Service," I felt awestruck and inspired. It left me with the idea (which I was struggling with) that perhaps there was a place for someone like me in this field. In that piece he talked about things like life being a spiritual journey, and that awareness of reality can only be attained by losing the conditioned ego and realizing the essence of our inner self. He explained how no amount of theorizing and rational thinking could teach us much about the truth—that in fact we should avoid the tenets of modern science in a new criminology, which should be inherently nonviolent. Unlike anything I had ever heard in any criminologically oriented, academic environment, he wrote how healing the belief in separation from one another is necessary for suffering to end. The willingness to serve others, he said, along with having hearts filled with love, will help us know what has to be done and how it needs doing.

Unexpectedly, I was finding continuity in my life. What Bo Lozoff had introduced me to in C-block, Richard was extending in my academic world. Several of the authors I had read after reading Bo's book were cited in Richard's chapter. Of course, their messages were fundamentally the same. That is, the way to a better world will be found as each of us becomes more aware, more awake, more compassionate, more loving, and more connected with everyone and everything.

"Everyday Life is the Source of Social Change and Transformation"

Hal

More than twenty years ago, Richard had established himself as a criminological friend of the underclass. He was a hero of the criminological left. He was acceptable reading among criminologists generally. He gave voice to the widespread recognition among many of us criminologists who felt pushed to become servants of the state. He invited us to question how we should respond. He became a darling of conflict theorists on the criminological left who hoped for political revolution/overthrow of the state or nurturance of rebellion by class enemies of the state.

In the 1970s, Richard became a darling of emergent critical criminologists. I distinguish *critical* from *radical*. Richard was radical. He radically disappointed critical criminologists with his 1978 book, *Providence*.

To me, *critical* signifies recognition that something is wrong with the established order. *Radical* signifies a determination to get to the roots of the social problem. Richard's greatest contribution to my own thinking, and I surmise to others, is that in a violent world one has to understand one's own self and one's capacity to respond as fully as one recognizes what Richard calls "suffering" and others call "injustice." To get to the roots of this issue, one needs to balance an awareness of social, political inequities with one's understanding of how one, oneself, bears responsibility. Conscious social change is fundamentally a matter of growing self-understanding of the difference between serving violence and serving peace.

Convict Criminology: Act III

Alan

The third act of our drama involves the internal machinations of the convict criminologist as prisoner. He has a visceral loathing for his own weakness and incompetence but understands conceptually that he is not solely to blame for his condition. How to reconcile the guilt of personal responsibility with the knowledge that his choices were few? How to reconcile a nascent understanding of the true, shared culpability for his crimes with the extant legal reality of his sole responsibility for doing the time? and How, in short, can you demand to be "right" when the cost is your life?

Chuck

I met Richard, Hal, Dennis Sullivan, Kay Harris, Larry Tifft, and other critical, proactive criminologists at an ASC panel. Richard used the allegory of the ox herder during his presentation to illustrate that peace can come to the world only when we come to know the peace within ourselves. He was brilliant. I felt elated and humbled in his presence. Here was a true teacher. Here was somebody, an academic criminologist at that, who really knew what was happening. I remember thinking that a clear understanding of his message should be a prerequisite for all criminologists. At the same time, I feared that few could be open to what he was saying. As a consequence, most would categorize his message as meaningless. Such is the paradox of Richard's work and, it seems to me, the paradox of the world.

Before long, Richard and I became friends. As well as meet at conferences, we occasionally communicated through letters sent in the regular mail. Once, in my hometown of Santa Barbara, he, Solveig, and I met at a restaurant by the beach for coffee. He has always been supportive and always encouraging of whatever I am doing.

By the time Richard was given a tribute at the 1998 ASC, I had become familiar with his widely accepted earlier work. By then I had also heard comments made by other criminologists about how he had "become strange." Once, in a class I was engaged in as a teacher's assistant, the instructor told the students about how good Richard used to be but that something unusual happened to him, like maybe he "got born again or something." At a conference, another indicated the same thing, that in earlier years his contributions were incredible but that somewhere along the way he had "lost it." By the time of the tribute I fully knew that many criminologists viewed his later work, work I see as the most real possible, as unreal.

Hal

If you are a prisoner, you are underclass. The world offers you fewer and fewer fair chances to join the power structure. How, then, do you survive? Do you surrender to your status, or do you try to transcend the "logic of commodities" in which you inevitably will live out your life?

When on my T-shirt I see Richard's reference to "an historical era in which all aspects of life are mediated by the logic of commodities," I infer that he (extraordinarily well-read as he is) is referring to Enlightenment thinking, in which heart and mind, spiritualism and rationalism, are separated. In *Providence*, Richard crossed the Enlightenment line. His reputation among leftist and mainstream criminologists alike suffered accordingly. He joined the academic underclass.

Now Richard is an avowed, exploring Buddhist. In his second spiritual book in 1982, *Social Existence*, he explored Taoist thought. Ironically, in the book that had leftist criminologists feeling betrayed and mainstream criminologists merely bewildered, he complemented Marx with Max Weber and Paul Tillich—a German social scientist and a U.S. Christian theologian. In *Providence*, Richard wrote that it is not enough to know what is wrong with the social order. One has to add meaning (Weber) and transcendent value to life (Tillich) to decide how to respond to oppression.

Convict Criminology: Postscript

Alan

When I read Quinney in *Peacemaking Criminology*, I was moved to read many of his other contemporary articles. I saw that he understood the conundrum of reconciliation, the paradox of living with oneself and within one's society. I suspect that he felt the tension himself in the context of his own work. His writings show that he recognized the frustration and pain systematically imposed on the dispossessed. He saw that criminological explanations of crime, at any level of analysis, only add to the pain. I believe that Quinney made up his mind to do no harm.

Although Richard knew that individual-level rationales for crime both attack and stigmatize the very humanness of offenders, social explanations take. They take some of the responsibility for law breaking, and they take some of the power that people, whether prisoners, need to build a life. It seems that the more we educate ourselves and cultivate an appreciation for the insights to be gained from abstraction, the less we are inclined to look within ourselves for answers or even to see if we are asking the right questions. On the other hand, the more we distain an elevated level of sociological explanation, the more naïve we come to seem. Such are the issues troubling the credentialed convict criminologist.

Chuck

During the small, celebratory gathering at ASC, Richard humbly accepted the symbols, a plaque and T-shirt, given to him as acknowledgments of his contributions. His simple words at the time still ring in my head. "It is not enough to be critical," he said. "We must also be proactive." I believe the proactiveness he advocates means, in part, that each of us work on ourselves and, as we do, we will become more aware of who we really are as human beings.

Richard's message and example give me continued strength and direction. As he and others have suggested throughout history, only the truth can set us free. Yet of itself, the truth can do nothing. Freedom and peace can only follow from an understanding of the truth, the truth that in reality we all are one. For this reason, I believe that, in time, Richard will be seen as the most real criminologist of this era, as he is to me now.

Whither Criminology?

Alan

Currently, the criminological disciplines claim a slightly better than chance ability to predict future criminality on the part of individuals with previous criminal histories. It's not that I'm unimpressed that a profession constituted of a group of folks with a combined 10,000 or so years of college education can surpass a monkey with a quarter in predicting crime, but after all this time wouldn't you think we could do better? What is it that holds us back? Why do we forward our agendas by endowing ourselves with such grand mantles of expertise, be they based on education, experience, or both, when our ability to accomplish what we set out to do is lacking?

Quinney suggests that it is our habitual ways of being that both hold us back and propel us forward with our ideas, our ambitions, and our careers. We continue to look for answers "out there" when all the data we will ever need reside within our hearts. Look within, he implores, and discover the roots of all suffering. Then, join action to understanding, engage with the world, and work for the cessation of all suffering, everywhere. Only then will criminology become an anachronism and the reality of crime no more.

"Everyday Life is Indeed, of Consequence"

Hal

Take yourself seriously. Even if you are a renowned criminologist, take time to examine yourself. Step off the treadmill of conformity. I think that in the early 1970s some people got caught in conformist thinking and made the mistake of taking Richard for a servant of Marxist theory. The mistake was that Richard was not a position in a single publication but a being in quest of (self-) understanding. The reality of class oppression did not tell him, by itself, how to respond.

"It is the Only Reality We Can Know"

Chuck

For those of us who have undergone change in our lives as an effect of self-discovery, Richard represents an essence of our own experience of transformation. The irony is that for the vast majority in the criminological mainstream, his work is regarded as not grounded in empirical reality. What does that denial, that judgment, say to me about the authenticity of my experience?

Hal

The Greek root of the term *empirical* is *empeirokos*, meaning experienced. Richard's approach to understanding crime and criminality has been supremely inductive. It has balanced an awareness of criminal justice as class warfare and social examination more generally with an attempt to become aware of self and of what allows one's compassion to open and close.

The most striking thing to me when I first met Richard, already a criminological hero of mine thirty years ago, was that he was interested in me. He wanted to know about me, not just intellectually. He was interested in my simple humanity. As a corollary, he was interested in himself—not just as a professional figure, but as a full being. He validated me, he encouraged me.

To me, this goes hand in hand with his works of self-reflection. He indeed shares with others, profoundly, meaningfully so.

In Zen Buddhist terms, every paradox is a *koan*, a riddle to be transcended through meditation. I believe that Richard has solved his koan, for himself and for so many of us who have been validated and encouraged by his work and personal friendship and mentorship. It is no mystery to me why many of us love all of Richard's work, whereas others dismiss his later work. Richard is in tune with a crucial side of ourselves—some call it the right brain—which other criminologists dare not touch for fear of losing objectivity. Richard teaches us that the only thing you lose when you lose objectivity is the dubious privilege of being a social object yourself. You gain, by sharing experience with others, the very stuff of cultural transformation. You gain compassion.

As I revisit lessons that I have learned from Richard, I think that he inspired me to a realization that I now make explicit with my students. In everyday life, we can seek chances to express all the repressed feelings, beliefs, and subservience that we have been forced to keep to ourselves. As criminologists, we can explore our own relation to the state. My criminal justice students can do the same. We can ask ourselves what criticisms of patriarchal order we have had to repress. We can take time to mourn our own structural traps. In that process, we stand to recognize and not rationalize the suffering of others. I have come to believe that this is the process by which people in my own country, the United States, can recognize how punitive and uncompassionate we have become as a people, and transform ourselves one by one.

In peacemaking theory as I have come to recognize it, as Richard has inspired it, the first question for change is not what others need to do or should do but what I myself, in everyday life, do next. That includes the question of what I do as a criminologist in the next moment of everyday life.

Alan

Richard Quinney is one of my favorite authors, and not because of his lyrical prose or brilliant insights. For me, Quinney stands out because he writes about one of my favorite topics: personal responsibility. Quinney's message, especially in later years, might properly distill down to the following: The conduct of everyone, the fate of everyone, and the needs of everyone are the personal responsibility of everyone.

Quinney's views are presently out of the mainstream, but they are hardly novel. They are based on wisdom traditions stretching back thousands of years. Our personal and social dilemmas today largely spring from our having accepted the validity of a quite different interpretation of our rights, responsibilities, and relationships. We have come to fear crime and even commit crimes because we suffer from the culturally induced delusions of separateness and scarcity. The cure, as always, is the truth: Whoever you think you are and whatever you think about others, the lived truth is that we are interconnected in myriad ways and none of us will ever be truly safe until we are all safe. As human beings we are obligated to one another. We are each other's personal responsibility.

Hal

The cruelty of making anyone "do time" is stark to me, even in making a child do a time-out, let alone "doing life." In *Journey to a Far Place* (1991), Richard sought to affirm the importance of that which had no manifest production value to him as a sociology professor. The gentle, open manner in which he documented his own everyday life gives us an opportunity to confront our own meaning systems, values, and stories. What have we learned along the way? Rather than focus on the criminal or the state, we are led to ask ourselves, How far have we come? What part do we play in creating the world we all share? I find tremendous comfort in the recognition that there is great consequence in the ways we get up and go about our daily business. I trust that Alan and Chuck made the time they did in prison of consequence.

Alan

Even though Richard's message of communal responsibility makes a lot of sense, accepting this truth and living in accordance with it is a real challenge. Such a way of being requires much dedication and practice. Maintaining a diligent practice is hard work, but the good news is that as we get better at embodying our values, by being patient with ourselves and gentle with others, our determination will make itself shown. Our prose will become more lyrical, our insights will attain brilliance, and we will come to know ourselves—and each other—as if for the first time.

Hal

For thirty years I have been in correspondence with many prisoners. I never ask them what their offense is or what they have done to get to prison. The main thing I want to know is how they are doing here and now. Pen pal–ships are made and broken based on how we interact on matters at hand, not on the past.

I imagine that the line "everyday life is of consequence" must be profoundly validating for all who have dramatically transformed their lives. The line suggests that it is not so much what we get done, how others see us, or what we gain, but how we lived that day. The direction it points to, it seems to me, is not to "be" a criminal, or "be" a professional, or anything else. Our task, instead, is to be as genuine, open, and honest as we can, and see others as doing the same. To me, these words of Richard's are a profound validation of my reality—

that whether a prisoner is worthy of my trust and friendship has nothing to do with the "seriousness" of the pretext for the imprisonment.

Everyday life is of criminological consequence in another respect. In the book Richard and Kevin Anderson recently edited on the work of Erich Fromm, one finds that Fromm's key insight was that our class warfare in the form of wars on crime is fueled by individual projection and the displacement of secret shame. We each feel isolation from having violated or been violated by others. In Quinney's Buddhist terms, it is only by acknowledging and sharing our daily personal existential suffering—in other words, by being compassionate with our own daily existence—that we can empathize with the suffering of others and thereby transform the urge to punish into compassion.

Among my criminal justice students, I find that as I encourage them to express their own honest feelings and opinions and experience about "justice," and as we together recognize their exploitation as a "student" class, they become noticeably more "liberal" about wars on crime. As their everyday lives become of consequence, their will to punish abates.

Alan

Recently, I attended a conference on leadership. It was organized by Tibetan Buddhists and attended by high-powered businesspeople, organization theorists, educators from all levels, and social service practitioners and administrators. I was the sole criminologist. As a criminologist I was of much interest, and with regard to civic leadership I was bemused to note that I held something of a middle ground. Others belonged to groups that had both much more and much less "relevance" to leadership in the organization of everyday life. What really struck a cord with the assemblage about me was not that I teach criminology or conduct research but that I teach meditation in prisons. A discussion arose based on a series of magazine and newspaper articles about a Zen monk and his students. The monk is a prison volunteer and his students reside in state prison.

The monk had been in communication with one of the more prominent conference presenters. We were told how the monk had expressed doubt as to whether meditation instruction in prison was "right" ethical practice. His worry was that by teaching prisoners how to be more contented in their daily lives he was in effect condemning them to social extinction. At the root of his concern was his feeling that prisons are wrong, prima facie, and that teaching convicts to be peaceful fed right into the hands of power. After all, few changes have come to the penal establishment in the absence of disruptive, violent uprisings.

The monk's paradox is one that is faced by many prisoner advocates and prison volunteers. Is it better to help ease immediate individual suffering or work toward structural change? Most of us try to avoid the question by posing another in its place and then leaving it unanswered: Can a small group of transformed individuals succeed in transforming an entire organization? Inevitably, it seems we want to have our cake and eat it too.

My experience tells me that the battle for systematic penal reform is a long and chancy proposition that entails much sacrifice and the potential for many casualties. Will our ends justify the means? Should the monk (and the rest of us) withdraw from prison work and leave the current mess to the "professionals" alone? Quinney is instructive here, I think. His message is one that I have tried to put into practice. It is that the direct easing of human misery is always a self-justifying "right" action. All the rest—the strategic maneuvering, political tactics, and public pressure—is indirect, abstract, and unreal. Changes on a grand scale may come to pass or, despite our best efforts, they may not. The germane point is perhaps best summed by Dennis Sullivan in his remarkable book *The Mask of Love*. Their message is unambiguous and, I think, exemplary: Means are ends. Easing human suffering is an end in itself. So is condoning pain, even in service to "higher" purposes.

We owe Richard Quinney our thanks for cultivating an awareness of the illusions of ego and the veils of grandiose abstraction, and for keeping it real. In the Zen tradition, life itself is seen as a paradox. The masters say that the answer to a paradox is never either/or but one liberally sprinkled with laughter.

Chapter 7

It's More Profitable to *Treat* the Disease than to *Prevent* it: Why the Prison Industrial Complex Needs Crime

Randall G. Shelden

"While arrests and convictions are steadily on the rise, profits are to be made—profits from crime. Get in on the ground floor of this booming industry now!"[1]

"It's like a hotel with a guaranteed occupancy."[2]

"In my mind there's no more recession-proof form of economic development. Nothing's going to stop crime."[3]

"There are no seasonal fluctuations, it is a non-polluting industry, and in many circumstances it is virtually invisible."[4]

"If crime doesn't pay, punishment certainly does..."[5]

During the past couple of decades one of the emerging perspectives in criminology is that of "restorative justice" (Sullivan and Tifft, 2001). Seeking to find alternatives to the usual punitive response to crime, restorative justice places emphasis on the needs of the victims, the offender and the community. Since the start of a "restorative justice movement" in Canada (with a case of two teenagers who went on a vandalism spree, which was handled via a direct meeting between the victims and the two teenagers), efforts to seek "peaceful" and "non-punitive" solutions have evolved all over the world (Bonita et al., 2002).

While marked by some success, restorative justice has apparently not had that much of an impact on the punitive tendency within modern American society. There are many reasons for this, but one that I'd like to explore here is the fact that there are many institutions (both public and private) that have a vested interest in maintaining a "get tough" approach to crime control. If we are serious about seeking restorative justice on a wide scale, we must know what we are up against, and what we are up against is a very large and powerful industry. Many have called the "crime control industry" (e.g., Christie, 2000; Shelden and Brown, 2000). This chapter is concerned mostly with one crucial component of this industry, thc "prison industrial complex," but first some problems of terminology should be addressed.

My idea is similar to what Lilly and Knepper, in a 1993 article, called the "correctional-commercial complex," which they describe as a sort of "sub-governmental policy-making" system consisting of an alliance between government and private enterprise. Lilly and Knepper noted that this system is quite similar to the "military industrial complex," since it consists of patterns of interrelationships known variously as "policy networks," "subgovernment" or the "iron triangle." They argued that such a system may not be legally a form of government, but nevertheless may exert greater influence than more formal structures of the government. In comparing this system to the military equivalent they note that within the military subgovernment there is an "iron triangle" of the Pentagon, private defense contractors, and various members of Congressional committees (e.g., armed services committees, defense appropriations committees). They noted further that the decision-making within any given policy arena "rests within a closed circle or elite of government bureaucrats, agency heads, interest groups, and private interests that gain from the allocation of public resources" (Lilly and Knepper, 1993, p. 152).

I am not the first to bring up such a subject as this one. One of the first to recognize this as a problem was Richard Quinney in his book *Class, State and Crime*, first published in 1977. In this book he wrote that there is what he termed a "social-industrial complex," of which a "criminal justice industrial complex" is a part. This much larger complex is "an involvement of industry in the planning, production, and operation of state programs. These state-financed programs (concentrating on education, welfare, and criminal justice), as social expenses necessary for maintaining social order, are furnished by monopolistic industries" (Quinney, 1980, p. 133). Large corporations, Quinney suggested, have found a new source of profits in this industry, with the criminal justice industry leading the way. Private industry, in short, has found that there is much profit to be made as a result of the existence of crime.

Examples include the educational system, with more than 3,000 thousands of criminal justice programs within colleges and universities. Educating people for occupations in criminal justice is a big business, given the large number of those majoring in "criminal justice" or "criminology" and planning on a career in this field. There are numerous examples of various businesses that may receive profits because of crime, such as hospitals and insurance companies (hospital emergency room visits, doctor's fees, insurance premiums on auto and other insurance covering crime, etc.) and the salaries of those who deal with the victims of crime (e.g., doctors, nurses, para-medics, insurance adjusters). Then, too, there are the profits from the sale of books (e.g., college textbooks, trade books), magazine and journal articles, newspaper coverage (and the advertisers who profit from crime stories), television crime shows (and their advertisers) and movies about crime (with the enormous salaries paid to actors and actresses who star in them). There is also the money collected by courts through various fines (especially traffic tickets), special courses defendants can enroll in as a condition of (or in lieu of) their sentence (e.g., traffic schools, petty larceny programs), plus a totally separate industry involved in the setting of bail (bail bondsmen and the insurance companies involved). Finally, we have to consider the private security industry, with profits almost impossible to estimate (ranging from companies that provide security guards to the makers of all sorts of security devices like locks and barbed wire, not to mention the security provided to gated communities). As you can clearly see, there are many different entities profiting in some way from the existence of crime.

The *prison industrial complex* represents an interconnection among the criminal justice system, the political system and the economic system—just like the military represents a connection with the political and economic system. Politics and economics go hand in hand—how do you think politicians get elected and whose interests do they serve? Think also of the large number of lobbyists in the nation's capital (not to mention the same thing at the local and state level—try to see your senator, congressman, city councilman or other representative and chances are you will have to wait in line until they see corporate lobbyists) (Parenti, 1999). Think for a moment about the building of prisons, jails, courthouses, police departments and furnishing them with everything they need to keep going (construction costs, electrical, furniture, toilet paper, etc.) and you get an idea of what I am talking about.

A recent illustration of this is revealed in an AP report called "7 Federal Prisons to Get Lethal Electrified Fences." According to this story seven "high-security" federal prisons will get to add "lethal electrified fences" costing around $10 million. A spokesperson for the Federal Bureau of Prisons stated that "This new technology will serve as new security and help us to deter potential escapes, allow us to operate more cost-effectively by reducing the guard towers, the staffing at some of our guard towers." The problem with this is that it is rare to find anyone attempting to escape from a federal prison. Judy Freyermuth, representing the Federal Prison Policy Project, a nonprofit prison reform group, questioned the savings, asking: "How many times have you read of an escape from a federal prison? None."[6] However, the "bottom line" is that there will be at least one company that builds such fences that will receive the bid.

Under Control of the Criminal Justice System

The most recent data show that as of June 30, 2005, there were 2,186,230 people behind bars. The overall incarceration rate was 738 per 100,000 population (up from 601 in 1995), placing the United States as number one in the world.[7]

It should be noted that our incarceration figures do not include all of those in various community-based facilities (e.g., work-release centers) and incarcerated juveniles. Exact number of those in these various community-based facilities are not available, but as of 2005 there were almost five million on probation and parole, up from about 1.3 million in 1980 (see Table 7.2). The number of juveniles incarcerated was about 109,000 as of 1999 (Chesney-Lind and Shelden, 2004).

Finally, there is the rather astonishing figure of forty-seven million American citizens (about one-fourth of the adult population) who have criminal records on file with some state or federal agency! This is a truly amazing statistic (Travis, 2002, p. 18). (Incidentally, the police made about 13 million arrests in 2002, according to FBI figures.) That brings the total of current and previous criminal justice "clients" to more than 65 million people, not counting juveniles on probation, parole or under some other form of supervision! It might be said without much exaggeration that *the criminal justice industrial complex reaches into every nook and cranny of American life.*

Looking more carefully at the past thirty years we find that while there have been some fluctuations in the overall crime rate, at this time the official crime rate ("index crimes") is about the same as it was in the early 1970s, yet the incarceration rate went up by about 500 percent. The rate of violent crime actually increased slightly during this period, but the rate of property crime had declined to offset that increase. During this same period of time, expenditures on the criminal justice system increased by 1500 percent (Shelden and Brown, 2003). Only one conclusion can be reached: increasing rates of incarceration and expenditures on the criminal justice system has had no impact on the crime rate. The absolute failure of the conservative, hard-line approach to crime is evident.

The Incarceration Boom: Expanding the Prison Industrial Complex

As already noted, the *prison industrial complex* represents an interconnection among the criminal justice system, the political system and the economic system. Politics and economics go hand in hand.

Looking at recent trends in the incarceration rates in the United States we can clearly see that we have the highest in the world. Table 7.1 shows changes in America's prison system during the past seventy-five plus years. Note that the most significant increases have occurred since 1975, roughly coinciding with the onset of the "war on drugs." We are way ahead of other industrial democracies, whose incarceration rates tend to cluster in a range from around fifty-five to 120 per 100,000 population, with some well below that figure, like Japan's rate of thirty-six, with an average incarceration rate for *all countries of the world* of around eighty. Thus, America's incarceration rate is almost nine times greater than the average country (Currie, 1998, p. 15). The Norwegian criminologist, Nils Christie, in the third edition of his ground-breaking book on the crime control industry, noted that there is a huge difference between the United States and our northern neighbor Canada. Canada's incarceration rate is about 129, about one-fifth our rate. He notes, by the way, that these two countries are essentially the same (in terms of the economic and political systems) except for one important exception: Canada has more of a "social safety-net" (various welfare benefits) than in the United States (Christie, 2000, p. 31).

Table 7.1. The Growing Prison Population, 1925–2005 (rates per 100,000 in state and federal prison)

Year	Number	Rate
1925	91,669	79
1935	144,180	113
1945	133,649	98
1955	185,780	112
1965	210,895	108
1975	240,593	111
1985	480,568	202
1995	1,085,363	411
2005	1,461,132	491
% increase (1975–2005)	507	342

Source: Maguire, K. and A. L. Pastore (eds.) (1997). *Sourcebook on Criminal Justice Statistics-1996.* Washington, DC: Department of Justice, Bureau of Justice Statistics, p. 518; Harrison, P. M. and A. Beck. (2006). "Prisoners in 2005." Washington, DC: Bureau of Justice Statistics, November. http://www.ojdp.usdoj.gov/bjs/pub/p05.pdf

For comparative purposes, Table 7.2 shows the increases in the four major components of the criminal justice system: prisons, jails, probation and parole. As noted here, between 1980 and 2005 each of these segments grew by over 270 percent. Prisons and jails led the way, having increased by 339 and 356 percent respectively. The number on probation went up by 272 percent, while the number on parole increased by 256 percent. All four together increased by 285 percent. What is perhaps most interesting from Table 7.2 is the fact that the overall adult population increased by about 18 percent during this period. Also, the number of arrests went up by only 41 percent, compared to an overall *decrease* in reported index crimes. What this clearly shows is that there has been a significant increase in the number of less serious offenders being arrested, with a corresponding increase in the number being convicted and sent to prison or jail.

The rising incarceration rate has done considerable damage to racial minorities and their communities. A few years ago, the Justice Department estimated that the average black child born in 1991 had a 28 percent chance of going to prison someday, compared to only a 4 percent chance for a white child. An updated survey found that a black male child born in 2001 had a 33 percent chance of going to prison someday (Younge, 2003). Back in 1995, the Sentencing Project estimated that about one-third of all black males in their twentiess was somewhere in the criminal justice system, either in prison, jail, on probation or on parole, up from 25 percent in 1990. Estimated for specific cities put the percentages even higher, for instance, about 60 percent in Washington, D.C. and Baltimore (Miller, 1996). Taking a longer view, whereas in the 1930s about 30 percent of all prisoners were racial minorities, by 2002 this percentage had climbed to 70 (Welch, 2005).

Table 7.2. Adults on Probation, in Jail or Prison, and on Parole, 1980–2005

Year	Total	Probation	Jail	Prison	Parole
1980	1,832,350	1,118,097	163,994	329,821	220,438
1985	3,011,500	1,968,712	254,986	487,593	300,203
1990	4,348,000	2,670,234	403,019	743,382	531,407
1995	5,335,100	3,077,861	499,300	1,078,545	679,421
2005	7,058,000	4,162,536	747,529	1,446,269	484,408
% increase (1980–2005)	285	272	356	339	256

Source: Glaze, L. E. and S. Palla (2005). "Probation and Parole in the United States, 2004." Washington, DC: Bureau of Justice Statistics, November 2005. http://www.ojp.us doj.gov/bjs/pub/pdf/ppus03.pdf

The latest numbers (June, 2005) show that African-Americans constitute more than half of the prison population, while their overall incarceration rate exceeds that for whites by a ratio of almost 8 to 1 (Harrison and Beck, 2006).

The incarceration rate for women has increased the most in recent years, going from a mere 8 per 100,000 in 1975 to 62 by 2003, a jump of more than 700 percent, compared to an increase of 400 percent for males. Not surprisingly, race enters the picture here, as African-American females have an incarceration rate that is almost eight times higher than their white counterparts (Shelden and Brown, 2003; Beck et al., 2002; Harrison and Beck, 2004; Austin et al., 2001, p. 26). Much of the increase in women's incarceration rate comes from the impact of *mandatory sentencing* laws, passed during the 1980s crackdown on crime. Under many of these laws, mitigating circumstances (e.g., having children, few or no prior offenses, non-violent offenses) are rarely allowed. One survey found that just over half (51 percent) of women in state prisons had none or only one prior offense, compared to 39 percent of the male prisoners (Donziger, 1996, p. 152). It should also be noted that drug convictions account for the bulk of these increases, as has been the case for all prisoners, as I will note below. What is of critical importance for women offenders is the fact that more than 80 percent of them have children and in most of these cases the women have sole responsibility to take care of them (how this has happened is another story and beyond the scope of this report; see Chesney-Lind and Pasko, 2004; and Owen, 1998, for further discussion of this issue).[8]

Prisons as a "Market" for Capitalism

A more complete understanding of the prison industrial complex requires placing it within the context of the overall economic system of capitalism. Within a capitalist society there tends to be an insatiable desire to continue "converting money into commodities and commodities into money." Everything, it seems, is turned into a "commodity"—from the simplest products (e.g., paper and pencil) to human beings (e.g., women's bodies, slaves). Indeed, within a capitalist society "daily life is scanned for possibilities that can be brought within the circuit of accumulation," since any aspect of society that can produce a profit will be exploited (Heilbroner, 1985, p. 60). Life itself has been "commodified."

The amount of money that flows into the coffers of the prison industrial complex from tax dollars alone is quite substantial. The budget for both state and federal correctional institutions came to $34.1 billion in fiscal year 2000, which represents an increase of almost 80 percent over 1992. The budgets for probation and parole have also been increasing. While in fiscal year 1992 the average budgets for both systems came to $23 million, in the year 2000 the average was $71 million, an increase of 209 percent. What is most interesting about the budgets for probation and parole is that the largest increases went to the parole system, with their average budgets going from $25.5 million in 1992 to $43.1 million in 2000, compared to a very modest increase for probation budgets from $55.7 million to $56.3 million. The total budgets for both probation and parole came to just over $1.7 billion in fiscal year 2000 (Camp and Camp, 2000, pp. 84,186). The costs per prisoner per day have been steadily increasing during the past decade, going from about $49 in 1991 to about $58 in 1999. That's about $21,170 per prisoner per year (Camp and Camp, 2000, p. 88).

A good illustration of how companies are "cashing in" on the boom in corrections is found in the amount of advertising done in journals related to this industry. One example comes from two major journals serving the prison industrial complex, *Corrections Today* and *The American Jail*, plus the American Correctional Association's annual *Directory*. (*Corrections Today* is the leading prison trade magazine and the amount of advertising in this magazine tripled in the 1980s.) I have sampled a few issues of these journals and the ACS Directory and found advertisements everywhere. Among the companies whose products are advertised here include the following:

> Prison Health Services, Inc., a company that has, since 1978, "delivered complete, customized healthcare programs to correctional facilities only. The first company in the U.S. to specialize in this area, we can deliver your program the fastest, and back it up with services that are simply the best"; Southwest Microwave, Inc., manufactures fence security, with their latest invention known as "Micronet 750" which is "more than a sensor improvement," it is "a whole new paradigm in fence detection technology"; Acorn Engineering, Inc., with their stainless steel fixtures known as "Penal-Ware" (lavatories, toilets, showers, etc.) and "Master-Trol" electronic valve system; Rotondo Precast, Inc. boasting "over 21,000 cells . . . and growing"; Nicholson's BesTea" with "tea for two or . . . two thousand. . . ." "Now mass-feeding takes

> a giant stride forward . . ."; Northwest Woolen Mills, manufacturing blanket with the slogan "We've got you covered"; and, "Prison on Wheels" from Motor Coach Industries, with their "Inmate Security Transportation Vehicle." Even insurance companies are getting in on the action, including U.S. Risk Underwriters, "with over 20 years combined experience in liability insurance for the criminal justice system." A company called Control Screening advertises its special Model 6040-M security parcel X-ray scanner with an ad that reads: "Don't allow suspicious packages into your facility." An example of a popular company that has entered the prison market is Western Union offering "an automated solution" for all sorts of payments, from court-ordered payments to commissary needs. Then there is one of the largest food service companies, Aramark, which says it will "trim the fat from your food service." While "your correctional officers are watching the food line, Aramark will be watching your budget." Then there is General Marine Leasing, a company that builds "portable, temporary and modular facilities." Their ad reads: "Overcrowded? Don't let overflow put them back on the street."[9]

This is a small sampling, for there are at least two web sites that list company ads aimed at the prison market. One is "corrections yellow pages" (www.corrections.com/vendor). This site contains more than 1000 different ads. Corrections.com organizes its web page by categories of vendors. For example, by clicking on the following (www.corrections.com/vendor/by_category) you will find under the heading "cleaning/sanitation" there are twenty companies, including Americhem Enterprises (they supply products like industrial degreasers, floor finishers, disinfectants, bowl cleaners, etc.), Champion Industries (specializing in "dishwashing machines for prison applications"), and Somat Corporation ("waste reduction systems for the correctional foodservice industry"). This web site also claims to be "Home to the Industry's Leading Organizations" and provides a list of thirty-four different organizations, including both the most popular national groups (e.g., American Correctional Association) and lesser-known regional groups (e.g., Kentucky Department of Juvenile Justice).

The American Correctional Association (ACA) is one of the largest national organizations in the country. Their annual meetings draw hundreds of vendors, usually taking up an entire floor of a hotel or convention center. On the ACA web site it mentions the $50 billion or so spent each year on prisons and jails and says to companies, "Don't miss out on this prime revenue-generating opportunity."

The trade journal of the American Correctional Association, *Corrections Today*, has a special issue every July in anticipation of the upcoming annual conference in August. There are more than 200 pages in this special issue. I have a copy of the July, 1999 issue, which includes descriptions from more than 200 different companies, selling everything imaginable. The list includes locks and other security devices, food service, hygiene kits, bedding, blankets, ceiling systems, communications equipment, clothing, weapons, and a wide assortment of architects, engineers and consultants used to build and maintain prisons and jails.

One section of this issue of the journal is devoted to advertising for the famous ACA Exhibit Hall, which they cleverly call the "County Fair Specialty Break." This ad was telling members about the previous winter meetings (these are held every January at various locations around the country) and reads as follows:

> The excitement of an old-fashioned County Fair was in the air in the Exhibit Hall Tuesday morning for the **1999 Winter Conference Exhibit Hall Specialty Break**. Attendees took a chance for prizes at **Correctional Healthcare Solutions, Inc.'s** Wheel of Fortune and at **Sverdrup Facilities, Inc.'s** Coke bottle ring toss. **Kenall** hosted a dart game for prizes and **HKS** provided a clown juggler who formed balloon animals. **Aramark Correctional Services'** tarot card reader foretold attendees' fortunes as did the palm reader **Norment Detention & Security Group** supplied.

The page shows photos of all sorts of people (including children) having a grand old time, just like an old fashioned "County Fair." While of course humorous, we must not forget that the bulk of the prisoners who make all this fun possible are poor blacks who, unwittingly, are making it possible for their masters to engage in this form of entertainment.

Not surprisingly, prison construction itself has become a booming business. During the 1990s a total of 371 new prisons opened. (About 92,000 new beds were added each year.) In 1999 alone, twenty-four new prisons were opened, at a total cost of just over $1 billion. The average cost of building a new prison came to $105 million (about $57,000 per bed, more than the starting salary of public school teachers and newly hired Assistant Professors and even some Full Professors). Also, in 1999 a total of 146 prisons were adding or renovating beds at a cost of $470 million (about $30,000 per bed). As of January, 2000 a total of 29 new institutions were under construction and another 137 institutions were being renovated or adding new beds. Most of the new beds will be in either maximum or medium security institutions, where the costs are the highest. The total estimated costs of these new building projects come to more than $2.2 billion (Camp and Camp, 2000, p. 76).

The construction of new prisons has become such a big business that there is a spccial newsletter called *Construction Report*, just to keep vendors up to date on new prison projects (Dyer, 2000, p. 13). A Google search on the Internet turns up dozens of companies advertising for prison construction. One example, among many, is Kitchell (http://www.kitchell.com) which, according to their web site, "has successfully delivered over 110,000 correctional beds, including over 130 criminal justice projects in 17 states." These projects include 42 state prisons, 29 adult jails, and 30 juvenile facilities. They also build police stations, courts facilities and camps.

Corporate Interests: the Role of ALEC

A little known fact about the prison industrial complex is an organization known as the American Legislative Exchange Council (ALEC). The mere existence of this organization demonstrates the classic connections between politics, economics and the criminal justice system. The membership consists of state legislators, private corporation executives and criminal justice officials. More than one-third of state lawmakers in the country (2400) belong and they are, not surprisingly, mostly Republicans and conservative Democrats. It was started in 1973 by Paul Weyrich (who also co-founded the Heritage Foundation and now is the head of a group called the Free Congress Foundation, a far right conservative group). Their mission is to promote "free markets," along with small governments, "states' rights" and, of course, privatization. Corporate membership dues range from $5,000 to $50,000 annually. Corrections Corporation of America is a member of this group, which is not surprising. However, members also include a veritable "who's who" of the Fortune 500, such as Ameritech, AT&T, Bayer, Bell Atlantic, BellSouth, DuPont, GlaxcoSmithKline, Merck & Co., Sprint, Pfizer, to name just a few. Among the companies that have supported ALEC through various grants include Ameritech, Exxon Mobil, Chevron and several corporate foundations, including the Proctor & Gamble Fund, Exxon Educational Foundation, Bell Atlantic Foundation, Ford Motor Company Fund, among many others (http://www.capitalresearch.org).

The web site of ALEC is an educational experience in itself. It proudly lists some of the bills it has been involved in getting passed, plus indicates some very important keynote speakers during the past three annual meetings. Among the notables giving speeches include Attorney General John Ashcroft, Secretary of Health and Human Services Tommy Thompson (see below), Secretary of Housing and Urban Development Mel Martinez, President and CEO of American Home Products Robert Essner, Chairman and CEO of Pfizer, Hank McKinnell, Florida Governor Jeb Bush, Secretary of Labor Elane Chao and ultra conservative syndicated columnist Cal Thomas (http://www.alec.org). This organization also puts together papers and policy statements on a wide variety of issues reflecting conservative ideas, including one about the "myth of global warming." Bill Berkowitz, who carefully follows conservative trends, has noted that ALEC sponsored more than 3,100 pieces of legislation between 1999 and 2000, with more than 400 of these bills passing (Berkowitz, 2002).

Within ALEC there is a "Criminal Justice Task Force." Among the duties of this group is to write "model bills" on crime and punishment. Among such "model bills" they helped draft include "mandatory minimum sentences," "Three Strikes" laws, "truth in sentencing" and the like. One member boasted that in 1995 alone they introduced 199 bills, including "truth in sentencing" bills, which passed in twenty-five states. Tommy Thompson, former Wisconsin Governor and current head of Health and Human Services in the Bush Administration, was once a member of ALEC. He was recently quoted as saying that "I always loved going to these meetings because I always found new ideas. Then I'd take them back to Wisconsin, disguise them a little bit, and declare that 'It's mine.'" Edwin Bender of the National Institute on Money in State Politics, says that: "Bayer Corporation or Bell South or GTE or Merck pharmaceutical company sitting at a table with elected representatives, actually hammering out a piece of legislation—behind closed doors, I mean, this isn't open to the public. And that then becomes the basis on which representatives are going to their state legislatures and debating issues" (www.americanradioworks.org). As everyone knows by now, these kinds of laws were a big reason for the swelling of the prison population, which in turn added new "markets" for capitalist profits.

More examples could be given and more reasons why we are in this state of affairs, but I will close with one glaring example of why spending seems to be constantly increasing for the criminal justice system. [10] Two words sum it up: politics and economics. Politics in the sense that elected officials want to be reelected and sounding "tough on crime" gets votes. Economics in the sense of not only the money to be made by businesses, but also the number of jobs created. Protecting those jobs is often done by strong unions representing criminal justice workers. [11]

Recycling Prisoners: The "Perpetual Prisoner Machine"

The police, the courts and the prison system have become huge, self-serving and self-perpetuating bureaucracies with a vested interest in keeping crime at a certain level. They need victims, they need criminals, even if they have to invent them, as they have throughout the "war on drugs" or else "recycle" them via the modern system of parole.

The "recycling" of prisoners through the system of probation and parole has been noted by several observers. A recent study demonstrates that rather than assist released prisoners in their adjustment to the outside world and help them "go straight," the probation and parole system almost guarantees failure (Richards, Austin and Jones, 2004). Increasing proportions of new commitments to prison are parole violators. Nationwide, in 2001 more than one-third (36 percent) of new prison commitments were parole violators, up from 29 percent in 1990 (Harrison and Karberg, 2003). In California, however, the percentages are even higher at 54 percent (Macallair, 2003). It is interesting to note that the recidivism rate is higher for prisoners released on parole than for those released outright, after serving their entire sentence (Richards, Austin and Jones, 2004; Austin and Hardyman, 2004). However, one must wonder if it is really a "failure" in the true sense of the word. It is almost seems like those controlling the criminal justice system view "success" as providing a steady stream of convicts. This writer once heard the director of a state parole system say "We train our parole agents to catch violators." A sign on the wall of one parole agent in California summed up this system very well. The sign read "Trail'em, surveil'em, nail'em, jail'em" (Miller, 1996, p. 131).

Just to give you an idea of the impact of probation and parole violations a recent survey by the Department of Justice found that almost 40 percent of those sent to prison in 1997 (latest figures available) were parole violators. At least half did *not* commit a new crime, but instead were sent back on what are called "technical violations," the most common being testing positive for drugs. Drug testing, by the way, has become a huge business. [12]

The growth in the building of prisons during the past couple of decades has had several unintended consequences, both political and economic. A close look at *where* most prisons have been built is revealing.

Rural Prisons: Uplifting Rural Economies?

In this country there are more prisoners than there are farmers. It would not be too much of an exaggeration to say that rural America has been pretty much destroyed by factory closings, corporate downsizing, the shift to service occupations and the build-up of chain stores like Wal-Mart. Many rural towns have become "dependent on an industry that itself is dependent on the continuation of crime-producing conditions" (Huling, 2002, p. 198).

Much of the building of American prisons during the past two decades have been in rural areas, largely because of the promises of economic stimulus to these areas coupled with the cost savings of the states. These figures tell the story: whereas during the 1960s and 1970s an average of four new prisons per year were built in non-metropolitan areas, during the 1980s this average increased four-fold to about 16 per year and during the 1990s went to an average of 24.5 per year. During the 1990s a new prison was opened about every 15 days. During this decade, 57 percent of all new prisons were in non-metropolitan counties, which have only 19 percent of the total population (Clement, 2002; Huling, 2002). By the end of the 1990s, there were about 235,000 prisoners and 75,000 workers in the new rural prisons built that decade. Between 1980 and 2000, "more than half of all rural counties added prison work to their available employment mix." Prisons, along with casinos and animal confinement units for raising or processing hogs and poultry have become the three leading industries in rural areas (Huling, 2002, p. 199).

There are many states that have several prisons built within a few miles of one another, described by one critic as "penal colonies." Tracy Huling reports that in the town of Ionia, Michigan (pop. 10,569) there are six state prisons, which ties it with Huntsville, Texas (pop. 35, 078) for the most prisons in any city in the country (Huling, 2002, p. 206–207). Speaking of Ionia, a story in the *Detroit News* was called "Ionia [Michigan] Finds Stability in Prison: Lockups Provide Fast Growing Community with Jobs" (Street, 2002, p. 40).

There are plenty of other examples. In the Wisconsin town of Stanley (population 1,898) a "spec" prison was completed in the year 2000, built by a company called Dominion Venture Group. The state finally purchased the facility for $75 million in October, 2001. The mayor of Stanley, David Jankoski, stated that "we needed something to bring back vitality to the community…" (Clement, 2002). An article in the *Chicago Tribune* (March, 2001) was titled: "Towns Put Dreams in Prisons," referring to many small towns in the southern part of Illinois, areas short on jobs.

In the rural "heartland" of Michigan, Wisconsin, Minnesota, Montana, North and South Dakota spending on prisons skyrocket during the past twenty years. Per capita spending in North Dakota, for instance, went from about $25 to about $75 between 1980 and 2000, while Michigan's per capita spending went from less than $50 to almost $200 during this time. The number of prisoners tripled in Montana and South Dakota and quadrupled in North Dakota and Wisconsin during these two decades. Incarceration rates for these states increased at about the same rate, with Michigan's rate going from about 150 to almost 500 and the rates in both Montana and South Dakota going from under 100 to more than 300 (Clement, 2002).

County and local leaders in these rural areas often engage in a vigorous campaign to get prisons built in their area. In Texas some towns "bombarded the [Texas Department of Prison] with incentives that range from country club memberships for wardens to longhorn cattle for the prison grounds" (Donziger, 1996, p. 94). In Rush City, Minnesota (pop. 2,102), civic leaders raised $700,000 in donations and another $40,000 from the city to buy the acreage for the site of the new prison. Tiny Shelby, Montana (pop. 3,216) used a $500,000 block grant and another $800,000 in federal grants to pay for the infrastructure so that Corrections Corporation of America (CCA) could build its prison, the Crossroads Correctional Facility (Clement, 2002).

Typical of such growth and overall impact can be seen in Michigan's "Upper Peninsula" where there are nine prisons and four minimum security prison camps; all but two of these were opened during the past two decades. While only 2 percent of the state's population lives there, about 18 percent of its prisoners are housed there (Clement, 2002).

Another example that can be cited is the Pelican Bay State Prison in Crescent City, California (pop. 4,006). Built with a cost of $277 million, it has become the largest employer in the county. Before it was built, Crescent City was a dying town, with most of its population living in poverty or near-poverty (20 percent unemployment rate). Of the county's 17 sawmills, only four were operating, while the fishing industry was dead. During the 1980s a total of 164 businesses went broke. In typical corporate-welfare fashion, local supporters, seeing a way out of their predicament, practically gave away land, water and power to get the prison built. The prison now provides around 1,500 jobs, a payroll of over $50 million and a budget of more than $90 million. The prison also indirectly created more business, such as a $130,000 contract to haul the garbage, a new hospital, a K-Mart and a new Safeway market. Housing starts doubled since then, as did the value of real estate, while collecting $142 million in real estate taxes, up from $73 million ten years earlier (Parenti, 1999, p. 212).

Politicians often seek assistance from private enterprise when it comes to building prisons. Faced with severe overcrowding in the 1980s, New York Governor Mario Cuomo found that real estate prices were far too high near the city of New York, where the majority of inmates are from. So he received help from a Republican state senator from the northern part of New York, who in turn arranged for low prices on land for prisons. What has been the result? While 25 years ago this area had only two prisons, today it has over 20. One prison now occupies land formerly used for the Olympic Village at Lake Placid, while others have opened in abandoned factories and sanatoriums (Schlosser, 1998, pp. 57–58; Dyer, 2000, p. 17). A total of thirty-six prisons have been built in this state since 1980 (Duke, 2000). This recent prison boom "has provided a huge infusion of state money to an economically depressed region." These prisons bring in about $425 million in annual payroll and operating expenses—in effect, an annual "subsidy" of more than $1,000 for each person in the area! The annual salary is around $36,000 for a correctional officer in this area, more than 50 percent higher than the average salary (Schlosser, 1998, pp. 57–58; Dyer, 2000, p. 17).

In yet another small town in upstate New York called Malone in the far northern end of the state (pop. 6,025), a $180 million "supermax" prison was recently built. According to one report, prior to its opening the plan called for holding around 1,500 prisoners in a fourteen by eight foot cell for 23 hours per day. The prison ostensibly was to create about 500 badly-needed jobs in this part of New York in order to replace the 750 jobs lost at a local shoe factory because of downsizing. And it's not that Malone needed more prisons, for they already had two medium-security institutions! The new prison will bring the prison population in Malone to around 5,000 (of a total population of 6,025). One writer notes that "prisons have become the North Country's largest growth industry. . . ." New businesses also tend to follow the building of new prisons—in the case of Malone, four new drugstores and eight new convenience stores (Wray, 2000, p. 52). A story in the *Washington Post* noted that "If crime doesn't pay, punishment certainly does, at least for isolated towns like Malone" (Duke, 2000).[13]

Most of the boom in upstate New York stems from the "Rockefeller drug laws" passed in the 1970s which set severe punishments for drug offenders. Prisons sentences have tripled since the passage of these laws and almost two-thirds (62.5 percent) were nonviolent drug offenders (Duke, 2000).[14]

This leads me to consider another aspect of the growth in rural prisons, a rather sinister and perhaps even fraudulent development. I am referring here to the use of prisoners to alter census counts in rural areas thereby allowing them to bring in federal dollars.

Exploiting Prisoners to Enhance Rural Populations

It was noted earlier that the increase in the number of prisoners has resulted in the disenfranchisement of large numbers of citizens, especially affected African-Americans. Even though prisoners cannot vote in almost every state, they are counted and this count is translated into federal dollars pouring into small towns all over the country. This is what one report called the "phantom" population of rural prisoners (Prison Policy Initiative, 2003). What is happening is that rural communities that have prisons are allowed to pay the U.S Census Bureau money to include prisoners in the census count, thereby adding substantial numbers to the local population.

A *Wall Street Journal* report details how this has happened in the small Arizona town of Florence, which has an "official" population of 17,054 according to the 2000 census (Kulish, 2001). What this census figure does not reveal is that 11,830 of these "residents" are prisoners, since Florence, like many other small towns with where prisons have been built, is looking to the census count to help them in these financially strapped times.

This began in Florence back in the 1980s and since then has expanded its borders no less than three times. On two occasions the town has paid the Census Bureau for special recounts. This is because for each dollar generated by local taxes and fees, they get $1.76 more because of the prison population. Florence now has "new town offices, a new park and a new senior center...The rebuilt little-league facilities boasts a digital score board and dugouts. New police and fire facilities are under construction, and officials are planning a $1 million community center with a pool—all without a local income tax or any substantial increases in sales or property taxes" (Kulish, 2001). In 2001 about $4 million additional federal funding was expected to be received by the end of the year, according to the *Wall Street Journal* report.

Not surprisingly, Arizona has one of the highest incarceration rates in the country (513 in 2002, ranked tenth in the country), with almost half being either black (14.7 percent) or Hispanic (33.7 percent) (Harrison and Karberg, 2003; Camp and Camp, 2000). After Corrections Corporation of America began housing prisoners from Washington, DC in its prison in Florence, the African-American population of the town more than doubled to over 1,500. Florence now has two state prisons, three private prisons, plus the U.S. Immigration and Naturalization Service detention center. This little town can now brag about having "the highest percentage of prison inmates of any U.S. town of more than 10,000" (Kulish, 2001).[15]

Another benefit of adding prisoners to the Census count is that it places many of these communities under the official poverty level, thereby qualifying for even more federal funds! Gatesville, Texas (pop. 15,591) qualified for poverty status with its 9,095 prisoners, resulting in the town receiving $4.2 million in state grants, which it used to upgrade water lines and build new roads. Another irony to all of this is the fact that while these prisoners are helping towns qualify for large sums of federal dollars, they are not included in the official unemployment figures. According to one recent study, by including African-Americans in the official unemployment figures, the unemployment rate for them increases to almost 40 percent (Western and Beckett, 1999), while adding about 2 to 3 percent to the official unemployment figures.

This is a form of "robbing Peter to pay Paul" since these federal dollars are following these prisoners from their original communities. One recent report noted that during the first decade of the twenty-first century about $2 trillion in federal funds will be distributed based upon the 2000 census count, so that a lot of money will be transferred from poor urban areas to small towns with prisons. Minnesota's state demographer Tom Gillaspy estimates that the census "directs $2,000–$3,000 per person counted to any given community each decade, *not including additional census-based funding distributed to poor communities*" (Maynard, 2000, emphasis added).

Finally, mention should be made of the impact rural prisons have had on redistricting. One result of the "phantom" increase in rural populations is in an increase in the voting power of rural districts, many of whom have added additional congressional seats, mostly Republican. The Prison Policy Initiative has argued that by allowing mostly white rural districts "to claim urban black prisoners as residents for purposes of representation resembles the old three-fifths clause of the Constitution that allowed the South extra representation for its slaves . . . ." Such a policy also means that legislators in rural areas "can devote more attention to their 'real constituents'" while at the same time those who support building new prisons in their rural areas have additional clout in state legislatures (Prison Policy Initiative, 2003). The state of Florida, already infamous for the 2000 election fraud, will soon have a significant redrawing of political boundaries, thanks to 79,144 (according to the Florida Department of Corrections web site) prisoners (over half are African-American). Gulf County has two prisons that contribute to its population numbers (13,332). The attorney general of Florida issued opinions in 2001 that said county commissions and school boards "*must* include prisoners when redistricting." One effect is that voting, in Florida and the other 48 states where prisoners are denied a vote, the voting power of large numbers of mostly minority urban communities are transferred to rural, mostly white areas—also, by the way, heavily Republican (Huling, 2002, p. 212, emphasis added). A statement from a former New York State legislator sums up the feelings of many politicians: "When legislators cry 'Lock'em up!' they often mean 'Lock'em up in my district'" (Huling, 2002, p. 213). I am tempted to conclude that locking up so many urban minorities is one part of a much larger conservative strategy to take over the country!

Todd Clear has noted that the increasing tendency to house prisoners in faraway rural communities amounts to what he calls "coercive mobility" that has a negative impact on informal methods of social control in poor communities. In many poor neighborhoods, up to 25 percent of the adult males are behind bars on any given day. This results in the removal of both *human capital* and *social capital* from these communities (Clear, 2002). Elsewhere he has estimated that as much as $25,000 per year leaves the community for every man who is incarcerated and this money goes directly to the communities that have the prisons (Clear and Rose, 1999).

Before leaving the subject of rural prisons I'd like to share a recent news item appearing in the *Los Angeles Times* on March 28, 2004. The story was about the small town of Clintwood, Virginia (pop. 1,549), tucked away in a relatively remote area of the far western edge of the state, close to the Kentucky border. The story is familiar in that a company called Travelocity (where you can make airline reservations), which was the largest employer in the area (250 jobs) and replaced the dying coal industry, was closing up shop and moving its operations to India by the end of the year.

In the middle of this article, which tells of the potential impact of the job losses that have typified the recent trend of "capital flight" to foreign countries, there's a passing reference to a prison in the area. The writer of the article notes that there is a joke around the town "that the only secure jobs are at the new state prison, because they are not going to be shipping the convicts to India anytime soon. There are several new lockups around the county, which a lot of people have mixed feelings about." The director of the local Chamber of Commerce stated, with somewhat bitter irony, "It's not quite as bad as being a nuclear waste dump site. But we're the dumpsite for human misery" (Streitfeld, 2004).

A check of the Virginia Department of Corrections web site reveals that there is a prison in the small town of Pound (about 10 miles from Clintwood, with a population of 1,089). The name of the prison is Red Onion State Prison which has an average daily population of 985 (http://www.vadoc.state.va.us/facilities/institutions/redonion.htm). This is a maximum security institution opened in August, 1998.

Conclusion

We live in times of great uncertainty as millions just barely eke out a living while a small minority become richer and richer, especially with Bush's latest round of tax cuts, not to mention the negative effects of the invasion and occupation of Iraq (Sklar, 2003; Piven and Cloward, 1997). We now find more and more of our citizens relegated to the ranks of what Marx once described as the "surplus population," a population rendered unneeded or "superfluous" as far as creating profits are concerned. One consequence is the disappearance of semi-skilled and unskilled jobs once filled by urban minorities, especially African-American males. But this group is still very much with us and their existence requires them to be "managed" in some way. One way that has been used to manage or control this population is to confine them to inner city ghettos, while another way is to use the prison system.

In a new edition of his *Crime Control as Industry*, Christie makes perhaps one of the strongest arguments in support of our own interpretation of the functions of the prison industrial complex:

> Societies of the Western type face two major problems: Wealth is everywhere unequally distributed. So is access to paid work. Both problems contain potentialities for unrest. The crime control industry is suited for coping with both. This industry provides profit and work, while at the same time producing control of those who otherwise might have disturbed the social process.
>
> Compared to most other industries, the crime control industry is in a most privileged position. There is no lack of raw-material; crime seems to be in endless supply. Endless also are the demands for the service, as well as the willingness to pay for what is seen as security. And the usual industrial questions of contamination do not appear. On the contrary, *this is an industry seen as cleaning up, removing unwanted elements from the social system.* (Christie, 2000, p. 13)

Part of the problem we are talking about here can be summed up by way of a parable, which originated with the famous social reformer and agitator of the early twentieth century, Saul Alinsky (reported in Bartollas, 2004, p. 354). Imagine a large river with a high waterfall. At the bottom of this waterfall hundreds of people are working frantically trying to save those who have fallen into the river and have fallen down the waterfall, many of them drowning. As the people along the shore are trying to rescue as many as possible one individual looks up and sees a seemingly never-ending stream of people falling down the waterfall and he begins to run upstream. One of his fellow rescuers hollers "where are you going? There are so many people that need help here." To which the man replied, "I'm going upstream to find out why so many people are falling into the river."

Now imagine the scene at the bottom of the waterfall represents the criminal justice system, responding to crimes that have been committed and dealing with both victims and offenders. If you look more closely, you will begin to notice that there are more people at the bottom of the stream, that they work in relatively new buildings with all sorts of modern technology and that those working here get paid rather well, with excellent benefits. And the money keeps flowing into this area, with all sorts of businesses lined up to provide various services and technical assistance. If you look upstream, you will find something far different. There are not too many people, the buildings are not as modern, nor are the technology that they use. The people working there do not get paid very much and their benefits are not as good as those provided down below, while the turnover is quite high.

Neither do they find businesses coming their way with assistance. They constantly have to beg for money. Moreover, you will often find more women working upstream, since their work in this culture is not as valued as the work men do (men are in charge downstream).

A researcher, writing about our health care system, observed that our economic system of capitalism "finds it more profitable to treat illness rather than prevent it." He notes that "preventive care measures, such as decent sewage and water systems, draining swamps near cities, education, regulated food handling, and universal vaccinations bring little in terms of profit for pharmaceutical companies or the larger capitalist system" (Engler, 2003, p. 34). The American medical industry has a financial stake in treating rather than preventing diseases.

If we pretend for a moment that crime is a disease (in a way it is), then this analogy makes perfect sense. Simply put, reacting to crime is far more profitable for business and other interests than preventing crime. Our criminal justice is designed to fail to reduce crime, because, although citizens would be greatly benefited from less crime (just as citizens would be greatly benefited from fewer health problems), the criminal justice industrial complex (and the prison industrial complex that is part of it) would not benefit. If you want a lower crime rate, then you must spend more money upstream, so to speak. In order to do this, however, the interests that now control the criminal justice system would have to be convinced that there is a larger profit to be made from investing upstream, rather than downstream.

Notes

1. An advertising brochure from an investment firm called World Research Group, cited in Silverstein, K. (1998). "America's Private Gulag." In Burton-Rose, D. and P. Wright (eds.). (1998). *The Celling of America: An Inside Look at the U.S. Prison Industry.* Monroe, ME: Common Courage Press, p. 156.

2. Ron Garzini, Private prison booster, quoted in Parenti, C. (1999). *Lockdown America: Police and Prisons in the Age of Crisis.* New York: Verso, p. 211.

3. City manager of Sayre, Oklahoma, which had just opened a prized new maximum-security prison. Kilborn, P. T. (2001). "Rural Towns Turn to Prisons to Reignite Their Economies." *New York Times,* August 1. Street, P. (2005). "Race, Place, and the Perils of Prisonomics." *Z Magazine*, July/August, 2005. http://zmagsite.zmag.org/JulAug2005/street0705.html.

4. A California Department of Corrections official explaining some of the benefits of putting a prison in a rural area. Quoted in Huling, T. (2000) "Building a Prison Economy in Rural America." In Mauer, M. and M. Chesney-Lind (eds.), *Invisible Punishment: the Collateral Consequences of Mass Imprisonment.* New York: New Press, p. 200.

5. Duke, L. (2000). "Prison Construction Boom Transforms Small Towns." *The Washington Post*, September 8.

6. "7 Federal Prisons to Get Lethal Electrified Fences." *Washington Post*, July 12, 2005.

7. Bureau of Justice Statistics, on line: www.ojp.usdog.gov/bjs/pub/pdf/pjim05.pdf. Not included in these figures are those detained under the jurisdiction of the Bureau of Immigration and Customs Enforcement (formerly the INS), which totaled 21,065 on December 31, 2002. This number represented a 46 percent increase over 1995. Additionally, there were 2,377 prisoners held under military jurisdiction, plus 16, 206 prisoners held in the custody of correctional authorities in U.S. territories. These numbers together add up to 39,648 (Harrison and Beck, 2004. The total number of prisoners comes to 2,072,979.

8. It should be noted that 13 percent of all adult African-American men are disenfranchised as a result of a felony conviction (1.4 million; one-third of all disenfranchised adults); in some states the percentage is more than 30 (e.g., Alabama and Florida), while in many more states over 20 percent are disenfranchised (The Sentencing Project/Human Rights Watch, 1998). No wonder some are calling imprisonment the "new American apartheid" (Shelden, Brown and Listwan, 2004).

9. These ads were selected from several issues of *Corrections Today*, spanning the past ten years.

10. Two additional examples would be telephone companies, many of whom have added surcharges to long-distance calls made by prisoners to their families and "bed brokers" who find empty jail or prison cells for a fee. For more detail see the following: http://www.sheldensays.com/Res-four.htm

11. There presently exists an extremely large and politically powerful union in California. Space does not permit a full discussion of the role of unions. For more detail see. http://www.sheldensays.com/Res-four.htm

12. Consistent with what seems to be a national obsession over drugs. A report called "Drug Monitoring and Abuse Testing Business" released in January, 1997 (produced by Business Communications Company, Norwalk, CT), noted that revenues for drug testing businesses grew as much as 15 percent annually during the first half of the 1990s. In 1996, the drug testing market took in around $628 million in revenues, increasing to about $737 million in 2001 (Hawkins, 2002). It has been estimated that about 61 percent of all major businesses test their employees, plus more than 500 school districts

test their students. An estimated 20-25 million Americans are tested for drugs each year, compared to around 7 million in 1996 (Hawkins, 2002). (Staples, 1997: 97)

13. A look at the web site for the New York State Department of Corrections (http://www.docs.state.ny.us/faclist.html) shows that there are five prisons in Franklin County (pop. 51,134) where Malone is. According to this web site, New York currently has 18 maximum security prisons, 37 medium security prisons, 13 minimum security prisons (4 are designated as "shock prisons"), three minimum security camps and one drug treatment "campus" (in Willard, pop. 600 in western New York, on the shores of Seneca Lake); the total is 72. A recent report notes that less than 40 percent of the population of New York State lives in what is considered the "upstate" area; over 70 percent of the prisoners are from the New York City area, while about 90 percent of the prisoners are incarcerated in upstate prisons (Prison Policy Initiative, 2003).

14. One downside to building all these prisons in upstate New York, however, is the fact that hundreds of families of inmates have to make the long bus ride in order to visit their relatives. Ironically, this fact has created yet another business, begun in 1973 by an ex-convict, who founded Operation Prison Gap, which operates a bus service for these families. They now have 35 buses and vans traveling on weekends and holidays (Schlosser, 1998: 58). Some rural residents have protested the locating of a prison in their counties. In the town of Braham, Minnesota (pop. 1,276), citizens rejected putting a prison there, with one local critic saying they would have to change their motto from "Homemade pie capital of Minnesota" to "Prison capital of Minnesota." The prison was located in nearby Rush City, over the objections of a few in that town. In Pembina County, North Dakota, local citizens are protesting the proposed building of a prison there. Opponents are concerned about the negative changes the prison would bring, such as impeding tourism; proponents talk about the jobs that would be created. One supporter hopes that a 500 bed prison will be built, claiming that the impact would be "tremendous," adding that "it's pretty much recession-proof" (Clement, 2002). Not all are "recession-proof" as it turns out. In Boone Terre, Missouri (pop. 4,039), a new prison was opened in 1995 (the most expensive in the state) and by 2001 the city was in debt with new businesses almost broke because state budget shortfalls delayed the opening of the prison, with an estimated loss of several million dollars (Huling, 2002: 204-205).

15. Florence is not the only small town to reap such benefits. Calipatria, California has an "official" population of 7,289, thanks to 4,095 prisoners; Ionia, Michigan has a population of 10,569 that includes 4,401 prisoners – they used some of the federal money to install laptop computers in the town automobiles and turn a National Guard armory into a community center (Kulish, 2001). Sussex County, Virginia appears to be the fastest growing county in the country, thanks mostly to the fact that between 1998 and 1999 two new prisons increased its population by 23 percent. According to the 2000 census, there are 12,504 "official" residents. Similarly, Coxsackie, New York received an increase in federal funding because its 1990 population was 27.5 percent prisoners. With a 2000 population of 2,895 it is no doubt set to receive more. Two small Arizona towns, Gila Bend (pop. 1,980) and Buckeye (pop. 6,537) competed to get both adult and juvenile prisons placed in their district. Buckeye won and stands to receive more than $10 million in federal subsidies (Huling, 2002). Malone, New York (mentioned above) has also benefited. The town may gain more federal dollars because one-third of the total population of 15,000 consists of prisoners (Duke, 2000).

References

Austin, J., Bruce, M. A., Carroll, L., McCall, P. L., & Richards, S. C. (2001). The use of incarceration in the United States. *Critical Criminology*, *10*, 17-41.

Austin, J., & Irwin, J. (2001). *It's about time: American's incarceration binge* (3rd ed.). Belmont, CA: Wadsworth.

Austin, J., & Hardyman, P. L. (2004). The risks and needs of the returning prisoner population. *Review of Policy Research*, *21*, 13-29.

Bartollas, C. (2004). *Juvenile delinquency* (6th ed.). Boston: Allyn and Bacon.

Beck, A. J., Karberg, J. C., & Harrison, P. M. (2002). Prison and jail inmates at mid-year, 2001. Washington, DC: Bureau of Justice Statistics.

Berkowitz, B. (2002). "Smart ALEC's." Working for Change. (www.workingforchange.com).

Bonita, J., Wallace-Capretta, S., Rooney, J., & Mcanoy, K. (2002). An outcome evaluation of a restorative justice alternative to incarceration. *Contemporary Justice Review*, *5*, 319-338.

Bureau of Justice Statistics, Key facts at a glance: Correctional populations, July 27, 2003. Online: www.ojp.usdoj.gov/bjs/

Burton-Rose, D. P., & Wright, P. (Eds.). (1998). *The celling of America: An inside look at the U.S. prison industry.* Monroe, ME: Common Courage Press.

Camp, C. G., & Camp, G. M. (2000). *The corrections yearbook 2000: Adult corrections.* Middletown, CT: Criminal Justice Institute.

Chesney-Lind, M. and Pasko, L. (2004). *The Female Offender: Girls, Women and Crime* (2nd ed.). Thousand Oaks, CA: Sage.

Chesney-Lind, M., & Shelden, R. G. (2004). *Girls, delinquency and juvenile justice* (3rd ed.). Belmont, CA: Wadsworth.

Christie, N. (2000). *Crime control as industry.* (3rd ed.). New York: Routledge.

Clear, T. (2002). Addition by subtraction. In M. Mauer, & M. Chesney-Lind (Eds.), *Invisible punishment: The collateral consequences of mass imprisonment.* New York: New Press.

Clear, T., & Rose, D. R. (1999). *When neighbors go to jail: Impact on attitudes about formal and informal social control.* Washington, DC: National Institute of Justice.

Clement, D. (2002). Big house on the prairie. *Fedgazette* (Federal Reserve Bank of Minneapolis), January. Online: www.minneapolisfed.org.pubs/fedgaz/02-01/house.cfm.

Currie, E. (1998). *Crime and justice in America.* New York: Metropolitan Books.

Donziger, S. (1996). *The real war on crime.* New York: HarperCollins.

Duke, L. (2000). Prison construction boom transforms small towns. *The Washington Post*, September 8.

Dyer, J. (2000). *The perpetual prisoner machine: How America profits from crime.* Boulder, CO: Westview Press.

Glaze, L. E. and S. Palla (2005). "Probation and Parole in the United States, 2004." Washington, DC: Bureau of Justice Statistics, November 2005. http://www.ojp.usdoj.gov/bjs/pub/pdf/ppus03.pdf

Engler, I. (2003, April). Selling drugs: Capitalist healthcare. *Z Magazine*, 32-35.

Harrison, P. M., & Beck, A. J. (2004). Prisoners in 2003. Washington, DC: Bureau of Justice Statistics.

Harrison, P. M., & Beck, A. J. (2006), Prison and jail inmates in mid-year 2005. Washington, DC: Bureau of Justice Statistics, May. http://www.ojp.usdoj.gov/bjs/pub/pdf/pjim05.pdf

Harrison, P. M. and J. C. Karberg. (2003). "Prison and Jail Inmates at Mid-Year 2002." Washington, DC: Bureau of Justice Statistics, April.

Hawkins, D. (2002). Tests on trial. Online: usnews.com. (drugtesting.freeservers.com).

Heilbroner, R. L. (1985). *The nature and logical of capitalism.* New York: W. W. Norton

Huling, T. (2002). Building a prison economy in rural America. In M. Mauer & M. Chesney-Lind (Eds.), *Invisible punishment: The collateral consequences of mass imprisonment.* New York: New Press.

Kilborn, P. T. (2001). "Rural Towns Turn to Prisons to Reignite Their Economies." *New York Times,* August 1

Kulish, N. (2001). Annexing the penitentiary. *The Wall Street Journal.* August 8.

Lilly, J. R., & Knepper, P. (1993). The correctional-commercial complex. *Crime and Delinquency*, *39*, 150-166.

Macallair, D. (2003). Flaws of justice behind bars: Reforming California's failed parole system. San Francisco: Center on Juvenile and Criminal Justice.

Maguire, K., & Pastore, A. L. (Eds). (1996). *Sourcebook on criminal justice statistics - 1995.* Washington, D.C.: Department of Justice, Bureau of Justice Statistics.

Maguire, K. and A. L. Pastore (eds.) (1997). *Sourcebook on Criminal Justice Statistics-1996.* Washington, DC: Department of Justice, Bureau of Justice Statistics

Maynard, M. (2000). Prison math. *City Beat,* 21. (citypages.com/databank/21/1309).

Miller, J. G. (1996). *Search and destroy: African-Americans males in the criminal justice system.* New York: Cambridge University Press.

Owen, B. (1998). *"In the mix": Struggle and survival in a women's prison.* Albany, NY: SUNY Press.

Parenti, C. (1999). *Lockdown America: Police and prisons in the age of crisis.* New York: Verso.

Piven, F. F. and R. Cloward (1997). *The Breaking of the American Social Compact.* New York: The New Press.

Prison Policy Initiative (2003). Diluting democracy: Census quirk fuels prison expansion. Springfield, MA: http://www.prisonpolicy,org.

Quinney, R. (1980). *Class, state and crime* (2nd ed.). New York: Longman.

Richards, S. C., Austin, J., & Jones, R. S. (2004). Kentucky's perpetual prisoner machine: It's about money. *Policy Review Journal*, *21*, 1, 93-106.

Schlosser, E. (1998). The prison-industrial complex. *The Atlantic Monthly* (December).

Shelden, R. G., & Brown, W. B. (2000). The crime control industry and the management of the surplus population. *Critical Criminology*, *8* (Autumn).

Shelden, R. G., & Brown, W. B. (2003). *Criminal justice in America: A critical view.* Boston: Allyn and Bacon.

Shelden, R. G., Brown, W. B., & Listwan, S. (2004). The new American apartheid: The incarceration of African-Americans. In R. R. Miller & S. L. Browning (Eds.), *The common good: A critical examination of law and social control.* Chapel Hill: Carolina Academic Press.

Silverstein, K. (1998). "America's Private Gulag." In Burton-Rose, D. and P. Wright (eds.). (1998). *The Celling of America: An Inside Look at the U.S. Prison Industry.* Monroe, ME: Common Courage Press.

Sklar, H. (2003). Working-class soldiers, upper-class tax cuts. *Progressive Populist*, 9 (May 15), 15-16.

Street, P. (2002, June). Class, color, and the hidden injuries of race. *Z Magazine*, 39-42.

Streitfeld, D. (2004). A town's future is leaving the country. *Los Angeles Times*, March 28.

Sullivan, D., & Tifft, L. (2001). *Restorative justice: Healing the foundations of our everyday lives.* Monsey, NY: Willow Tree Press.

Travis, J. (2002). Invisible punishment: An instrument of social exclusion. In Mauer and Chesney-Lind, *Invisible punishment.*

Welch, M. (1999). *Punishment in America: Social control and the ironies of imprisonment.* Thousand Oaks, CA: Sage.

Welch, M. (2005). *Ironies of Imprisonment.* Thousand Oaks, CA: Sage.

Western, B., & Beckett, K. (1999). How unregulated is the U.S. labor market? The penal system as a labor market . *American Journal of Sociology*, *104*, 1030-1060.

Wray, L. R. (2000). "New Economic Reality: Penal Keynesianism." *Challenge* 43, 5, p. 52.

Younge, D. (2003). HEADLINE: 30% of black men in the US will go to jail. *The Guardian*, August 19 (www.cjcj.org/press/black_men.html).

Part II

Peacemaking Themes

Chapter 8

Toward a Theoretical Model of Peacemaking Criminology: An Essay in Honor of Richard Quinney

John F. Wozniak

In previous research, core peacemaking criminology themes addressed by authors within the Pepinsky and Quinney reader were examined. These peacemaking criminology themes are types of crimes/social harms embedded in current social structure, types of theoretical frameworks/perspectives guiding peacemaking criminology, and types of peacemaking alternatives to confront the social injustices underlying crimes/social harms in today's society. Building on this previous research as well as a survey of peacemaking authors, this article illustrates how elements of a peacemaking criminology theoretical model come into view. The article then explores the basic nature and connections of the elements in this peacemaking criminology theoretical model. The analysis concludes with suggestions of ways this peacemaking criminology theoretical model can be adapted toward future crime research and policies.

During the past ten years, I have been greatly interested in the origins and development of peacemaking criminology. One of my first experiences with peacemaking criminology occurred while I served as the coordinator of the critical criminology division for the 1994 Annual Meeting of the Academy of Criminal Justices Sciences in Chicago. At this meeting, I invited Richard Quinney, Lila Rucker, Kay Harris, and Harold Pepinsky to speak on topics about peacemaking criminology to illustrate "New Voices in Critical Criminology." While I moderated this session, I became intrigued with not only the progressive ideas expressed by each of these panelists but also the engaging comments offered by various individuals in the audience. I also had the good fortune of being one of more than 150 participants at the 1997 International Conference on Justice Without Violence, Peacemaking Criminology, and Restorative Justice at Albany, New York. Here, my desire to study peacemaking criminology was further influenced by compelling testimonies of these conference participants that peacemaking and restorative justice are most promising and very much needed paths to take in criminology.

This article is built on the hopeful views about what to do about crime shared by people at these conference sessions in Chicago and Albany. More specifically, I have undertaken two research projects to heighten discourse about peacemaking criminology as a theoretical perspective in criminology. First, I surveyed authors who have written about peacemaking criminology as it approaches the study of crime, punishment, and justice (Wozniak, 2000b). Second, I did a content analysis of how Harold Pepinsky and Richard Quinney's *Criminology as Peacemaking* (1991) reader tends to exhibit core peacemaking theories in regard to crime and its control.

These studies of peacemaking criminology have provided a foundation for me to write this current article. Essentially, the central objective of this article is to illustrate basic elements of a peacemaking criminology theoretical model. Before introducing the elements of this theoretical model, it seems beneficial to first review how peacemaking criminology has been treated in recent literature. The second part of this article then briefly notes key findings in my survey of peacemaking criminology authors. The third part of this article delineates peacemaking criminology themes that help to form a basis of a peacemaking criminology theoretical model. After that, this article identifies this peacemaking criminology theoretical model in terms of its basic nature and connections. The article concludes with suggestions of ways that this peacemaking criminology theoretical model can be adapted toward future crime research and policies.

Treatment of Peacemaking Criminology Within Readers and Textbooks

This part of the article demonstrates how peacemaking criminology has been characterized in criminological writings. Hence, it will be shown that many current criminological authors have not formulated the basic premises and policies of peacemaking criminology in as broad of a way as it could be done.

For example, during the past 5 years, various criminologists (e.g., Cordella & Siegel, 1996; Cullen & Agnew, 1999; Henry & Einstadter, 1998; Paternoster & Bachman, 2001; Simpson, 2000) have edited books of readings to illustrate major developments in current criminological theories. Arrigo's (1999) book of readings is unlike the others, given that each featured reading focuses on a current theoretical development in critical criminology. Notably, in Arrigo's (1999) book, the "Peacemaking Primer" chapter of Harold Pepinsky explores peacemaking criminology assumptions, principles, perils, and prospects. However, the other collections of readings listed above are designed to explore how issues and controversies emanating from classic theoretical approaches within criminology have been reformulated with respect to the changing context of contemporary society.[1] It is apparent on review of this latter literature that criminologists today are often engaged in the application of a very wide variety of theoretical approaches toward the study of unlawful behavior. In this light, it is instructive to further note that peacemaking criminology is a theoretical perspective that is not given (except by Arrigo and Cullen and Agnew) general attention in these most recent examples of criminology theory readers.

One reason that peacemaking criminology is not always given prime emphasis by criminologists today lies in the manner in which this theoretical approach is treated in criminology and crime theory textbooks. In more specific terms, of thirty criminology textbooks published since 1990, eighteen touched on peacemaking criminology and the other twelve made no mention of peacemaking criminology at all.[2] An analysis of these latter eighteen criminology textbooks reveals five general limitations in the way that peacemaking criminology is discussed as a theoretical perspective.

First, some of these textbooks tend to offer commentary of peacemaking criminology in a very brief manner, such that at times there is often not more than just a few paragraphs or so of coverage.[3] Second, some criminology textbook authors define peacemaking criminology in a favorable way but with terms included that are not necessarily self-explanatory and in need of more precise elaboration. For instance, Beirne and Messerschmidt (2000) asserted that peacemaking criminology is "a critical perspective that examines the essence of the person charged with a crime and emphasizes cooperation, compassion, and respect for all others" (p. 512). Similarly, Barkan (2001) defined peacemaking criminology as "an approach that combines several humanistic strains of thought to view crime as just one of the many forms of suffering that characterize human existence" (p. 526). Likewise, Sacco and Kennedy (1996) conceptualized peacemaking criminology as "a process that involves reducing punishment/imprisonment and promoting programs that encourage treatment, rehabilitation, alternatives to incarceration, mediation, and enhanced social justice" (p. 385). Schmalleger (1996) maintained that peacemaking criminology is "a perspective which holds that crime-control agencies and the citizens they serve should work together to alleviate social problems and human suffering and thus reduce crime" (p. 516). In addition, Siegel (1998) wrote that peacemaking is "a branch of conflict theory that stresses humanism, mediation, and conflict resolution as a means to end crime" (p. 561).

Third, several criminology textbook authors trace peacemaking criminology to the body of research found within the *Criminology as Peacemaking* (1991) book of readings edited by Harold Pepinsky and Richard Quinney.[4] On one hand, these latter textbook authors are to be credited for acknowledging the important influence of Pepinsky and Quinney on the development of the peacemaking criminology approach as a whole. On the other hand, there is more need of an elaboration on the origins, foundations, and reformulations of peacemaking criminology than what is commonly offered in such recent criminology textbooks. Along these same lines, another criminology textbook provided a citation of the Pepinsky and Quinney peacemaking criminology reader yet failed to utilize the term *peacemaking criminology* in the textbook discussion.[5]

Fourth, a few criminology textbook authors point out that peacemaking criminology is best understood as one of the recent examples of critical/new criminology.[6] However, these latter textbook authors generally fail to clearly show how peacemaking criminology is similar or not to other critical/new criminologies. Usually, these authors position peacemaking criminology as a critical/new approach without taking more steps to address possible interconnections between peacemaking criminology and other critical/new criminology theories. Parenthetically, it is quite rare to find textbooks, which treat peacemaking criminology as a critical theory, expanding on the origins and possible reformulations of peacemaking as a broad theoretical paradigm.

A fifth tendency within current criminology textbooks is to begin discussion of peacemaking criminology in a favorable manner but then proceed to observe a grave flaw in applying this approach to the study and control of crime in general. As an illustration, Beirne and Messerschmidt (2000) showed how peacemaking criminology has key policy applications such as reconciliation and conflict resolution but at the same time stated that peacemaking criminology has an "eclectic theoretical basis of which lies in a loose mixture of religious humanism and feminism" (p. 233). Like Beirne and Messerschmidt (2000, p. 233), Maguire and Radosh (1999, p. 256) showed the importance of distinguishing between "negative peace" (i.e., criminal justice system responds to crime) and "positive peace" (i.e., sources of crime such as poverty, inequality, racism, and alienation are no longer present). Furthermore, Maguire and Radosh indicated to their textbook readers that peacemaking criminology has a set of core components and central thrusts that could be potentially linked to ideas/variables within the mainstream criminology proposal of adopting a "social support paradigm" (Cullen, 1994; Cullen, Wright, & Chamlin, 1999) toward the study of crime and its control. Nonetheless, Maguire and Radosh also asserted, "As a scientific enterprise, however, peacemaking criminology is less impressive" and has "little to say about *how* the grand scale changes they produce might be achieved" (p. 256). Beirne and Messerschmidt (2000) tended to concur with these authors as follows: "Although laudable in its ideology, peacemaking criminology as yet offers no blueprint for achieving a humanistic criminal justice system" (p. 237).

Along with depicting peacemaking criminology in a favorable light, some other criminology textbook authors tend to feel the need to caution the use of peacemaking criminology in the times ahead. As an example, Berger, Free, and Searles (2001) suggested that peacemaking criminology is "not a programmatic response that all injustices and social problems of the world can be solved" (p. 435). Similarly, Schmalleger (1996) stated, "Peacemaking criminology has been criticized as being naive and utopian, as well as failing to recognize the realities of crime control and law enforcement" (p. 490).

Along with these limitations, it would be remiss to fail to point out that a number of criminology textbook authors have evaluated peacemaking criminology in a very favorable light. For example, Siegel (1998) summarized the premises of peacemaking criminology as follows: "Peace and humanism can reduce crime; conflict resolution strategies can work" (p. 248). In one of the most elaborate discussions of peacemaking criminology in a criminology textbook, DeKeseredy and Schwartz (1996, pp. 268–276) identified the origins of peacemaking criminology along with its principles and practical applications. Generally, DeKeseredy and Schwartz's assessment of peacemaking criminology is complimentary, such that "this perspective can help us think through 'our facile acceptance of violence against others'" (p. 273).

Likewise, Quinney and Wildeman (1991) wrote a criminology textbook that advocated a "peacemaking criminology" approach in its analysis of crime. Like DeKeseredy and Schwartz (1996), Quinney and Wildeman (1991) elaborated on the origins, principles, and practical applications of peacemaking criminology. As one might expect, this latter textbook was quite optimistic about the prospects of peacemaking criminology as it is stated:

> This is a criminology that is based necessarily on human transformation in the achievement of peace and justice. Human transformation takes place as we change our social, economic, and political structure. And the message is clear: Without peace within us and in our actions, there can be no peace and justice in our results. Peace is the way. (p. 110)

Such wordings, often found in other peacemaking writings as well (e.g., Braswell, 1990; Pepinsky & Quinney, 1991), seem to connote the potential value of seeking peace over violence as a general standpoint to approach criminology. Interestingly, some very recent crime-related textbooks conclude their analysis that it is most desirable to now proceed toward the study and handling of crime/criminals with a "peacemaking criminology" perspective (Berger et al., 2001; Fuller, 1998; Shelden, Tracy, & Brown, 2001). However, as will be demonstrated in the discussion ahead, there are fundamental themes of peacemaking criminology that have not been systematically examined within these recent criminology textbooks. The same can be said of recent crime theory textbooks. Again, of 11 crime theory textbooks published since 1990, nine dealt with peacemaking criminology and the other two made no mention of peacemaking criminology at all.[7]

There are several patterns in the way that crime theory textbooks tend to overview peacemaking criminology on the whole. For example, one way of visualizing how current crime theory textbook authors observe the general value of peacemaking criminology is to note their place on a continuum. This continuum can be thought of as those less favorable of peacemaking criminology on one side and those more favorable of peacemaking criminology on the other side. Notably, it can be argued in this way that Akers (2000) ranks as least favorable, followed by Gibbons (1994) and Bohm (2001). Vold, Bernard, and Snipes (1998) tend to be moderate on this issue. Einstadter and Henry (1995) seem to be most favorable to peacemaking criminology, followed by Moyer (2001); Williams and McShane (1999); Lilly, Cullen, and Ball (2002); and White and Haines (1996). More specifically, Akers (2000) wrote of the various contributions of Pepinsky and Quinney toward the development of peacemaking criminology, and then moved on to state,

> Peacemaking criminology does not offer a theory of crime or of the criminal justice system that can be evaluated empirically . . . this is a highly laudable philosophy of criminal justice, but it does not offer an explanation of why the system operates as it does or why offenders commit crime. It can be evaluated on other grounds but not on empirical validity. (p. 214)

Akers (2000) further took issue with this perspective's challenge of mainstream criminology by stating,

> The assertion by peacemaking criminologists that no "traditional" criminologist or no one in the criminal justice system recognizes the real suffering created by crime or that none has advocated peaceful, non-violent ways of dealing with crime, is simply inaccurate. None of the policy implications of peacemaking criminology is unique to those who self-consciously identify themselves with this perspective . . . all these policies, such as the non-punitive treatment of offenders, mediation, restitution, offender reintegration, rehabilitation, and so on, have long been mainstays of the policy recommendations from "traditional" criminology. (p. 215)

Gibbons (1994) considered peacemaking criminology as one of the forms of "new criminologies" along with left realism, feminism, and postmodernism. However, Gibbons's (1994) skepticism of peacemaking criminology is evident as follows:

> The representative sample of essays in the Pepinsky and Quinney volume does suggest that modest steps toward a more humane society and more positive approaches to lawbreaking, in the form of reductions of sexual violence and other forms of abuse of women, alterations in the severity of incarceration, and wider use of mediation strategies in the criminal justice machinery, are possible. But massive overhaul of American society is another matter. Many persons would argue that the huge federal deficit, runaway entitlement program costs, and a host of other problems plaguing the economy and society make it almost impossible to restructure the social order. On this point, both Currie's book and the Pepinsky and Quinney volume have little to say about how the grand scale changes they propose might be achieved. (p. 172)[8]

Bohm (2001), on the other hand, was not as derogatory in his treatment of peacemaking criminology. Yet he posited that

> peacemaking criminology can be criticized for its extreme idealism and emphasis on the transformation of individuals (as a way of transforming society) rather than the transformation of society (as away of transforming individuals). It has also been criticized for not providing a blueprint of how such transformations can be achieved. (p. 121)

Vold et al. (1998) opted to subsume peacemaking criminology as a variant of postmodernism, with Pepinsky and Quinney as influential contributors to this theory. The parting words of Vold et al. about these latter theorists were

> Ultimately, these criminologists have come to the conclusion that the violence of punishment can only perpetuate and increase the violence of crime. Only when criminologists and the public give up their belief in the effectiveness and appropriateness of violence can we reasonably expect criminals to do the same thing. (p. 274)

Williams and McShane (1999) offered an elaboration, without criticism, of peacemaking criminology themes such as relief of suffering; restraining violence in the community; transformation of social, economic, and authority structures; and criminal justice that integrates the community into policing, courts, and corrections. Lilly et al. (2002) summarized peacemaking criminology origins, assumptions, traditions, policies, and links to restorative justice. Einstadter and Henry (1995) and Moyer (2001) presented the most favorable analyses of peacemaking criminology with respect to authors of crime theory textbooks. For instance, they identified links to peacemaking criminology such as humanism, feminism, anarchism, and left realism. And for the purposes of this article, Einstadter and Henry (1995, p. 296) reported insights of a few chapters in the Pepinsky and Quinney (1991) peacemaking reader. All in all, according to Einstadter and Henry (1995),

> Peacemaking as replacement discourse offers a different means of framing and thinking about crime that breaks out of the current punitive context. At the same time it brings into its discourse the voice of the victim, currently the mostly neglected element in the established justice system. (p. 297)

Moyer (2001) provided a cultural and historical background for peacemaking criminology that features the lives and contributions of Mahatma Gandhi, Jane Addams, and Martin Luther King, Jr. This crime theory textbook also includes a table depicting the emergence of peacemaking criminology as well as a detailed discussion of authors working in the spiritual/religious tradition (Quinney; Gibbs; Cordella; and Barak), feminist tradition (Brocke-Utne; McDermott; Harris; Knopp; and Warren and Cody), and critical tradition (Pepinsky; Caulfield; Sanzen; Scimecca; Lozoff and Braswell; and Fuller) of peacemaking criminology. Moyer concluded her chapter on peacemaking criminology as follows:

> It is hoped that this emerging theoretical perspective will be more widely read and will lead to positive policy changes in approaches to education and to a more peaceful and compassionate response to individuals who are defined as criminals during the twenty-first century. (p. 338)

In summation, this overview of recent criminology literature (book of readings, criminology textbooks, and crime theory textbooks) indicates a central point: Peacemaking criminology has attained increased coverage in crime-related textbooks. As a disseminator of knowledge, this broad set of literature has enabled an opportunity for discourse on "making peace, not war" to be blended with other criminological approaches to criminality.

As the discussion shows above, many criminology authors have taken issue with the general and practical usefulness of peacemaking criminology as an approach for criminal justice. This article does not agree with authors who develop a skeptical stance on the potential of peacemaking criminology. Nor does this article support a conclusion that the summaries of peacemaking criminology found in recent criminology textbook literature are cogent appraisals of the promise of peacemaking criminology as a paradigm of research and policy application. This latter conclusion is not supported particularly in light of an analysis of the survey responses of peacemaking authors about peacemaking criminology on the whole. The next section of this article summarizes these survey responses in detail.

Key Findings of the Survey of Peacemaking Criminology Authors

As reported in my article (Wozniak, 2000b), authors of peacemaking criminology writings provided responses to survey questions about what is distinctive about the peacemaking perspective in relation to mainstream criminology and how peacemaking criminology can contribute to policies and practices of the criminal justice system. The results of this survey indicate that peacemaking criminology authors tend to envision three differences between peacemaking criminology and mainstream criminology. The first difference between these perspectives is evident in their views about the relationship between social structure and crime:

> Peacemaking criminology begins with the premise that existing political, economic, and social structures and their underlying ideologies, that is, the status quo, should be questioned, not accepted as legitimate. Mainstream criminology is prone to ignore how structural injustices and definitions of "crime" are rooted in power and not somehow natural manifestations of the social order. A task of peacemaking criminology is thus to articulate how existing arrangements are the source of harm in society and to show how much of this harm, which serves the interests of the rich and powerful, is potentially avoidable. (Wozniak, 2000b, p. 273)

In this survey, a second difference between peacemaking criminology and mainstream criminology pertains to their approaches to "causes of crime," as exhibited in the following:

> Mainstream criminologists accept existing legal categories and then seek to use the scientific method to define, oversee, study, and control the "criminals" specified by law and to explore the cause of crime within that framework. Peacemaking criminology is less interested in such a narrow view of the etiology of "crime." Such inquiry, inevitably value-laden, must start by asking not what is "crime" but what is social harm and what are the political, economic, and social arrangements that bring about such harms. Ultimately, the peacemaking perspective maintains there is limited value in accumulating "causes of crime" that focus on individual failings and ignore the larger structures of power in which we are all enmeshed. (Wozniak, 2000b, p. 273)

In the following, a third difference shown in this survey between peacemaking criminology and mainstream criminology can be seen in their stances about solving crime within the criminal justice system:

> The tendency of mainstream criminologists is to seek solutions to crime within the confines of the existing criminal justice system. Their goal, so to speak, is to act as mechanics who operate and fix the machinery of the system so that it can run more efficiently and effectively. Peacemaking criminology, in contrast, believes that the answers to violence and social harm, and the injustices that are associated with such harm, lie largely outside the criminal justice system or, at least, in a justice system whose structures and processes are radically transformed. Solutions to the harms we do to each other are to be found in restorative processes that help heal those who have been hurt and thereby foster community. (Wozniak, 2000b, p. 274)

It is further demonstrated in this survey that peacemaking criminologists have specific recommendations for improving policing, the courts, and corrections (Wozniak, 2000b, p. 276). In a nutshell, these peacemaking survey respondents note the need to transform the police from "crime fighters" to "peace officers" who "would be trained more in human relations to find non-formal means to resolve disputes." In addition, police officers "would focus much of their effort on preventing crime" in the peacemaking criminology policy framework. Similarly, peacemaking criminologists "reject the idea that courts have to be instruments of adversarial justice." Instead, they feel that "courts should be places devoted to conflict resolution through processes such as peer mediation and victim-offender reconciliation" (i.e., restorative justice). On corrections, peacemaking criminologists have "recognized the need to abandon ill-advised policies rooted in punitiveness. Inflicting more harm—not doing peace—is counterproductive. The challenge is to humanize the prison environment."

In sum, the survey of peacemaking criminology authors further maintained that:

> at its core, peacemaking criminology reveals that, instead of waging a war on crime, we can create social arrangements in which the needs of all are taken into account. In particular, peacemaking criminology calls upon us to refuse to invest in a social ethic that separates us from one another and instead to visualize all people—including those responsible for serious harms—as being connected. (p. 283)

It is a key contention of this article that such views of crime and its control as commonly expressed within the survey of peacemaking criminology authors are important pieces of the puzzle enabling the formulation of a peacemaking criminology theoretical model. As will be demonstrated later in this article, ideas emanating from authors who responded to the peacemaking criminology survey provide one set of guideposts to build a peacemaking criminology theoretical model. A second set of guideposts to evolve a peacemaking criminology theoretical model lies in the analyses of pertinent themes in the Pepinsky and Quinney (1991) reader. It is to this latter issue that our discussion will now turn.

Three Salient Themes of Peacemaking Criminology

For the purposes of this article, it is useful to begin with Harold Pepinsky's concluding chapter in the Pepinsky and Quinney reader, *Criminology as Peacemaking* (1991). Most important, Pepinsky's conclusion offers a detailed commentary about how each chapter in this reader contributes to the peacemaking criminology approach. Here, Pepinsky's writing also offers background information about what led the authors in this reader to adopt a peacemaking criminology framework as a foundation for addressing the topics of interest in their chapters.

On reading Pepinsky's conclusion to the peacemaking criminology reader, it is possible to acquire a keener grasp and appreciation of what all the authors of this book were attempting to accomplish in their particular chapters. More specifically, Pepinsky (1991) maintained that there are many ways to conduct research in peacemaking criminology, but there are "three categories of tradition that stand out in this collection—religious traditions, feminist or women's traditions, and critical traditions" (p. 299). Notably, Pepinsky's discussion of ways authors in this reader fit into each of these traditions makes it apparent that peacemaking criminology has not only multiple influences and variants but also salient themes woven into its general analysis of social issues.

That is, it is fruitful to explore, as Pepinsky suggested, peacemaking criminology writings as part of religious, feminist, and critical traditions. It is important as well to examine three salient themes that are commonly addressed in peacemaking criminology writings. These salient themes are (a) types of crimes/social harms drawing the attention of peacemaking criminology authors, (b) types of peacemaking frameworks/perspectives guiding the analysis of peacemaking authors, and (c) types of peacemaking alternatives provided by peacemaking criminology authors to confront the social injustices within today's society.

Types of Crime/Social Harms

When all five chapters in religious traditions are examined together, it is evident that there is a tendency among peacemaking criminologists to address various crimes (i.e., violation of a law) in the same context of a myriad of other social harms (i.e., physical, mental, or social damages or injuries that are not violations of law in the strictest sense). For example, a main subject in Richard Quinney's (1991) analysis centered on solving the problem of crime. For Quinney, "crime is suffering" (p. 4) that is invariably linked with social harms such as poverty, hunger, homelessness, pollution, destruction of the environment, war, threat of nuclear destruction, and oppression. Similarly, in his comparison of Gandhian and Marxian humanism, Kevin Anderson (1991) considered crimes such as juvenile delinquency, robberies, assault, theft, assassinations, and government crime along with social harms such as alienation, oppression, slavery, exploitation of peasants, imperialism, and fetishism of commodities. Likewise, in Peter Cordella's (1991) chapter on mutualist religious communities, crimes such as theft, robbery, and assault are juxtaposed with social harms such as religious persecution, alienation, addiction, poverty, and unemployment. Furthermore, Gregg Barak's (1991) chapter on homelessness posed crimes such as vagrancy, physical abuse of mothers and babies, sexual abuse, runaways, and street crimes along with social harms such as alcoholism, addiction, AIDS victimizations, alienation, detachment, violent punishment, displacement of deinstitutionalized persons, decline in workers' purchasing power, increases in bankruptcies, and trade and budget deficits. And in Russ Immarigeon's (1991) chapter on movement toward reconciliation in the United States, crimes such as theft, robbery, and assault are explored along with social harms such as alienation, addiction, social problems, religious persecution, theological offenses, poverty, and unemployment.

In this light, peacemaking criminologists such as those in religious traditions just alluded to tend to broaden the outcomes of study in empirical research. These peacemaking criminologists are indeed calling for a grander array of dependent and intervening variables than some sort of crime (i.e., a violation of a law). For many peacemaking criminologists, then, it is practically inconceivable to analyze crime without simultaneously considering how it is linked with other social harms.

For the most part, this latter tendency was found again to be the case for seven authors addressing feminist traditions in the Pepinsky and Quinney reader. The one exception of note here is Maria Volpe's (1991) discussion of mediation in the criminal justice system. Harold Pepinsky (1991) observed about Volpe's work that "all the enterprises in doing mediation are not necessarily peaceful or successful" (p. 315). Thereby, Volpe's research was not geared to identifying a broad list of crimes/social harms in her analysis. Rather, Volpe took a different approach to peacemaking by highlighting the fact that "people involved in tense situations may find their actions can lead to criminal charges and further processing in the legal system" (p. 194). Furthermore, Volpe asserted that there is evidence of widespread interest in the use of mediation in the criminal justice system.

However, the other six authors in the Pepinsky and Quinney reader who wrote in terms of feminist traditions made it a point to address various crimes along with a host of social harms. For example, like Volpe (1991), Lila Rucker (1991) wrote about an intervention program in a prison that was based on numerous peacemaking principles. Yet, while formulating the main points of her study, Rucker emphasized that the prison setting is filled with persons who have committed many types of crimes in an atmosphere filled with social harms such as negative stereotyping, poor health, abnormal physical aggression, distrust, hopelessness, anger, and hostility.

Similarly, in her chapter that outlines a feminist view of justice, Kay Harris (1991) built her points in light of crimes such as murder, rape, and assault, and social harms such as prisoner overcrowding, demoralization, isolation, danger, despair, social inequality, terrorism, ecological damage, resource shortages, arms buildup, and nuclear holocaust. Notably, the other authors of the feminist tradition in the Pepinsky and Quinney reader all primarily examine violence against women. That is, in their study of sexual assault in Kalamazoo, Michigan, Susan Caringella-MacDonald and Drew Humphries (1991) explored assault, robbery, murder, and rape, along with negative gender role stereotyping; economic, social, and sexual inequality; and psychological and verbal violence. Likewise, in her chapter about community solutions to sexual violence, Fay Honey Knopp (1991) considered crimes in general and especially rape, child molestation, and nuisance offenders (exhibitionists, voyeurs, obscene phone calls), along with the social harm of general prejudice against women and children.

In this same vein, Walter DeKeseredy and Martin Schwartz (1991) showed how left realist principles can be used to better understand abuse of women. Here, they considered burglary, theft, and elite crime, along with violence against women, children, and ethnic groups; sexual harassment; working-class and female victimization; victims of unnecessary surgery; and workplace death and injury. Furthermore, in their chapter that shows similarities between battering women and battering central Americans, Larry Tifft and Lyn Markham (1991) delved into child abuse, sexual abuse, marital rape, abuse of elderly, robbery, assault, and property destruction along with social harms such as intimidation, exploitation, dependency diminishment, marginalizing women, sexism, racism, hunger, poverty, religious condemnation, torture, terrorism, and warfare invasions.

In addition, there are seven chapters designated as examples of critical traditions in the Pepinsky and Quinney reader. Like Volpe's (1991) work, Dragan Milovanovic's (1991) chapter was not designed to address an array of crimes/social harms in his analysis. Instead, Milovanovic explored images of unity and disunity with the master-slave relationship and "draws on," as Pepinsky (1991) noted, "Nietzsche of all people to infer the antithesis of war making" (p. 317). Similarly, the six other chapters cited as examples of critical traditions in the Pepinsky and Quinney reader do not tend to address many types of crime in their analyses. In specific terms, Susan Caulfield (1991) alluded to battering and interpersonal crime; Peter Sanzen (1991) and Joseph Scimecca (1991) considered crime in relation to the death penalty; John Galliher (1991) featured murder, rape, sexual assaults, and kidnapping; Robert Elias (1991) touched on crime in general; and Klein, Luxenburg, and Gunther (1991) made observations on burglary, arson, vandalism, and illegal selling of drugs. However, within these writings in the critical tradition of peacemaking criminology, a varied display of social harms are apparent as follows: alienation, racism, genocide, war, violations of human rights, and slaughter in Third World countries (Caulfield, 1991); alienation, poverty, hostility, segregation, suppression, exploitation, and police and prison repression (Sanzen, 1991); racism, humiliation, torture, and war (Galliher, 1991); poverty, hunger, homelessness, racism, sexism, inequality, repression, war, and totalitarianism; divorce, loss of jobs, terrorism, and totalitarianism (Scimecca, 1991); and racial discrimination, frustration, social injustice, underemployment/unemployment, and political repression (Klein et al., 1991).

As the discussion in this section of the article tends to indicate, writings in the Pepinsky and Quinney (1991) reader commonly focus on investigating crime in connection with social harms, which was shown earlier to be also a prime concern in the responses of authors to the peacemaking criminology survey. Moreover, this section illustrates that writings in the Pepinsky and Quinney reader, as a body of literature, are concerned with studying varying types of crime (e.g., street, white collar/corporate, organized, victimless, political) in juxtaposition with diverse kinds of social harms (e.g., interpersonal, such as negative stereotyping, aggression, hostility, despair, and alcoholism/addiction; social structural, such as alienation, poverty, religious persecution, sexism, and racism; and international, such as imperialism, terrorism, nuclear destruction, trade deficits, and ecological damage). Again, it is worthwhile to note that this latter approach of studying unlawful behavior is very much in keeping with the sentiments expressed about the nature of peacemaking criminology within the peacemaking criminology survey. In short, one of the main tenets in formulating a foundation to build a peacemaking criminology theoretical model is to recognize how various types of crime are inextricably linked with various types of social harms.

Types of Peacemaking Frameworks/Perspectives

It is not possible in this limited space to discuss in detail all of the various theoretical frameworks and perspectives underlying each of the chapters in the Pepinsky and Quinney (1991) reader. Nonetheless, it may be noted that central influences, indicated by selected authors regarding their chapter in this peacemaking criminology reader, are apparent as follows: Quinney (1991): Buddhism; Anderson (1991): Marx and Gandhi; Cordella (1991): mutualist model of community; Barak (1991): humanist sociology/criminology and constitutive criminology; Immarigeon (1991): Nils Christie; Harris (1991): feminist orientation toward justice and humanism; Tifft and Markham (1991): anarchism; DeKeseredy and Schwartz (1991): left realism, feminism, socialism, Marxists, and penal abolitionists; Rucker (1991): Quakers and feminism; Knopp (1991): abolitionism, Quakerism, feminism, socialism, and Gandhi; Milovanovic (1991): Nietzsche, Hegel, and Weber; Caulfield (1991): Chomsky, Foucault, Schwendingers, Gouldner, and anarchism; Galliher (1991): theory of communication breakdown and humanist criminology; Elias (1991): human rights enforcement perspective; Scimecca (1991): Maslow and the Burton approach to conflict resolution; and Klein et al. (1991): Durkheim, Reiman, Cullen and Gilbert, Lemert, Flacks, and Galper.

A general review of this listing shows that such peacemaking criminology authors tend to gravitate away from mainstream criminology theories as guides to conduct research. Again, consistent with the views of authors who responded to the peacemaking criminology survey, writers in the Pepinsky and Quinney reader generally choose to adopt perspectives of a critical/progressive nature, which are more often the type of theories that "begins with the premise that existing political, economic, and their underlying ideologies, that is, the status quo, should be questioned, not accepted as legitimate," and "believes that answers to violence and social harm, and the injustices that are associated with such harm, lie largely outside the criminal justice system" (Wozniak, 2000b, pp. 273–274).

It is equally important to note the diversity of theoretical standpoints influencing writers in the Pepinsky and Quinney (1991) reader. As such, peacemaking criminology is, by its very nature, not only a multivaried but also an optimistic approach that "could open up to criminal justice workers the possibility that society could be organized differently—including their places of work—and that human reactions could be conducted in a different, more humane way" (Wozniak, 2000b, p. 275). Be that as it may, another of the main tenets in formulating a foundation to build a peacemaking criminology theoretical model is to recognize how the diverse set of critical/progressive theoretical frameworks/perspectives driving peacemaking criminology has the potential to "articulate how existing social arrangements are the source of harm in society and to show how much of this harm, which serves the interests of the rich and powerful, is potentially avoidable" (Wozniak, 2000b, p. 273).

Types of Peacemaking Alternatives

Space limitations again do not permit a detailed discussion of the ways in which authors in the Pepinsky and Quinney (1991) reader formulated peacemaking alternatives to confront crimes and social harms. Hence, a careful reading of the chapters in this reader will afford a better vantage point than this article to grasp the nature and essence of the peacemaking alternatives proposed here. Nonetheless, let us briefly identify selected types of peacemaking alternatives displayed in the Pepinsky and Quinney (1991) reader.

Quinney (1991), for example, alluded to Buddhist principles of mindfulness, kindness, and right understanding. Similarly, Anderson (1991) suggested the adoption of the concept of *satyagraha*, which involves an active but nonviolent cooperation with an oppressor, Gandhi's disciplined nonviolent tactics, and *panchayats*, which are village councils for settling disputes. In the same vein, Barak (1991) recommended nonviolent responses to the homeless, such as Hesed house. Cordella (1991) called for reconciliation, mutual affection, and a mutualist ethic as strategies for healing and growth of the entire community. Likewise, Immarigeon (1991) advocated the Vera program, which promotes unpaid service at a community work site.

Authors in the feminist tradition of peacemaking criminology, such as Harris (1991), believed social injustice might be confronted through the creation of humane structures predicated on reconciliation, harmony, nurturance, empathy, compassion, forgiveness, and nonviolent conflict resolution. Caringella-MacDonald and Humphries's (1991) study of sexual assault led them to highlight the promise of community "Take Back the Night" marches, sexual assault centers, rape crisis programs, "Men and Women Committed to Stopping Violence Against Women," and watchdog programs that monitor the treatment of victims through the criminal justice system. Tifft and Markham (1991) urged the replacement of processes of militarization and a working against power whether it be parental, interpersonal, organizational, or at the state level.

DeKeseredy and Schwartz (1991) supported the development of a new system that will incorporate women's interests in justice as well as the use of local crime surveys to formulate humane policies rather than to control policies of crime. Rucker (1991) directed attention toward the "Alternatives to Violence Project" for prisoners and the transformation of the correctional center to the healing center and a general teaching of nonviolent techniques. A "Safer Society" program was prompted by Knopp (1991), who worked toward incorporating strategies of moratorium, decarceration, excarceration, and restraint of the few within communities experiencing increased sexual assault. Along these same lines, Volpe (1991) wrote of the value of mediation programs as alternatives to criminal prosecution and dispute resolution within communities.

Reflecting the critical tradition of peacemaking criminology, Milovanovic (1991) singled out transpraxis, which involves a "humanist transfiguration of man/woman and for visions for movement toward the peacemaking community" (p. 209). Caulfield (1991) promoted the development of peace groups, witnesses for peace, and the Committee in Solidarity with the People of El Salvador (CISPES), an organization that supports El Salvador. Peace education, humanist education, and cooperative living are high on the policy agenda list of Sanzen (1991). This list of policies for Galliher (1991) consisted of rehabilitation, conciliation, mediation, and compromise. Elias (1991) desired the achievement of positive peace (providing of political, economic, and social justice) and negative peace (absence of violence and war), and a general enforcement of human rights. Scimecca (1991) wrote of five ways to attain conflict resolution as a peacemaking possibility. Klein et al. (1991) stressed locality development, social planning, and a collective approach to crime prevention and community organizations.

Like the listing of crimes/social harms and peacemaking frameworks/perspectives, the scope of peacemaking alternatives is equally diverse. It is useful to note the varying levels of society (interpersonal, group, organizational, national, and international) on which the writers in the Pepinsky and Quinney (1991) reader propose to incorporate peacemaking alternatives to lessen crimes/social harms. Again, these peacemaking alternatives are very much in keeping with the responses of authors within the peacemaking criminology survey (Wozniak, 2000b). Thereby, a third tenet in formulating a foundation to build a peacemaking criminology theoretical model is to recognize the diversity of peacemaking alternatives that commonly shape peacemaking criminology research.

Peacemaking Criminology Theoretical Model

Up to this point of the article, it has been demonstrated that core peacemaking criminology themes are generally apparent within responses to the peacemaking criminology survey as well as writings in the Pepinsky and Quinney (1991) reader. Most important, as alluded to earlier, it was reported that peacemaking criminology calls upon us to refuse to invest in a social ethic that separates us from one another and instead to visualize all people—including those responsible for serious harms—as being connected" (Wozniak, 2000b, p. 283).

Figure 8.1. Peacemaking Criminology Theoretical Model

In keeping with these principles, along with the general discussion provided so far in this article, Figure 8.1 portrays a peacemaking criminology theoretical model. Here, the theory, research, and policy of peacemaking criminology consist very much of a connected endeavor on the whole.[9] By this it is meant that peacemaking criminologists tend to examine the connections among social structure, crimes, social harms, the criminal justice system, and peacemaking alternatives. In other words, peacemaking criminology research, in its strictest sense, will opt to examine how people in our present times become affected by and, in turn, affect these five basic elements within the peacemaking criminology theoretical model. Leaving out an element would lead, in a peacemaking criminology view, to an incomplete understanding of crime and how to address crime in a humane way.

At this point, it is instructive to further note that according to Pepinsky (1991), "A common belief among peacemaking traditions is that understanding runs in circles than in straight lines" (p. 324). As such, the use of circles is a way of conveying the interconnection between elements in the peacemaking criminology theoretical model.[10] In this way of thinking, linear models are not as useful of a metaphor to characterize how life actually works. Instead, the peacemaking criminology theoretical model emphasizes seeing the world in terms of its interconnections that cannot be reduced down.

In an earlier discussion in this article, it was demonstrated that peacemaking criminologists tend to study varying types of crime (e.g., street, white collar/corporate, organized, victimless, and political) in juxtaposition with diverse kinds of social harms (e.g., interpersonal, such as negative stereotyping, aggression, and hostility; social structural, such as alienation, poverty, sexism, and racism; and international, such as imperialism, terrorism, and nuclear and ecological damage). It was also pointed out before that within peacemaking criminology it is a central goal to transform the present criminal justice system through greater humanization of police work, court processing, and correctional environment. It was also noted previously that peacemaking criminologists have been apt to propose peacemaking alternatives at varying levels (interpersonal group, organization, national, international) to lessen crimes/social harms.

The discussion presented in this article, however, has not yet made clear the specific manner in which peacemaking criminologists might conceptualize social structure. In a very broad sense, writers in the Pepinsky and Quinney (1991) reader have been identified as utilizing theoretical frameworks that can enable a lens to view developments in the social structure (i.e., institutions such as economy, government, military, family, religion, and education) of society. For example, in the Pepinsky and Quinney reader, the peacemaking criminology authors reported influences ranging from Marx to humanist sociology to constitutive criminology to feminist criminology to anarchist criminology to left realism to penal abolitionism to Weber to Durkheim. Certainly, each of these theoretical perspectives enables research of social structure in relation to crimes, social harms, the criminal justice system, and peacemaking alternatives. In other words, the many theoretical influences on the writers in the Pepinsky and Quinney reader provide fruitful guideposts to build further knowledge about the operation of elements in the peacemaking criminology model depicted in Figure 8.1.

Yet it seems reasonable to also point out some more specific theoretical stances that can be employed in relation to this peacemaking criminology model. At this point, it is helpful to note Dennis Sullivan's view (Wozniak, 2000b) that peacemaking criminology offers:

> A needs-based alternative to the prevailing deserts-based market economy and an alternative to the state where needs are defined in terms of equal distribution or equal rights. Peacemaking criminologists offer a conception of justice defined in terms of equal well-being for all, where the needs of all are met equally but differentially, that is, according to the unique needs of each. Hence, peacemaking criminologists talk of justice defined as equal well-being and of creating social arrangements in which all are treated equally not only in terms of the results achieved but also in terms of the means. All are encouraged to enjoy full participation in the design of the social arrangements that affect one's life, in the definition of one's needs, in the production of goods and services to satisfy those needs, and in the evaluation of the satisfaction of those needs. (p. 271)

With this observation in mind, it is possible to propose that peacemaking criminologists might build on anarchist criminology analyses that address the social structuring of unmet social needs within our current society (e.g., see Sullivan & Tifft, 1998, 2001; Sullivan, Tifft, & Sullivan, 1999; Tifft, 1993; Tifft & Sullivan, 1980). Similarly, the social structuring of unmet social needs in relation to crime can be applied to the work of Erich Fromm (Wozniak, 2000a). For example, Fromm (1955) maintained that five social needs—relatedness, transcendence, rootedness, sense of identity, and frame of orientation—are common in the human situation. However, "Erich Fromm's theory of alienation proposes that the conditions of human existence arising from the nineteenth and twentieth centuries often make it difficult to satisfy these five social needs" (Wozniak, 2000a, p. 46; see also Quinney, 2000).

Another approach potentially applicable to the study of elements in the peacemaking criminology model lies in Simon's (2002, p. 35) analysis of elite deviance, which referred to acts by elites and/or organizations that result in physical harms, financial harms, or moral harms. Also, of use for our purposes of study here is how

> Simon links together a relationship between C. Wright Mills' concepts of higher immorality and the dominance of elite social institutions (i.e., economy, government, military). As such, the imbalancing of power within our economic, governmental and military institutions has, in the Mills/Simon scheme, types of deviance (i.e., political corporate white collar, organized crime, street crime) occurring with much regularity across the spectrum of our current social structure. (Wozniak, 2001, p. 469)

One other likely way to approach elements in the peacemaking criminology model is to address the social structure of gender inequality as exhibited in the research of Caulfield (1991, 1999), McDermott (1994, 1999), and Radosh (2000). And of course, other variants of critical criminology (i.e., Marxist and radical) seem well suited for application to the peacemaking criminology model as well (e.g., see Kauzlarich & Kramer, 1998; Lynch, Michalowski, & Groves, 2000).

Suggestions for Future Research

The main limitation of this article is that its analysis was based primarily on two major sources: responses of peacemaking authors to a peacemaking criminology survey and a content analysis of the Pepinsky and Quinney (1991) reader on peacemaking criminology. Hence, analyses and findings undertaken by peacemaking criminologists outside of the peacemaking survey/ reader are left out of this present article.

However, the main advantage of this article is that a close examination of the peacemaking survey/reader has uncovered core themes (i.e., types of crimes/social harms, types of theoretical frameworks, and types of peacemaking alternatives) that augment the development of a theoretical model of peacemaking criminology. A key challenge underlying this peacemaking criminology model is to systematically organize and analyze future research in keeping with each of the elements identified in this model. Given the possibilities of social turmoil in our current domestic and international climate, it is also problematic that peacemaking alternatives can be readily applied and analyzed on a timely and more regular basis.

Nevertheless, some beneficial directions to take in respect to peacemaking criminology is to adapt this model to attitudinal and behavioral research of various segments of people across the criminal justice system and social structure of society. It would be very interesting to conduct cross-cultural analyses of this peacemaking model in this same regard.

A generally untapped set of studies in peacemaking criminology research lies with the development of data to conduct evaluation research on the host of peacemaking alternatives illustrated in this article's formulation of the peacemaking criminology theoretical model. For that matter, crimes and social harms in relation to peacemaking alternatives, the criminal justice system, and the social structure might be more coherently studied than in the past and perhaps in relation to policies and programs linked to mainstream criminology. One specific direction of research that could be considered here is to attempt to blend insights of peacemaking criminology with those arising from recent research on rehabilitation in corrections settings (e.g., Andrews et al., 1990; Gendreau, 1996; Gendreau, Little, & Goggin, 1996; Gendreau & Ross, 1987). It might prove beneficial to also work on a blending of restorative justice and rehabilitation in keeping with the spirit of the peacemaking criminology model (e.g., see Levrant, Cullen, Fulton, & Wozniak, 1999). More specifically, prison research can be devised with peacemaking themes to work toward "restorative rehabilitation" (Cullen, Sundt, & Wozniak, 2001).

One development that has received increasing attention in current criminological research is the integration of theories (e.g., Bohm, 2001; Cullen & Agnew, 1999; Lilly et al., 2002; Paternoster & Bachman, 2001; Shoemaker, 2000). Bohm (2001, pp. 134–136) posited that there are four types of integrated theory: One type "synthesizes concepts from different theories within the same discipline," another involves theories that "combine theories or concepts from different disciplines within the same paradigm," other "life course" theories "posit that different factors (sometimes from different disciplines and different levels of analysis) affect people's propensity for crime at different points in their lives," and a fourth type refers to theories that "attempt to integrate theories or concepts from different paradigms or to combine all of the different types of integration." The noteworthy implication here is that it would be interesting to observe how this peacemaking criminology model might compare and contrast with all four types of this latter integrated format. At this point, it seems beneficial to recall from previous discussion (Maguire & Radosh, 1999, p. 256) that peacemaking criminology has the potential to be linked with a "social support paradigm" (Cullen, 1994; Cullen et al., 1999), especially because the latter perspective contains propositions that are quite consistent with peacemaking alternatives in the peacemaking criminology theoretical model.

As a way to bring this discussion to a close, it is instructive to note how peacemaking authors responded to questions about the value of teaching peacemaking to students. Hence, it was found that peacemaking criminologists "want students to see—indeed to believe—that there is a different way of organizing social life and practices of justice. Peacemaking offers away to achieve less harm in the world, including harm from crime and violence" (Wozniak, 2000b, p. 279). But as also reported in the peacemaking criminology survey (Wozniak, 2000b, p. 280), when students are taught about peacemaking criminology, they are to be urged to assume "personal responsibility" and to practice "responsiveness." That is, peacemaking criminology is a perspective that calls for each individual to strive to become involved in the personal and social process of peacemaking. As further reported in the peacemaking criminology survey,

> In the end peacemaking criminology is not something that emerges after some kind of gigantic social transformation has taken place but is a means to such transformation. It must be pursued by people—including students—wherever they are—one person at a time. (Wozniak, 2000b, p. 280)

In Richard Quinney's view, crimes and social harms are forms of suffering. "To begin to end suffering," Quinney (1991) stipulated that "we must be aware of the causes of suffering within ourselves and search for the reasons that make us suffer" (p. 9).Within this sentiment lies an ultimate policy implication of peacemaking criminology as well as the most important suggestion for policies and research in the future.

Notes

1. For example, Cordella and Siegel's (1996) book of readings features essays about recent insights emerging within criminological theories ranging from rational choice to labeling/shaming to biosocial to neuropsychological to ecology/routine activities to anomie/strain to integrated to critical to left realist to feminist. Henry and Einstadter's (1998) reader also covers these latter theories and additionally examines new developments in theories such as subcultural, differential association, social learning, neutralization, social control, social constructionist, postmodernist, and constitutive. Similarly, Simpson's (2000) edited anthology of readings portrays newer developments in theories such as differential association, feminist, social disorganization, anomie/strain, labeling/shaming, rational choice, and routine activity, while additionally characterizing latest insights arising from critical race theory, hegemonic theory, and developmental theory. Moreover, the Cullen and Agnew (1999) set of readings examines most of the criminological theories listed above. However, this latter reader adds a further twist to this issue: The foundation readings of a theory are systematically explored in relation to the reformulations that have emerged in the past two decades. In particular, the Cullen and Agnew reader looks at the following criminological theories in this latter way: biosocial/psychological, social disorganization, differential association, subcultural, social learning, anomie/strain, control, integrated, rational choice, routine activities, labeling/shaming, critical, and feminist. In their reader, Paternoster and Bachman (2001) covered these same theories.

2. The eighteen criminology textbooks that address peacemaking criminology are Adler, Mueller, and Laufer (2001a, 2001b); Barak (1998); Barkan (2001); Beirne and Messerschmidt (2000); Berger, Free, and Searles, (2001); DeKeseredy and Schwartz (1996); Ellis and Walsh (2000); Hagan (1998); Maguire and Radosh (1999); Quinney and Wildeman (1991); Reid (1997); Sacco and Kennedy (1996); Schmalleger (1996); Siegel (1998); Sheley (1995); Vito and Holmes (1994); and Voigt, Thornton, Barrile, and Seaman (1994). The 12 criminology textbooks that do not address peacemaking criminology are Barlow (1996); Brown, Esbensen, and Geis (1991); Conklin (1998); Gibbons (1992); Gilsinan (1990); Glick (1995); Jackson and Griffiths (1995); Jeffery (1990); Livingston (1996); Masters and Roberson (1990); Sykes and Cullen (1992); and Yablonsky (1990).

3. These textbooks include Adler et al. (2001a, 2001b), Barkan (2001), Ellis and Walsh (2000), Maguire and Radosh (1999), Reid (1997), Sacco and Kennedy (1996), Siegel (1998), and Vito and Holmes (1994).

4. These criminology textbook authors include Adler et al. (2001a, 2001b), Barak (1998), Barkan (2001), Ellis and Walsh (2000), Hagan (1998), Sacco and Kennedy (1996), Schmalleger (1996), and Siegel (1998).

5. This textbook is Sheley (1995).

6. Such textbooks include Barkan (2001), Beirne and Messerschmidt (2000), Hagan (1998), Reid (1997), and Vito and Holmes (1994).

7. The nine crime theory textbooks that address peacemaking criminology are Akers (2000); Bohm (2001); Einstadter and Henry (1995); Gibbons (1994); Lilly et al. (2002); Moyer (2001);Vold, Bernard, and Snipes (1998); White and Haines (1996); and Williams and McShane (1999). The two crime theory textbooks that do not address peacemaking criminology are Curran and Renzetti (1994) and Winfree and Abadinsky (1996).

8. Here, Currie's (1985) book is *Confronting Crime.*

9. It is instructive to note that in regard to "Criminology and Public Policy as Peacemaking," Quinney (1993) stated, "Criminologists are encouraged to support and engage in a 'compassionate criminology' that recognizes the interrelatedness of everything; that everyone is connected to each other and to their environment" (p. 3).

10. On peacemaking circles, see also Stuart (2001) and Pranis (2001).

References

Adler, F., Mueller, O.W.G., & Laufer, W. S. (2001a). *Criminology* (4th ed.). New York: McGraw-Hill.

Adler, F., Mueller, O.W.G., & Laufer, W. S. (2001b). *Criminology and the criminal justice system* (4th ed.). New York: McGraw-Hill.

Akers, R. L. (2000). *Criminological theories: Introduction, evaluation, and application* (3rd ed.). Los Angeles: Roxbury.

Anderson, K. (1991). Radical criminology and the overcoming of alienation: Perspectives from Marxian and Gandhian humanism. In H. E. Pepinsky & R. Quinney (Eds.), *Criminology as peacemaking* (pp. 14-29). Bloomington: Indiana University Press.

Andrews, D.A., Zinger, I., Huger. D., Bonta, J., Gendreau, P., & Cullen, F. T. (1990). Does correctional treatment work? A clinically relevant and psychologically informed meta-analysis. *Criminology*, *28*, 369-404.

Arrigo, B. A. (Ed.). (1999). *Social justice/criminal justice: The maturation of critical theory in law, crime, and deviance*. Belmont, CA: West/Wadsworth.

Barak, G. (1991). Homelessness and the case for community-based initiatives: The emergence of a model shelter as a short-term response to the deepening crisis in housing. In H. E. Pepinsky & R. Quinney (Eds.), *Criminology as peacemaking* (pp. 47-68). Bloomington: Indiana University Press.

Barak, G. (1998). *Integrating criminologies*. Boston: Allyn & Bacon.

Barkan, S. E. (2001). *Criminology: A sociological understanding* (2nd ed.). Upper Saddle River, NJ: Prentice Hall.

Barlow, H. D. (1996). *Introduction to criminology* (7th ed.). New York: HarperCollins.

Beirne, P., & Messerschmidt, J. (2000). *Criminology* (3rd ed.). Boulder, CO: Westview.

Berger, R. J., Free, M. D., Jr., & Searles, P. (2001). *Crime, justice, and society: Criminology and the sociological imagination*. New York: McGraw-Hill.

Bohm, R. M. (2001). *A primer on crime and delinquency theory* (2nd ed.). Belmont, CA: Wadsworth.

Braswell, M. C. (1990, May/June). Peacemaking: A missing link in criminology. *Criminologist*, *15*, 3-5.

Brown, S. E., Esbensen, F.-A., & Geis, G. (1991). *Criminology: Explaining crime and its context*. Cincinnati, OH: Anderson.

Caringella-MacDonald, S., & Humphries, D. (1991). Sexual assault, women, and the community: Organizing to prevent sexual violence. In H. E. Pepinsky & R. Quinney (Eds.), *Criminology as peacemaking* (pp. 98-113). Bloomington: Indiana University Press.

Caulfield, S. L. (1991). The perpetuation of violence through criminological theory: The ideological role of subculture theory. In H. E. Pepinsky & R. Quinney (Eds.), *Criminology as peacemaking* (pp. 228-244). Bloomington: Indiana University Press.

Caulfield, S. L. (1999). *Creating peaceable schools*. Paper presented at the annual meeting of the American Society of Criminology, Toronto, Canada.

Conklin, J. E. (1998). *Criminology* (6th ed.). Boston: Allyn & Bacon.

Cordella, J. P. (1991). Reconciliation and the mutualist model of a community. In H. E. Pepinsky & R. Quinney (Eds.), *Criminology as peacemaking* (pp. 30-46). Bloomington: Indiana University Press.

Cordella, P., & Siegel, L. (Eds.). (1996). *Readings in contemporary criminological theory*. Boston: Northeastern University Press.

Cullen, F. T. (1994). Social support as an organizing concept for criminology: Presidential address to the Academy of Criminal Justice Sciences. *Justice Quarterly*, *11*(4), 527-559.

Cullen, F. T., & Agnew, R. (Eds.). (1999). *Criminology theory: Past to present*. Los Angeles: Roxbury.

Cullen, F. T., Wright, J. P., & Chamlin, M. B. (1999, April). Social support and social reform: A progressive crime control agenda. *Crime & Delinquency, 45*, 188-207.

Cullen, F. T., Sundt, J., & Wozniak, J. F. (2001). The virtuous prison: Toward a restorative rehabilitation. In H. N. Pontell & D. Schichor (Eds.), *Contemporary issues in crime and criminal justice* (pp. 265-286). Upper Saddle River, NJ: Prentice Hall.

Curran, D. J., & Renzetti, C. M. (1994). *Theories of crime*. Boston: Allyn & Bacon.

Currie, E. (1985). *Confronting crime*. New York: Pantheon.

DeKeseredy, W. S., & Schwartz, M.D. (1991). British left realism on the abuse of women: A critical appraisal. In H. E. Pepinsky & R. Quinney (Eds.), *Criminology as peacemaking* (pp. 154-171). Bloomington: Indiana University Press.

DeKeseredy, W. S., & Schwartz, M. D. (1996). *Contemporary criminology*. Belmont, CA: Wadsworth.

Einstadter, W., & Henry, S. (1995). *Criminology theory: An analysis of its underlying assumptions*. New York: Harcourt Brace.

Elias, R. (1991). Crime control as human rights enforcement. In H. E. Pepinsky & R. Quinney (Eds.), *Criminology as peacemaking* (pp. 251-262). Bloomington: Indiana University Press.

Ellis, L., & Walsh, A. (2000). *Criminology: A global perspective*. Boston: Allyn & Bacon.

Fromm, E. (1955). *The sane society*. New York: Holt, Rinehart and Winston.

Fuller, J. R. (1998). *Criminal justice: A peacemaking perspective*. Boston: Allyn & Bacon.

Galliher, J. F. (1991). The Willie Horton fact, faith, and commonsense theory of crime. In H. E. Pepinsky & R. Quinney (Eds.), *Criminology as peacemaking* (pp. 245-250). Bloomington: Indiana University Press.

Gendreau, P. (1996). Offender rehabilitation: What we know and what needs to be done. *Criminal Justice and Behavior, 23*, 144-161.

Gendreau, P., Little, T., & Goggin, C. (1996). A meta analysis of the predictors of adult offender recidivism: What works! *Criminology, 34*(4), 575-607.

Gendreau, P., & Ross, R. R. (1987). Revivification of rehabilitation: Evidence from the 1980's. *Justice Quarterly, 4*, 349-407.

Gibbons, D. C. (1992). *Society, crime, and criminal behavior* (6th ed.). Englewood Cliffs, NJ: Prentice Hall.

Gibbons, D. C. (1994). *Talking about crime and criminals: Problems and issues in theory development in criminology*. Englewood Cliffs, NJ: Prentice Hall.

Gilsinan, J. F. (1990). *Criminology and public policy: An introduction*. Englewood Cliffs, NJ: Prentice Hall.

Glick, L. (1995). *Criminology*. Boston: Allyn & Bacon.

Hagan, F. E. (1998). *Introduction to criminology: Theory, methods, and criminal behavior* (4th ed.). Chicago: Nelson-Hall.

Harris, M. K. (1991). Moving into the new millennium: Toward a feminist vision of justice. In H. E. Pepinsky & R. Quinney (Eds.), *Criminology as peacemaking* (pp. 83-97). Bloomington: Indiana University Press.

Henry, S., & Einstadter, W. (Eds.). (1998). *The criminology theory reader*. NewYork: NewYork University Press.

Immarigeon, R. (1991). Beyond the fear of crime: Reconciliation as the basis for criminal justice policy. In H. E. Pepinsky & R. Quinney (Eds.), *Criminology as peacemaking* (pp. 69-80). Bloomington: Indiana University Press.

Jackson, M. A., & Griffiths, C. T. (1995). *Canadian criminology: Perspectives on crime and criminality* (2nd ed.). Toronto, Canada: Harcourt Brace.

Jeffery, C. R. (1990). *Criminology: An interdisciplinary approach*. Englewood Cliffs, NJ: Prentice Hall.

Kauzlarich, D., & Kramer, R. C. (1998). *Crimes of the American nuclear state: At home and abroad*. Boston: Northeastern University Press.

Klein, L., Luxenburg, J., & Gunther, J. (1991). Taking a bite out of social injustice: Crime control ideology and its peacemaking potential. In H. E. Pepinsky & R. Quinney (Eds.), *Criminology as peacemaking* (pp. 280-296). Bloomington: Indiana University Press.

Knopp, F. H. (1991). Community solutions to sexual violence: Feminist/abolitionist perspectives. In H. E. Pepinsky & R. Quinney (Eds.), *Criminology as peacemaking* (pp. 181-193). Bloomington: Indiana University Press.

Levrant, S., Cullen, F. T., Fulton, B., & Wozniak, J. F. (1999, January). Reconsidering restorative justice: The corruption of benevolence revisited. *Crime & Delinquency*, *45*, 3-27.

Lilly, R. J., Cullen, F. T., & Ball, R.A. (2002). *Criminological theory: Context and consequences* (2nd ed.). Thousand Oaks, CA: Sage.

Livingston, J. (1996). *Crime and criminology* (2nd ed.). Upper Saddle River, NJ: Prentice Hall.

Lynch, M., Michalowski, R., & Groves, W. B. (2000). *The new primer in radical criminology: Critical perspectives on crime, power and identity*. Monsey, NY: Criminal Justice Press.

Maguire, B., & Radosh, P. F. (1999). *Introduction to criminology*. Belmont, CA: Wadsworth.

Masters, R., & Roberson, C. (1990). *Inside criminology*. Englewood Cliffs, NJ: Prentice Hall.

McDermott, M. J. (1994). Criminology as peacemaking, feminist ethics, and the victimization of women. *Women and Criminal Justice*, *5*(2), 21-44.

McDermott, M. J. (1999). From a peacemaking perspective: Is personal change more important than social change? No. In J. R. Fuller & E.W. Hickey (Eds.), *Controversial issues in criminology* (pp. 119-126). Boston: Allyn & Bacon.

Milovanovic, D. (1991). Images of unity and disunity in the juridic subject and movement toward the peacemaking community. In H.E. Pepinsky & R. Quinney (Eds.), *Criminology as peacemaking* (pp. 209-227). Bloomington: Indiana University Press.

Moyer, I. L. (2001). *Criminological theories: Traditional and nontraditional voices and themes*. Thousand Oaks, CA: Sage.

Paternoster, R., & Bachman, R. (Eds.). (2001). *Explaining criminals and crime: Essays in contemporary criminological theory*. Los Angeles: Roxbury.

Pepinsky, H.E. (1991). Peacemaking in criminology and criminal justice. In H.E. Pepinsky & R. Quinney (Eds.), *Criminology as peacemaking* (pp. 299-327). Bloomington: Indiana University Press.

Pepinsky, H. E., & Quinney, R. (Eds.). (1991). *Criminology as peacemaking*. Bloomington: Indiana University Press.

Pranis, K. (2001). Restorative justice, social justice, and the empowerment of marginalized populations. In G. Bazemore & M. Schiff (Eds.), *Restorative community justice: Repairing harm and transforming communities* (pp. 287-306). Cincinnati, OH: Anderson.

Quinney, R. (1991). The way of peace: On crime, suffering, and service. In H. E. Pepinsky & R. Quinney (Eds.), *Criminology as peacemaking* (pp. 3-13). Bloomington: Indiana University Press.

Quinney, R. (1993). A life of crime: Criminology and public policy as peacemaking. *Journal of Crime and Justice*, *16*, 3-9.

Quinney, R. (2000). Socialist humanism and the problem of crime: Thinking about Erich Fromm in the development of critical/peacemaking criminology. In K. Anderson & R. Quinney (Eds.), *Erich Fromm and critical criminology: Beyond the punitive society* (pp. 21-30). Urbana: University of Illinois Press.

Quinney, R., & Wildeman, J. (1991). *The problem of crime: A peace and social justice perspective.* Mountain View, CA: Mayfield.

Radosh, P. F. (2000). Gender, social character, cultural forces, and the importance of love: Erich Fromm's theories applied to patterns of crime. In K. Anderson & R. Quinney (Eds.), *Erich Fromm and critical criminology: Beyond the punitive society* (pp. 59-82). Urbana: University of Illinois Press.

Reid, S. T. (1997). *Crime and criminology* (8th ed.). Guilford, CT: Brown and Benchmark.

Rucker, L. (1991). Peacemaking in prisons: A process. In H. E. Pepinsky & R. Quinney (Eds.), *Criminology as peacemaking* (pp. 172-180). Bloomington: Indiana University Press.

Sacco, V. F., & Kennedy, L. W. (1996). *The criminal event: An introduction to criminology.* Belmont, CA: Wadsworth.

Sanzen, P. L. (1991). The role of education in peacemaking. In H. E. Pepinsky & R. Quinney (Eds.), *Criminology as peacemaking* (pp. 239-244). Bloomington: Indiana University Press.

Schmalleger, F. (1996). *Criminology today.* Englewood Cliffs, NJ: Prentice Hall.

Scimecca, J. A. (1991). Conflict resolution and a critique of "alternative dispute resolution." In H. E. Pepinsky & R. Quinney (Eds.), *Criminology as peacemaking* (pp. 172-180). Bloomington: Indiana University Press.

Shelden, R. G., Tracy, S. K., & Brown, W. B. (2001). *Youth gangs in American society* (2nd ed.). Belmont, CA: Wadsworth.

Sheley, J. F. (1995). *Criminology: A contemporary handbook* (2nd ed.). Belmont, CA: Wadsworth.

Shoemaker, D. J. (2000). *Theories of delinquency: An examination of explanations of delinquent behavior.* New York: Oxford University Press.

Siegel, L. J. (1998). *Criminology* (6th ed.). Belmont, CA: West/Wadsworth.

Simon, D. R. (2002). *Elite deviance* (7th ed.). Boston: Allyn & Bacon.

Simpson, S. S. (Ed.). (2000). *Of crime & criminality: The use of theory in everyday life.* Thousand Oaks, CA: Pine Forge.

Stuart, B. (2001). Guiding principles for designing peacemaking circles. In G. Bazemore & M. Schiff (Eds.), *Restorative community justice: Repairing harm and transforming communities* (pp. 219-241). Cincinnati, OH: Anderson.

Sullivan, D., & Tifft, L. (1998, February). The transformative and economic dimensions of restorative justice. *Humanity and Society, 22*, 38-54.

Sullivan, D., & Tifft, L. (2001). *Restorative justice: Healing the foundations of our everyday lives.* Monsey, NY: Willow Tree Press.

Sullivan, D., Tifft, L., & Sullivan, K. (1999). *Justice without violence: Exploring the transformative and economic dimensions of the restorative justice movement.* Paper presented at a meeting of the Catholic Worker Community, Albany, NY.

Sykes, G. M., & Cullen, F. T. (1992). *Criminology* (2nd ed.). New York: Harcourt Brace Jovanovich.

Tifft, L. L. (1993). *Battering of women: The failure of intervention and the case for prevention.* Boulder, CO: Westview.

Tifft, L. L., & Markham, L. (1991). Battering women and battering Central Americans: A peacemaking synthesis. In H. E. Pepinsky & R. Quinney (Eds.), *Criminology as peacemaking* (pp. 114-153). Bloomington: Indiana University Press.

Tifft, L., & Sullivan, D. (1980). *The struggle to be human: Crime, criminology, and anarchism*. Sanday, Orkney Islands: Cienfuegoes Press.

Vito, G. F., & Holmes, R. M. (1994). *Criminology: Theory, research and policy*. Belmont, CA: Wadsworth.

Voigt, L., Thornton, W. E., Jr., Barrile, L., & Seaman, J. M. (1994). *Criminology and justice*. New York: McGraw-Hill.

Vold, G. B., Bernard, T. J., & Snipes, J. B. (1998). *Theoretical criminology* (4th ed.). New York: Oxford University Press.

Volpe, M. R. (1991). Mediation in the criminal justice system: Process, promises, problems. In H. E. Pepinsky & R. Quinney (Eds.), *Criminology as peacemaking* (pp. 194-205). Bloomington: Indiana University Press.

White, R., & Haines, F. (1996). *Crime and criminology: An introduction*. Melbourne, Australia: Oxford University Press.

Williams, F. P. III, & McShane, M.D. (1999). *Criminology theory* (3rd ed.). Upper Saddle River, NJ: Prentice Hall.

Winfree, L. T., Jr., & Abadinsky, H. (1996). *Understanding crime: Theory and practice*. Chicago: Nelson-Hall.

Wozniak, J. F. (2000a). Alienation and crime: Lessons from Erich Fromm. In K. Anderson & R. Quinney (Eds.), *Erich Fromm and critical criminology: Beyond the punitive society* (pp. 43-58). Urbana: University of Illinois Press.

Wozniak, J. F. (2000b). The voices of peacemaking criminology: Insights into a perspective with an eye toward teaching. *Contemporary Justice Review*, *3*(3), 267-289.

Wozniak, J. F. (2001, Fall). Assessing contemporary white collar crime textbooks: A review of common themes and prospects for teaching. *Journal of Criminal Justice Education*, *12*, 455-475.

Yablonsky, L. (1990). *Criminology: Crime and criminality* (4th ed.). New York: Harper and Row.

Chapter 9

The Relevance of Richard Quinney's Writings on Peacemaking Criminology: Toward Personal and Social Transformation

John F. Wozniak

As internationally renowned criminologist, Richard Quinney, retired from Northern Illinois University in 1998 as a professor emeritus, authors have continued to cite the relevance of his writings toward the understanding of crime and its social consequences in these troubled times of the early twenty-first century. For example, Richard Quinney very recently ranks among the top ten most-cited scholars in criminology (Wright, 2000, p. 119). Hence, highly adopted current textbooks in introductory sociology (i.e., Kendall, 2005; Macionis, 2005; Schaefer, 2005) and criminology (Barlow and Kauzlarich, 2002; Beirne and Messerschmidt, 2006; Siegel, 2007) feature how his work is linked to conflict theory. Similarly, some latest textbooks on criminological theories (Akers and Sellers, 2004; Lilly et al., 2007; Williams and McShane, 2004) indicate his contribution to the origins and development of not only Marxist criminology but also peacemaking criminology. Moreover, several recent crime-related textbooks (Berger et al., 2001; Elias, 1993; Fuller, 1998 and 2006; Shelden et al., 2004; Shelden and Brown, 2003) conclude that, at present, it is most desirable to proceed toward the study and handling of crime/criminals with a "peacemaking criminology" perspective.

In this regard, it is instructive to further note that in a recent survey of peacemaking criminology authors, there was widespread consensus that Quinney's works have provided the basis of the peacemaking perspective (Wozniak, 2000, p. 270). While this peacemaking perspective in criminology has gained increased attention among contemporary criminological theorists and researchers, there has not been a systematic analysis, at this point in time, which synthesizes Quinney's collection of writings on peacemaking criminology (i.e., Quinney, 1989; 1991c; 1993; 2000b; 2000c; Quinney and Wildeman, 1991).

Hence, it is the central objective of this chapter to synthesize Quinney's writings on peacemaking criminology, with a particular focus on how this literature can be adapted toward personal and social transformation of crime and social justice in our society today. As Quinney (2000a, p. 21) aptly observes: "The struggle is to create a humane existence, and such an existence comes only as we act peacefully toward ourselves and one another."

Essentially, this chapter is divided into four parts. It begins with a discussion of how the peacemaking perspective has been conceived within the discipline of criminology and then identifies some of Quinney's writings that can be viewed as precursors or building blocks toward his development of a peacemaking criminology theoretical framework. The third part of this chapter shows that when Quinney's peacemaking criminology writings are examined together, it becomes apparent that he has provided many pertinent insights in regard to general peacemaking assumptions about crime, peacemaking ways to bring about personal and social transformation, and the role of the peacemaking criminologist as teacher, researcher, and policy-maker. The final part of this chapter explores future directions of peacemaking criminology in keeping with the work of Quinney and others who are building upon this area of study.

Conceptions of the Peacemaking Perspective within the Discipline of Criminology

Upon concluding their synopsis of Richard Quinney as one of the pioneers in criminology, Martin and colleagues (1990, p. 402) maintain: "When Quinney first wrote the *Social Reality of Crime*, he moved the discipline forward in its thinking and at the very least caused many to question their own perceptions of the justice system." As the analysis unfolds in this chapter, it will be illustrated how Quinney's works on peacemaking criminology again have raised important criminological questions, many of which have been posed in an unprecedented way.

Like other scholars who reflect upon their life-long theories and research, Quinney tends to view his body of written works throughout his career as very connected and progressive from theme to theme and from publication to publication. Thereby, he (2000a, pp. x–xi) contends:

> My own travels through the 1960s, the 1970s, the 1980s, and the 1990s were marked by a progression of ways of thinking and acting: from the social constructionist perspective to phenomenology, from phenomenology to Marxist and critical philosophy, from Marxist and critical philosophy to liberation theology, from liberation theology to Buddhism and existentialism. And then to a more ethnographic and personal mode of thinking and being. It is necessary to note that in all of these travels nothing was rejected or deleted from the previous states; rather each new state of development incorporated what had preceded it. Each change was motivated by the need to understand crime in another or more complex way, in a way excluded from a former understanding. Each stage incorporated the changes that were taking place in my personal life. There

was to be no separation between life and theory, between witnessing and writing.

Of course, a case can be made that all of Quinney's scholarly (and even autobiographical—see Quinney, 1991a; 1998) works have led to or are in some way associated with his views of the peacemaking perspective in criminology. However, given limitations of space, this chapter will pinpoint examples of Quinney's writings that do not have "peacemaking" in the title, yet address, often in a preliminary way, core themes and concerns of interest within the peacemaking criminology paradigm of study.

Before embarking upon the identification of these latter writings that will be shown to be precursors of Quinney's peacemaking criminology, it seems fruitful to offer basic summations of how the peacemaking perspective is generally conceived within the discipline of criminology. As such, these basic summations are furnished to augment understanding of both the precursors and direct writings of Quinney's peacemaking criminology.

First, although there are various approaches to peacemaking criminology including religious, humanist, feminist, and critical traditions (i.e., Pepinsky and Quinney, 1991; Pepinsky, 1999; Fuller, 1998; Fuller and Wozniak, 2006; Sullivan and Tifft, 1998), three principle themes of peacemaking criminology are *connectedness*, *caring*, and *mindfulness*. Notably, Braswell (1990, p. 4) asserts:

> Understanding that we are *connected* to each other, the best and the worst of us, and to our environment should give us pause to reconsider both our world view and our view of criminal justice. The theme of *care* provides us with a context from which we can respond in ways to correct the imbalance between seeking justice and restoring both victims and offenders to community. *Mindfulness* allows us to become more aware of how we as persons can contribute to and encourage peacemaking. Mindfulness recognizes that personal and social peace comes from the inside out, not from the top down or outside in. (My emphases.)

Friedrichs (1991, p. 102) describes these same themes more directly in regard to crime as follows:

> *Connectedness* refers to our recognition of our bonds with each other and our environment, and the need for reconciliation; *caring* refers to the privileging of a traditionally feminine concern with nurturance over other objectives for the correctional system; *mindfulness* refers to the cultivation of inner peace as a fundamental point of departure for our responses to crime and to those we designate as criminals. (Again, my emphases.)

Another commonality within peacemaking criminology, no matter the specific approach or tradition undertaken, is that it offers an alternative to the "war on crime" model within criminal justice. According to Bohm (2001, p. 121), peacemaking criminology:

> rejects the idea that predatory criminal violence can be reduced by repressive state violence. In this view, "wars" on crime only make matters worse. Consisting of a mixture of anarchism, humanism, socialization, and Native American

> and Eastern philosophies, peacemaking criminology suggests that the solution to all social problems, including crime, is the transformation of human beings, mutual dependence, reduction of hierarchical structures, the creation of communities of caring people, and universal social justice.

Fuller (1998, p. 60) likewise stresses:

> The peacemaking perspective does something else that the war on crime model does not. It takes a broader look at human interaction and proposes that human worth and dignity be emphasized in all associations between people. The dynamics between parents and children, wives and husbands, bosses and workers, professors and students, and institutions and citizens can all be guided by the peacemaking perspective.

A third commonality within peacemaking pertains to the notion of personal and social transformation. As Pepinsky (1999, p. 59) views it: "Peacemaking is the art and science of weaving and reweaving oneself with others into a social fabric of mutual love, respect, and concern." Fuller (1998, pp. 42–43) extends this theme with these imageries:

> The peace perspective, with its more inclusive view of the crime problem, looks to transform both the individual criminal and the institution that produced this type of criminal . . . the important message that people fail to understand about the peace perspective is that it demands justice not only on the part of the individual but also on the part of the institution . . . by requiring social justice, the peace perspective does not excuse crime, but rather looks both at the individual's culpability and at the contribution of the institutions of society. Only by transforming both can we hope to develop effective, fair, and humane responses to the problem of crime.

Bohm (2001, p. 121) purports that in peacemaking criminology: "Emphasis is placed on the transformation of human beings, on an inner rebirth or spiritual rejuvenation (inner peace) that enables individuals to experience empathy with those less fortunate and respond to other people's needs."

A fourth commonality within peacemaking criminology can be seen in its critique of theories and policies proposed within mainstream criminology. Moyer (2001, p. 313), for example, states: "Peacemaking in criminology that has emerged during the 1990's rejects mainstream traditional criminological theory and policy as based on a hierarchical military model that seeks to return violence with violence." By contrast, according to Moyer (2001, p.313), "the peacemaking perspective seeks to understand the suffering that causes crime and to extend compassion, harmony, and social justice to the persons who have been identified as deviants or criminals." Echoing this theme, a survey of peacemaking criminologists (Wozniak, 2000, p. 274) reveals they believe:

> The tendency of mainstream criminologists is to seek solutions to crime within the confines of the existing criminal justice system. Their goal, so to speak, is to act as mechanics who operate and fix the machinery of the system so that it can run more efficiently and effectively. Peacemaking criminology, in contrast, believes that the answers to violence and social harm, and the injustices that are

> associated with such harm, lie largely outside the criminal justice system or, at least, in a justice system whose structures and processes are radically transformed. Solutions to the harms we do to each other are to be found in restorative processes that help heal those who have been hurt and thereby foster community.

Be that as it may, Friedrichs (1991, p. 102) elicits: "peacemaking criminology is a heresy of the first order." Because it proposes to "turn the criminological enterprise on its head, to challenge the most fundamental premises of this enterprise." And "the very name 'peacemaking criminology' appears to take exception to the typical positivist assumption that the principal mission of criminology is dispassionate analysis."

Along with these four commonalities of peacemaking criminology, it is possible to visualize peacemaking criminology through the lens of a theoretical model (Wozniak, 2002b, p. 221) in which:

> The theory, research, and policy of peacemaking criminology consist very much of a connected endeavor on the whole. By this it is meant that peacemaking criminologists tend to examine the connections among social structure, crimes, social harms, the criminal justice system, and peacemaking alternatives. In other words, peacemaking criminology research, in its strictest sense, will opt to examine how people in our present times become affected by and, in turn, affect these five basic elements within the peacemaking criminology theoretical model.

In more specific terms, this peacemaking criminology theoretical model (Wozniak, 2002b, p. 222) illustrates that peacemaking criminologists tend to study varying types of crime (from street to white collar to political) in juxtaposition with diverse kinds of social harms (from interpersonal to social structural to international). In order to lessen these crimes/social harms, peacemaking criminologists propose peacemaking alternatives (from group to organization to national to international) while also striving to transform the present criminal justice system through greater humanization of police work, court processing, and the correctional environment.

In light of this discussion of primary thrusts within peacemaking criminology, let us next consider writings that Quinney produced before he authored a series of works primarily focused upon peacemaking criminology.

Precursors of Richard Quinney's Peacemaking Criminology

This part of the chapter will examine six examples of precursors of Quinney's peacemaking criminology which are:

1. "The Production of Criminology" (1979)
2. *Class, State, and Crime* (1980)

3. "Nature of the World: Holistic Vision for Humanist Sociology" (1982)
4. "Myth and Art of Criminology" (1985)
5. "Beyond the Interpretive: The Way of Awareness" (1988)
6. "Oneness of All: The Mystical Nature of Humanism" (1991b)

Again, although peacemaking criminology is neither listed in the title nor directly addressed in these writings, it is evident that Quinney was striving to identify theoretical assumptions and policy objectives to be used toward the formation of a "peace and social justice" perspective in criminology (i.e., Quinney and Wildeman, 1991).

If we proceed in chronological order, Quinney's (1979, p. 445) "Production of Criminology" article was particularly designed: "to think about and act upon the production of a socialist future." Yet, a further examination of this article reveals Quinney addressing four peacemaking themes as early as 1979. For instance, in regard to transformation, he (1979, p. 445) states:

> The objective material conditions of the time provide the setting for the possibilities of creation, change, and revolution. While our daily struggle is one of transforming the existing order, of removing conditions of oppression and making an authentic existence, the old social order will not perish until all the productive forces and contradictions of that order have become obstacles to its further development.

Parenthetically, Quinney (1979, p. 447) visualizes a potential sense of connectedness among people working within criminology and criminal justice as he writes:

> Criminology continues to bring together in a very amorphous manner people who do the following (not necessarily mutually exclusive) kinds of work: (1) academicians (often sociologists) who teach students a subject called criminology, including those criminologists who also do research and write on the subject; (2) teachers who train other people for professional roles in crime control and criminal justice work; (3) those who are involved in policy research within the criminal justice system; and (4) those who "apply" criminology, that is, all the people who are employed in criminal justice agencies, ranging from policemen to lawyers to prison wardens to correctional workers.

Like Pepinsky (1999, p. 59), Quinney refers to criminology as an "art." According to Quinney (1979, pp. 452–453): "Criminology resembles the art form" and that "art suggests how the world could be." It is a form of knowledge that has at its objective a transcendence of the everyday life of the existing order. However, in Quinney's (1979, p. 451) view, it can be difficult for criminologists to help society to move progressively ahead given that they are commonly employed to operate as the "petty bourgeoisie" rather than to engage in the class struggle for socialism.

A second example of a precursor to peacemaking criminology pertains to Quinney's textbook titled *Class, State, and Crime*. This textbook is broad in scope and includes one chapter about crime during the development of capitalism and another chapter on crime within advanced capitalist society. The other three chapters focus upon crime in relation to justice in terms of its meaning, link to political economy, and societal implications. So many salient observations about crime within the context of the social structure of U.S. society are made by Quinney in this writing. Interestingly, he (1980, p. 177) posits the "war on crime . . . gave birth to the criminal justice movement," which is closely tied to the interests of the state in controlling "threatening social behavior."

For the purposes of this chapter, it is especially instructive to note that the final chapter of *Class, State, and Crime* is devoted to "the struggle for social justice." Hence, this final chapter begins with a discussion about the difficulties underlying the transition from capitalist society to socialism, with the role of criminologists as part of this transition demarcated again. In congruence with peacemaking criminology, particularly in regard to its religious tradition, Quinney devotes a section of this final chapter to the issue of "Marxism and theology." For example, Quinney (1980, p. 183) begins this section with:

> Our understanding of the world and our struggle within it nevertheless require a depth that comes only in a union of the material and the spiritual. The dialectic in our thought and action takes place most fully and essentially with an apprehension of that which is transhistorical and eternal. The Marxism known to social theorists is a philosophy confined to the secular world, no matter how prophetic the philosophy may be within that world. Although Marx did not write much about religion, his rejection of it is absolutely clear: religion is a fantasy of alienated humanity.

Yet, by the end of this chapter, to borrow a phrasing from Friedrichs (1991, p. 102), Quinney (1980, p. 193) "turns the criminological enterprise on its head" by supporting these words of a noted theologian:

> The problem is not whether we are Christians or Marxists, but whether—as Christians, Marxists or whatever—our lives point beyond themselves and are united with others struggling for justice. The radical immanence of Marxism and the transcendent power or Christianity are the integral parts of an infinite design of divine providence—realized in and through our human history.

As a third precursor to peacemaking criminology, Quinney (1982) wrote an article which directs attention toward the value of a "holistic vision for humanist sociology." Although he does not directly link this writing to crime, there are connections made in this analysis to peacemaking criminology. Personal transformation is considered as he (1982, p. 322) observes: "We are all on a pilgrimage, searching for a meaning in the self. The human need is to understand life and death in terms that transcend the self and the concrete events of social existence." Relatedly, Quinney's (1982, p. 323) notion of a "holistic vision" as a path to be taken by humanist sociologists involves a "new way of seeing" and a "new way of speaking" about our social world. That is, he (1982, p. 323) evokes the peacemaking "connectedness" theme in a holistic vision that recognizes: "We are within the whole material world, participating in all that is and ever has been . . . in a mystical sense, because of being enveloped in the universal process of creativity, we are traveling to eternity." Therein, as Quinney (1982, p. 336) concludes: "The critical objective as humanist sociologists is to promote that which will assure the survival of the natural world and to be a part of the struggle in transforming our own human history."

A fourth precursor of peacemaking criminology can be seen in "Myth and the Art of Criminology," which Quinney presented upon receiving the Edwin H. Sutherland Award at the annual meeting of the American Society of Criminology in 1984. In this talk, Quinney (1985, p.295) provides two peacemaking-oriented assumptions about crime: "Crime is one of the predominant myths of our contemporary culture . . . in the myth of crime, we today are cautioned in a way; we are told about the character of the social world in which we must travel. In the daily stories of crime, we measure our existence." Likewise in this regard, he (1985, p. 296) maintains: "crime is a homelessness in the world, physically and spiritually. We will eliminate crime only when we find a way to travel home—only when we can be at home in this world of universal consequence."

In this conference talk to his fellow criminologists, Quinney (1985, pp. 294; 296–297) further eludes to peacemaking criminology themes of mindfulness, connectedness, transcendence, and social transformation as follows:

> Our travel—our journey toward home—is a journey through the modern era and an attempt to go beyond it . . . the question for us then is this: In what way do we choose to tell the story? . . . The way we describe the myth is important . . . thought of such kind necessarily leads us beyond traditional boundaries of criminology . . . As criminologists we tend to do little more than explicate, elaborate, and synthesize the obvious. . . Our task, it seems to me, is to see things exactly as they are and to live our lives accordingly. And to see things as they are requires an openness and an awareness—a mindfulness—that comes with a new practice, a practice that involves not only collective struggle, but also personal stillness. This is a practice that is unclouded by unconventional thought, by the illusion of self, by the mythology of crime. This is a journey to the sacred, to that part of humanity that is beyond all thought . . . with awareness we may go beyond myth to a new creation—to a world, among other things, free from crime. We are traveling into a new territory.

Quinney's article "Beyond the Interpretive: The Way of Awareness" is his fifth precursor of peacemaking criminology. In this article, he (1988, p. 100) blends two peacemaking criminology themes—personal transformation and mindfulness—as follows:

> The path to awareness involves a transformation in our being, a transformation which allows a healing of the separation between the observer and the observed. To enter into this realm requires a mind that is unattached and compassionate. In mindfulness—in attention to our oneness with all things—we become aware of things as they are, here and now.

A key implication of Quinney's (1988, p. 107) analysis is that he calls for sociologists (and criminologists, presumably) to work toward developing more of an interpretive sociology, a "sociology-with-awareness." And what is awareness predicated upon? In his (1988, p. 114) analysis, it involves an understanding that: "Growing in wisdom and compassion is our work—and helping all others in their suffering."

The sixth example of a precursor of Quinney's peacemaking criminology is titled "Oneness of All: The Mystical Nature of Humanism." Here, he (1991b, p. 115) extols the importance for humanist sociologists and criminologists to grasp the meaning of mysticism (i.e., belief that direct knowledge of God, of spiritual truth is attainable through intuition). For Quinney, a humanism infused with mysticism can provide an alternative awareness about how to live in a world in which alienation of humans from each other is a daily occurrence. The objective of mystical humanism, according to Quinney (1991b, p. 116) is:

> We be kinder to one another, that we break down the barriers between ourselves and others. That we realize and live moment-to-moment our connection to all that is. Such is the objective . . . of humanism, and of a social theory that is humanist. The peace and social justice we seek comes in the awareness of our interconnectedness—our oneness.

With themes of these precursor writings in mind, let us turn attention to Quinney's vision of what is central to focus upon in the development of a peacemaking perspective in criminology.

Richard Quinney's Peacemaking Criminology Writings: A Synthesis

This part of the chapter examines Quinney's peacemaking criminology writings which are:

1. "The Theory and Practice of Peacemaking in the Development of Radical Criminology" (1989)
2. *The Problem of Crime: A Peace and Social Justice Perspective*, Third Edition (1991)
3. "The Way of Peace: On Crime, Suffering, and Service" (1991c)
4. "A Life of Crime: Criminology and Public Policy as Peacemaking" (1993)
5. "Criminology as Moral Philosophy, Criminologist as Witness" (2000b)
6. "Socialist Humanism and the Problem of Crime: Thinking About Erich Fromm in the Development of Critical/Peacemaking Criminology" (2000c)

Quinney wrote each of his peacemaking criminology writings as an individual author except for the *Problem of Crime* textbook, which he co-authored with John Wildeman. This textbook contains six chapters of which two focus upon the conceptualization and study of crime and another two are concerned with the origins and development of criminology from the 1700s to the late 1900s. The final two chapters support and illustrate the adoption of the peacemaking perspective in relation to crime and its control. Here, it may be noted that peacemaking themes are touched upon throughout this textbook. However, the core of the peacemaking criminology discussion is presented at the end of the fifth chapter and throughout the final chapter.

The 1989 article on "The Theory and Practice of Peacemaking in the Development of Radical Criminology" is one page and thus can be easily distributed as a class or public presentation handout. As will be noted shortly, a number of key peacemaking criminology themes are made in this 1989 writing and it covers much ground even though it consists of a total of ten paragraphs.

Quinney included "The Way of Peace: On Crime, Suffering, and Service" as the first chapter in the Pepinsky and Quinney (1991) *Criminology as Peacemaking* book of readings. The discussion in this chapter centers upon an developing understanding of awareness of human suffering, compassion, and service in keeping with a peace and social justice perspective in criminology.

Quinney's 1993 article "A Life of Crime: Criminology and Public Policy as Peacemaking" encourages criminologists to engage in a compassionate criminology of peacemaking in their personal and professional agenda. The discussion in this article raises how crime can be re-examined in relation to notions of wisdom, love, kindness, and nonviolence.

Similar views are elaborated upon in "Criminology as Moral Philosophy, Criminologist as Witness" which is a chapter in Quinney's book, *Bearing Witness to Crime and Social Justice*. This chapter (2000b, p. 194) explores the importance of "witnessing to all that is associated with crime and criminal justice." In this analysis, such witnessing is linked to phenomenology, Judeo-Christian theology, Marxist analysis, Buddhism, socialist humanism, and peacemaking criminology.

Quinney's (2000c) chapter "Socialist Humanism and the Problem of Crime: Thinking about Erich Fromm in the Development of Critical/Peacemaking Criminology" proposes that Fromm's socialist humanism has implications for peacemaking criminology. This is because this humanism has a "conviction that the urgent task for humanity is the establishment of peace" (Quinney 2000c, p. 24). The relevance of Buddhism, existentialism, and Gandhi for peacemaking criminology is also considered in this chapter.

Upon review of the discussion about the precursors of Quinney's peacemaking criminology, it can be surmised that his writings on peacemaking criminology similarly exhibit a wide variety of general tendencies. Peacemaking criminology, no matter if it is espoused by Quinney or other criminologists of like mind, needs to be absorbed in its diverse manifestations. The synthesis provided below of Quinney's works on peacemaking criminology is thereby undertaken not to be seen as a dissection or revision of his original thoughts. With that caveat in mind, it should be noted that this synthesis is primarily done to pull all the broad themes of Quinney's peacemaking criminology writings into focus within this single chapter. This chapter is also done to potentially bring about even more interest and desire among teachers, students, researchers, and policy makers within criminology and criminal justice to engage in the peacemaking criminology paradigm.

As such, it will be demonstrated throughout the discussion ahead that Quinney's peacemaking research has provided a multitude of pertinent criminological insights. As noted earlier, these insights involve general peacemaking assumptions about crime, peacemaking ways to bring about personal and social transformation in relation to crime and its control, and the role of the peacemaking criminologist as teacher, researcher, and policy-maker. Most importantly, each of Quinney's peacemaking criminology writings connect to these themes often in similar ways and at other times in terms of some different set of imageries and contexts. This is the dimension of Quinney's peacemaking criminology research that is most illuminating, highly compelling, and very invigorating to work through from piece to piece.

Therefore, as we consider "The Theory of Practice of Peacemaking in the Development of Radical Criminology," it is worthwhile to note that although this writing is very short, it offers a useful blueprint to explore the various parameters of peacemaking criminology. That is, at this point, Quinney (1989, p. 5) defines peacemaking as a "criminology that seeks to alleviate suffering and thereby reduce crime." Here, he (1989) also makes these assumptions about crime: "Crime is a form of suffering," which, "is the condition of our existence. The forms of suffering are all around us" such as "tensions, anxieties, physical pains in our bodies, psychological hurts in our hearts and minds, violence of one kind or another, poverty, violence, hunger, homelessness, destruction of the environment, nations at war, and threat of nuclear warfare." (These imageries are recounted again in the Quinney and Wildeman textbook to be addressed just ahead.) Quinney (1989) observes: "interpersonal relations are carried out in violence of one kind or another" and "the criminal justice system is founded on violence. It is a system which assumes violence can be overcome by violence." In this light, he (1989) thereby assumes "our lives are within a realm that demands a *spiritual* as well as material existence" (his italics).

What are we do to as citizens given these assumptions are true? Quinney suggests both personal and social transformation. In regard to personal transformation, he (1989) stipulates "care has to be given to the inner life of each of us" and "without peace within us and in our actions, there can be no peace in our results. Peace is the way." In respect to social transformation, he (1989) contends "human transformation takes place as we change our social, economic, and political structure." Furthermore, according to Quinney (1989):

> Rather than attempting to create a good society first, and then trying to make ourselves better human beings, we have to work on the two simultaneously. The inner and the outer are the same.

Thus, the implication for the role of the criminologist in personal and social transformation is to come to see that establishing justice involves ending both suffering and crime, which comes out of peace.

As one might surmise, Quinney and Wildeman's (1991) textbook expands the basic assumptions and views about personal/social transformation emanating from the peacemaking perspective in criminology. Yet, it is instructive to additionally note that although the views of peacemaking criminology are broadened in this textbook, the messages about the analysis of crime and suffering and the goals of peacemaking criminology are strikingly similar but more fleshed out in terms of social context. Thus, Quinney and Wildeman (1991, p. viii), conceive peacemaking criminology as "a nonviolent criminology of compassion and service," that, "seeks to end suffering and thereby eliminate crime." Added to that conception of peacemaking criminology is the notion that peacemaking criminology is:

> An orientation that dovetails with a progressive social agenda that strives to alleviate both the terrible suffering of the citizens who make up the underclass in America as well as the inner anguish and meaninglessness we all experience from time to time in our lives, an anguish and emptiness that easily breeds greed and selfishness (Quinney and Wildeman, 1991, p. 41).

In effect, with this definition of peacemaking criminology, the scope of attention is heightened through its emphasis on not only the suffering of the underclass but also the general anguish and stress arising for people living in contemporary society.

The range of social relations and social structure is also expanded in regard to the general assumptions about crime presented in the Quinney and Wildeman textbook. For instance, they (1991, p. 50) maintain "human suffering, and hence crime, arise out of disunity and separation—Durkheim was to . . . call it anomie, and Marx was to call it alienation." It is also conjectured (1991, p. 40) that:

> Our social institutions wreak violence on all of us. But more on some of us than others; and we in turn react violently to one another. Our institutions separate and isolate us from one another instead of binding us together. The sources of suffering are within each of us, as well as within the larger social institutions and systems we construct to try to solve our common problems of living. Crime can be dealt with effectively only with the ending of suffering, which is to say, only when there is peace and justice among us.

Therefore, it is in Quinney and Wildeman's (1991, p. 107) way of thinking to view the problem of crime and criminals as not simply a matter of flawed individuals but more due to a deficient social system. Their analysis (1991, p. 115) offers hope that we can eventually move our society to truly eradicate crime because "we are all interrelated—and 'not just people, but animals too, and stones, clouds, trees'."

The notion of personal transformation first comes into Quinney and Wildeman's (1991, p. 39) analysis in this way—awareness is moving beyond conditioned thought such that we begin:

> To live in a way that takes us beyond the problems and destructions of contemporary existence, beyond the problem of crime. We would not, then, leave society but transcend it, not withdraw from fellowship with others but renounce the appearances of reality in order to live fully in a spiritual life of love, union, and compassion with all beings. We would be part of the process of creating a world without crime.

And how might such personal transformation come about? For Quinney and Wildeman (1991, p. 113), we all would do well to take paths toward *right understanding*, which involves working toward gaining an awareness of the limitations that result when our actions are motivated by greed, hatred or delusion. Thus, "being on the simple path of right understanding," in their view (1991, p. 113), "we create thought, words, and deeds that will end suffering."

On the matter of social transformation, Quinney and Wildeman (1991, p. 110) conceive of peacemaking criminology as a direct framework to heighten the possibilities of changing our social, economic, and political structure. Further in this regard, they (1991, p. 111) suggest "the reconstruction of our existence—the ending of suffering—begins by giving attention to the mind." Within their (1991, p. 116) vantage point, the mind of a human being that comes to understand its own suffering and therefore the suffering of others can come to know peace and be peaceful. Here, they (1991, p. 116) support the views of Mahatma Gandhi's philosophy (Gandhi, 1948; Fischer, 1962; Anderson, 1991) of *satayagraha* which is thought to be a truth force in which "social action comes out of the informed heart, out of the clear and enlightened mind." Illustrating this philosophy, they (1991, p. 116) ask: "If we ourselves cannot know peace, *be* peaceful, how will our acts disarm hatred and violence?" But again their positive hope for humanity is seen as they (1991, pp. 116–117) indicate further: "Without *inner* peace in each of us, without peace of mind and heart, there can be no *social peace* between people and no peace in societies, nations, and in the world." Their peacemaking perspective (1991, p. 117) is thereby predicated upon the belief that: "Rather than attempting to create a good society first and then trying to make ourselves better human beings, we have to work on the two simultaneously. The inner and outer are the same."

To shift the discussion somewhat, it is also very apparent that Quinney and Wildeman (1991) address policy objectives for teachers, researchers, and practitioners very much in keeping with a peacemaking criminology framework. The implication of their analysis for teaching is teachers might strive to recognize the need to take steps toward an ending of suffering. That is, teachers might engage their instruction more in practices of "loving-kindness," "caring and connectedness," and "compassion" rather than generally applying "theories of science and the calculations of conditioned thought" among their students (Quinney and Wildeman, 1991, pp. 115–116).

For crime researchers, Quinney and Wildeman (1991, p. 108) recommend a movement toward more studies of needs assessment than evaluative research. That is, the study question is not so much what did the crime program accomplish for the offender or not, but rather "What is lacking in the lives of our fellows that gives them no alternative but a life of crime and violence?" (Quinney and Wildeman, 1991, p. 108). For criminology/criminal justice practitioners, their textbook advocates peacemaking alternatives to be applied to criminals within the community. Hence, they (1991, p.107) maintain: "Treatment, rehabilitation, alternatives to prisons, mediation, the realization of social justice, giving all people decent and real life chances: These are the ways of peacemaking." In their policy framework for peacemaking, they (1991, pp. 107–108) also support more employment of "problem-oriented" policing; mediation and reconciliation among offenders, parents, adolescents, victims; informal justice (i.e., out-of-court settlements); and rejection of capital punishment practices within society.

At this point, it is important to discern that the third example of Quinney's peacemaking criminology writings, titled "The Way of Peace: On Crime, Suffering, and Service," is predominantly the same wording found in the final chapter of the Quinney and Wildeman textbook. It should also be noted that the synthesis of this textbook provided just above covered this final chapter along with parts of other chapters in this textbook as well.

In so many ways, *The Problem of Crime* textbook offers the broadest treatment of peacemaking criminology of any of Quinney's writings about the peacemaking perspective in criminology. The analysis of this present writing did not attempt to isolate the final chapter of this textbook from what was written about peacemaking in the other chapters. Thus, the discussion in this chapter was broadened by examining and then reporting what was being said about peacemaking criminology in every chapter of this textbook (not just the final chapter).

Keeping this in mind, one might wonder what are the main thrusts of "Way of Peace: On Crime, Suffering, and Service" especially since it is the lead chapter of Pepinsky and Quinney's (1991) *Criminology as Peacemaking* book of readings. In other words, what is the message of this chapter when it is read alone—not in relation to other chapters in *The Problem of Crime*—as a representation of Quinney's work on peacemaking criminology?

In his "Way of Peace" chapter, Quinney (1991c, p. 3) boldly argues: "No amount of thinking and no amount of public policy have brought us any closer to understanding and solving the problem of crime." And then he (1991c, p. 3) observes further: "In recent years, we have floundered desperately in reformulating the law, punishing the offender, and quantifying our knowledge." Yet the U.S. "remains one of the most crime-ridden nations." (Both sets of observations originally appeared in the preface of Quinney and Wildeman's textbook.)

As presented in the preface, Quinney (1991c, pp. 3–4) lists a series of assumptions linked toward the rationale for a need to develop and implement a "criminology of peacemaking." Examples of such crime-related assumptions, some mentioned previously in this chapter, include: "crime is suffering . . . crime can be ended only with the ending of suffering . . . a criminology of peacemaking, the nonviolent criminology of compassion and service, seeks to end suffering and thereby eliminate crime." Paralleling his other peacemaking criminology writings, he (1991c, p. 4) makes further assumptions such as "suffering is the condition of our existence . . . our interpersonal relations are carried out in violence of one kind or another."

Again, in "the Way of Peace" chapter, Quinney (1991c, p. 8) emphasizes making ourselves better as human beings must be done simultaneously without attempting to create a good society (i.e., inner peace and social peace must come about together at the same time). Hence, social transformation is to consist of: "the transformation of our human being. Political and economic solutions without this transformation inevitably fail" (Quinney, 1991c, p. 4).

It is fruitful to note further in "the Way of Peace" chapter, Quinney (1991c) seems to be making a concerted effort to inform his fellow criminologists of the value and potential of studying and altering the effects of crime in relation to the emerging spiritual frameworks. For example, on Buddhism, he (1991c, p. 4) cites "all that we are is a result of what we have thought." His (1991c, p. 5) discussion turns to the relevance of Hinduism to crime and peacemaking in the following: "Truth can be known only through that which is beyond the ego-self and its attempt at purely rational thought." Borrowing from a Zen master, he (1991c, p. 5) writes in relation to gaining more awareness of human suffering and crime that: "If your mind is empty, it is always ready for anything; it is open to everything . . . when our mind is open and thus compassionate toward all things, it is boundless in understanding." Likewise, a Buddhist principle can again be applied to the problem of crime and suffering as follows: "In the practice of loving-kindness, what the Buddhists call metta, there is developed the feeling of caring and connectedness . . . in comparison, the suffering of others is recognized out of one's own suffering, and the suffering is shared" (Quinney, 1991c, p. 9).

For criminologists, the teaching—research—policy considerations become apparent in these Quinney (1991c, pp. 7–8) statements:

> Oppression in the world is caused by selves that are not spiritually aware . . . you cannot have peace without charity . . . seeing the truth . . . sets us on a path that promotes a humane and peaceful existence . . . a life devoted to criminology cannot avoid the importance of this truth. Care has to be given to the inner life of us. That we criminologists are to be engaged in spiritual work in order to eliminate crime may require further reflection. To be fully human presupposes the development within oneself that transcends material existence. It is a quality that is not acquired automatically, but one that develops slowly and needs to be tended carefully.

Quinney's fourth peacemaking criminology writing, "A Life of Crime: Criminology and Public Policy as Peacemaking" offers a challenge to criminologists to reexamine their personal and professional agenda. He (1993, p. 3) encourages criminologists to support peacemaking criminology as a "compassionate criminology" that "recognizes the interrelatedness of everything; that everyone is connected to each other and to their environment." Thereby, "compassion, wisdom, and love," according to Quinney (1993, p. 3), "are essential to understanding the suffering of which we are all a part and to practicing a criminology of nonviolence."

In this article, Quinney's (1993, p. 5) assumptions about crime are that the U.S. "has one of the highest crime rates in the world" and "our official ways of responding to crime are similar to those of most repressive nations." What is the peacemaking alternative? For Quinney (1993, p. 6), again it is a matter of personal and social transformation through a compassionate, peacemaking criminology whose: "objective is quite simple: to be kind to one another, to break down barriers that separate us from one another, to live moment-to-moment our connection to all that is . . . our oneness." On personal transformation, he (1993, p. 7) adds: "We have to become one with all who suffer from lives of crime and from the sources that produce crime." Great care is then given to our response to crime because in this compassionate criminology, there is no separation of the outer world and inner world such that: "Suffering on the social level can be ended only with the ending of the suffering on the personal level—the two realms are one and the same" (Quinney, 1993, p. 7).

In Quinney's analysis (1993, p. 8), criminologists as teachers, researchers, and policymakers are to be "peacemakers of the world" who are of "sound mind and gentle heart" and we are developing "ways of thinking, speaking, and writing that foster peace." These peacemaking ways consist of "alternatives that go beyond the criminal justice system," which in his (1993, p. 8) view would include: "quality education for children, physical and mental health services, family support programs, employment and job security, and the allocation of resources for the reduction of poverty." As Quinney (1993, p. 8) puts it: "Instead of a war on crime (on 'criminals'), we need to be waging peace on the economy, in the society, and within ourselves."

A fifth example of Quinney's peacemaking criminology work is "Criminology as Moral Philosophy, Criminologist as Witness." This chapter begins with Quinney making observations about his experiences traveling on a train from Chicago to Albany, New York, to eventually taking part in a "Justice Without Violence" conference. (I also participated in this conference and journeyed by plane from Macomb, Illinois, to Albany.) One of the novel dimensions of this writing is that it explores how "varieties of moral philosophy" can be thought to "inform contemporary criminology." Before offering the main points of his argument, Quinney (2000b, p. 194) makes this central assumption:

> A realization has been developing for some time and the conference I was attending confirmed it: Whatever else we do as criminologists, we are engaged in a moral enterprise. Simply stated, our underlying questions are these: How are we human beings to live? Who are we, and of what are we capable? And how could things be different?

Quinney's second major assumption is that criminologists need to be concerned about not only "how we humans might live" but also "what we think we are doing." According to Quinney (2000b, p. 194), a major part of what criminologists are doing "is witnessing to all that is associated with crime and justice." That is, criminologists tend to witness sufferings such as poverty, exploitation, violence, hate, greed, brutality, prejudice, and inequality. But at the same time, criminologists are witnesses who promote attempts to lessen suffering. All in all, "witnessing is an active vocation, one that is grounded in a particular moral stance toward human existence" (Quinney, 2000b, p. 194).

Thereby, Quinney takes readers through a discussion of a variety of moral philosophies that tend to build insights for peacemaking criminology. More specifically, these moral philosophies range from a social constructionist perspective to the prophetic meaning of justice, Marxist analysis, Buddhism, and socialist humanism. Space limitations do not permit an in-depth depiction of the broad discussion of Quinney in this chapter. However, in keeping with the design of this chapter, it is instructive to point out how it imparts insights about personal and social transformation and the role of criminologists as teacher, researcher, and policy maker.

Thus, for Quinney, (2000b, p. 195) social constructionism "assumes that reality—our perception of reality—is a mental construction rather than a direct apprehension of the world." The social constructionist, in his (2000b, p. 195) terms, "is interested not in the correspondence between 'objective reality' and observation, but in the utility of observations in understanding our own multiple, subjective realities." It can be thought that Quinney (2000b, pp. 195–196) is writing about social constructionism to illustrate that its questioning of the process by which we know (see Quinney, 1973), instead of taking it for granted can be applied to transcendent goals of peacemaking criminology. Expanding this notion, he (2000b, p. 196) states: "Social constructionists give us the beginnings for explaining multiple versions of reality, allowing us to transcend the official reality, and ultimately, our current existence."

In a similar light, the prophetic meaning of justice is a "form of address that calls for human beings to an awareness of their historic responsibility and challenges them to act in ways that will change the existing human condition" (Quinney, 2000b, p. 197). Seemingly, Quinney is writing about prophetic justice to influence criminologists to perceive the value of linking a concern about crime and its control with the prophetic justice notion that all of history involves a struggle between justice and injustice. Further on this point, he (2000b, p. 197) contends: "We the people in a covenant with God—are responsible for the character of our lives and our society, for the pursuit of righteousness, justice, and mercy." It also is apparent that Quinney (2000b, p. 197) is seeking for peacemaking criminologists to perceive the applicability of these words: "moral comprehension . . . is rooted in the depth of the divine." This is a sense of justice, according to Quinney, "that goes far beyond our modern liberal and legalistic notions of justice. For the prophets, the worldly virtue of justice is founded on the understanding that oppression on earth is an affront to God."

Consistent with his earlier Marxist-oriented writings (Quinney, 1974; 1980), Quinney (2000b, p. 200) supports Marxist theory given that it is "a form of thought that allows us to transcend in theory and practice the oppression of the capitalist order." The implications of Buddhism that he (2000b, p. 202) links to peacemaking criminology pertain, on the one hand, to the idea that "rational thought alone cannot answer the important existential questions of being human in relation to the whole world." On the other hand, Buddhist principles are very much in keeping with creating a world without crime. In fact, according to Quinney (2000b, p. 203), a Buddhist way of awareness "places us in the proper position to know the world," to pursue a *criminology with awareness*.

Socialist humanism's contribution to peacemaking criminology is two fold. First, peacemaking criminology's opposition to violence is bolstered by Mahatma Gandhi's concept of satyagraha, which Quinney (2000b, p. 204) associates here with truthful action; the refusal to do harm; compassion and self-constraint grow in the effort not to harm; and one who opposes what seems wrong and attempts to accept whatever may be right and just. Within socialist humanism, he (2000b, p. 205) derives concepts of negative peace "its purpose being to deter or process acts of crime through threat and application of force." According to Quinney (2000b, p. 205), deterrence and punishment have little to do with positive peace, in which "there is neither overt violence nor structural violence and attention is given to those things that cause crime and happen before crime occurs such as poverty, inequality, racism, and alienation."

Quinney's "Socialist Humanism and the Problem of Crime: Thinking about Erich Fromm in the Development of Critical/Peacemaking Criminology" is the sixth example of his peacemaking criminology writing. At the beginning of this chapter, Quinney notes at the time of this writing, his work was influenced by humanist, existentialist, Buddhist, pacifist, and socialist frameworks. In keeping with these frameworks, Quinney (2000c, p. 21) states that he attempts to "envision a world without crime" and to "imagine a world that would not produce crime." He suggests that the writings of Fromm can be used to explore these issues. For example, in *Socialist Humanism*, Fromm expresses that the establishment of peace is a central task for humanity (Quinney, 2000c, p. 24). However, as illustrated by Quinney (2000c, p. 24), Fromm draws attention to the fact that the economic contradictions of capitalism "promote the *having* mode of existence over the *being* mode." Further, creation of individuals and societies based on the having mode (rather than the being mode) lead toward obstacles of building love, compassion, and peace for humanity (Quinney 2000c, p. 24). Similarly, Quinney (2000c, p. 24) suggests that Fromm's popular *Art of Loving* book has a linkage to peacemaking criminology given Fromm's arguments that "love is the essence of being human" but "love is difficult to find and to practice in contemporary society. Love disintegrates in such a world."

In terms of personal and social transformation, Quinney (2000c) offers images that parallel what is found in his other peacemaking writings. As an illustration, he (2000c, p. 26) states in peacemaking criminology, "the objective is clear: to be kind to one another, to transcend the barriers that separate us from one another and to live every day life with a sense of independence." Regarding policies in respect to teaching, researching and servicing from a peacemaking perspective, Quinney (2000c, pp. 24–25) shows that Fromm's work is a combination of socialist humanism, Zen Buddhism, and mysticism. It seems reasonable to suggest that Quinney was striving in this writing to demonstrate for criminologists how Fromm endeavored to make his research oriented toward peace and peacemaking. That is, as Quinney (2000c, p. 27) reports, Fromm was a lifelong activist for movements of peace.

This essay of Quinney (2000c) also illustrates how ideas arising in relation to Gandhi can be linked with those of Fromm. Hence, Quinney (2000c, p. 27) suggests that Fromm's work and research was oriented against "continued war and violence and further bureaucratization and automatization of man." As a result, Fromm's legacy can be seen in his personal and professional efforts to "go in the direction of life, peace and political and spiritual renewal" (Quinney, 2000c, p. 28). According to Quinney (2000c, p. 28), Gandhi was also firm in his belief that since absolute truth is not easily arrived at or possibly known, how can we come to conclusions as humans that anyone is competent to punish offenders?

Quinney (2000c, p. 28) completes this work by discussing other differences between *negative peace* ("its purpose being to deter or process acts of crime through the threat and application of force") and *positive peace* which is a condition "other than deterrence or punishment of crime," and "more than merely the absence of crime and violence—of war." Instead positive peace, in Quinney's (2000c, p. 28) view, tends to minimize exploitation and "is the attention given to all things, most of them structured in the society, that causes crime, that happens before crime occurs." In addition, according to Quinney (2000c, p. 28), "positive peace exists when the sources of crime—poverty, inequality, racism, and alienation—are not present." In sum, punishment (negative peace) is not the way of peace; positive peace (i.e., striving to eliminate the structure of violence and crime) is the objective of peacemaking criminology (Quinney, 2000c, p. 28).

Conclusion

In light of the analysis of this chapter, let us now stand back from Quinney's writings on peacemaking criminology (both the precursors and direct writings) and proceed to draw some summary points and implications for future research in this area of study. In respect to tendencies within this literature, there are four which stand out. First, Quinney's peacemaking writings are very consistent with those commonly found within criminology and his approach to peacemaking criminology is very much like that of others who carry out the study of crime in this way. That is, Quinney's peacemaking criminology: is in keeping with the three principle themes of peacemaking—connectedness, caring, mindfulness; consistently offers an alternative to the "war on crime" within criminal justice; progressively addresses the value of society moving more toward personal and social transformation of crime and social justice; and comprehensively strives to critique theories and policies within mainstream criminology. Furthermore, Quinney's peacemaking criminology raises broad and very humane peacemaking assumptions about crime, develops peacemaking alternatives to the ineffectual way of violence which looms within our criminal justice system, and contributes ongoing innovations to build the role of the peacemaking criminologist as teacher, researcher, and policy-maker.

Given the work of Quinney and others who share the path in developing peacemaking criminology, it is useful to consider what steps need to be taken to gain further understanding about the alleviation of crime and social harms through the lens of the peacemaking criminology paradigm. First, for those teachers, researchers, and policy-makers who continue to take on a daily basis the bold steps of social activism called for in the peacemaking criminology supported by Quinney, peace indeed is the way. It is extremely rewarding to move along the path of positive peace. As Quinney and Wildeman (1991, pp. 117, 118, 119) write:

> In peacemaking, we attend to the ultimate purpose of our existence—to heal the separation between all things and to live harmoniously in a state of unconditional work. When our hearts are filled with love and our minds with willingness to serve, we will know what has to be done and how it is to be done . . . everything is done out of compassion to lessen the suffering of others.

This is one of Richard Quinney's greatest legacies in criminology. He made it a consistent point to inspire criminology and criminal justice toward a way of peace. It seems reasonable to suggest there is no one in this field of study who builds insights about crime in the way that Quinney regularly does with such vigor. In this profession, he can be seen as a leading criminologist who continually lofts attention toward how to bring about connectedness, compassion, oneness, mindfulness, loving-kindness, transcendence, spirituality, holism, and transformation for both the individual and society.

Second, a promising peacemaking path for criminologists and criminal justice practitioners to take part in involves socially progressive teaching/research/service pursuits along the lines of what Maguire calls "the applied dimension of radical criminology." That is, according to Maguire (1988, p. 133), "radical criminology is known mostly for its theoretical focus. Though less attended to, there is a practical side to the perspective" (see also Lynch and Michalowski, 2006; Lynch et al., 2006; Wozniak, 2002b). More specifically, this practical side can be conceived as "applied criminology," which refers to "programmatic politics which have the potential for altering events in the real world which bear on crime and justice" (Maguire, 1988, p. 134). According to Maguire (1988, p. 149), "radical criminology is in need of an applied program capable of embracing grass roots practices and national, and even international, planning." In this light, peacemaking criminology would do well to move toward these paths suggested by Quinney and Maguire.

A third path is one suggested by Cullen (1994) which is a movement against criminogenic policies and social conditions by advancing a social support paradigm of teaching, research and service within criminology and criminal justice. This path could potentially be taken by criminologists and criminal justice practitioners who are sympathetic with the peacemaking perspective in criminology but might feel less ease or affinity in carrying out the social activist side or the radical applied side of peacemaking. For example, adapted from three steps needed for the social support paradigm (i.e., Cullen, 1994, pp. 550–551; see also Cullen et al., 1999), peacemaking criminology could also move in these directions in the future:

- peacemaking criminology researchers need to conceptualize and study which forms of peacemaking are implicated most deeply in diminishing criminal involvement and social harms.
- peacemaking criminology researchers need to identify the precise mechanisms by which peacemaking objectives decrease criminal behavior and social harms.
- to advance the peacemaking criminology paradigm, criminologists should incorporate measures of peacemaking and social harms into their crime research designs.

Whenever possible, it would be beneficial for peacemaking criminology research to merge with other possible progressive research projects to advance peacemaking criminology studies into generally untrodden territory within the discipline. Peacemaking criminology, for example, could extend more studies in relation to rehabilitation in correctional settings (e.g., Andrews et al., 1990; Cullen, 2002; Cullen and Gendreau, 2003; Gendreau, 1996; Gendreau et al., 1996; Gendreau and Ross, 1987) and the integration of theories (e.g., Bohm, 2001;

Cullen and Agnew, 2006; Lilly et al., 2006; Paternoster and Bachman, 2001; Shoemaker, 2000). For that matter, it would be refreshing to attend a national or regional conference and see a peacemaking criminology paper presented (and hopefully seriously listened to) on the same panel as a mainstream theory (e.g., strain, control, social disorganization, learning, rational choice, life course, routine activities) and vice versa.

In sum, as Quinney (2000c, p. 21) states in his tribute to Fromm on peacemaking:

> What is important in the study of crime is everything that happens before crime occurs. The question of what precedes crime is far more significant to our understanding the act of crime itself. Crime is the reflection of something larger and deeper.

A prominent question now facing us is what happens in the study of peacemaking criminology in the future after its forerunners, like Quinney, have laid out its encompassing foundation? It is hoped peacemaking criminology will continue to flourish and that this chapter and the work of Richard Quinney play some part in bringing about the positive peace called for in peacemaking criminology.

References

Akers, R. L., & Sellers, C. S. (2004). *Criminological theories: Introduction ,evaluation, and application* (4th ed.). Los Angeles: Roxbury.

Anderson, K. (1991). Radical criminology and the overcoming of alienation: Perspective from Marxian and Gandhian humanism. In H. E. Pepinsky & R. Quinney (Eds.), *Criminology as peacemaking* (pp. 14-29). Bloomington: Indiana University Press.

Andrews, D. A., Zinger, I., Hoge, R. D., Bonta, J., Gendreau, P., & Cullen, F. T. (1990). Does correctional treatment work? A clinically relevant and psychological informed meta-analysis. *Criminology*, *28*, 369-404.

Barlow, H. D., & Kauzlarich, D. (2002). *Introduction to criminology* (8th ed.). Upper Saddle River, NJ: Prentice Hall.

Berger, R. J., Free, M. D. Jr., & Searles, P. (2001). *Crime, justice and society: Criminology and the sociological imagination*. New York: McGraw-Hill.

Beirne, P., & Messerschmidt, J. W. (2006). *Criminology* (4th ed.). Los Angeles: Roxbury.

Bohm, R. M. (2001). *A primer on crime and delinquency theory* (2nd ed.). Belmont, CA: Wadsworth.

Braswell, M. C. (1990). Peacemaking: A missing link in criminology. *The Criminologist*, *15* (3), 1, 3-5.

Cullen, F. T. (1994). Social support as an organizing concept for criminology: Presidential address to the Academy of Criminal Justice Sciences. *Justice Quarterly*, *11* (4), 527-559.

Cullen, F. T. (2002). Rehabilitation and treatment programs. In J. Q. Wilson & J. Petersilia (Eds.), *Crime: Public Policies for Crime Control* (pp. 253-289). Oakland, CA: Institute for Contemporary Studies Press.

Cullen, F. T., & Agnew, R. (Eds.) (2006). *Criminology theory: Past to present: Essential readings* (3rd ed.). Los Angeles: Roxbury.

Cullen, F. T., & Gendreau, P. (2003). Assessing correctional rehabilitation: Policy, practice, and prospects. In J. Horney (Ed.), *Criminal Justice 2000: Vol. 3 Policies, Processes, and Decisions of the Criminal Justice System* (pp. 109-175). Washington, D.C.: National Institute of Justice, U.S. Department of Justice.

Cullen, F. T., Wright, J. P., & Chamlin, M. B. (1999, April). Social support and social reform: A progressive crime control agenda. *Crime & Delinquency*, 45, 188-207.

Elias, R. (1993). *Victims still: The political manipulation of crime victims*. Newbury Park, CA: Sage.

Fischer, L. (Ed.) (1962). *The essential Gandhi*. New York: Vintage.

Friedrichs, D. O. (1991). *Introduction: Peacemaking criminology in a world filled with conflict*. In B. D. MacLean & D. Milovanovic (Eds.), *New directions in critical criminology* (pp. 101-110). Vancouver, Canada: Collective Press.

Fromm, E. (Ed.) (1965). *Socialist humanism*. Garden City, NY: Doubleday.

Fromm, E. (1976). *To have or to be*. New York: Harper and Row.

Fromm, E. (1989). *The art of loving*. New York: Harper and Row.

Fuller, J. R. (1998). *Criminal justice: A peacemaking perspective*. Boston: Allyn and Bacon.

Fuller, J. R. (2006). *Criminal justice: Mainstream and crosscurrents*. Upper Saddle River, NJ: Pearson Prentice Hall.

Fuller, J. R., & Wozniak, J. F. (2006). Peacemaking criminology: Past, present, and future. In F. T. Cullen, J. P. Wright & K. R. Blevins (Eds.), *Taking stock: The status of criminological theory, advances in criminological theory*, Vol. 15 (pp. 251-273). New Brunswick, NJ: Transaction.

Gandhi, M. (1948). *Autobiography: The story of my experiments with truth.* New York: Dover.

Gendreau, P. (1996). Offender rehabilitation: What we know and what needs to be done. *Criminal Justice and Behavior, 23*, 144-161.

Gendreau, P., Little, T., & Goggin, C. (1996). A meta analysis of the predictors of adult offender recidivism: What works! *Criminology, 34*(4), 575-607.

Gendreau, P., & Ross, R. (1987). Revivification of rehabilitation: Evidence from the 1980's. *Justice Quarterly*, 4, 349-407.

Kendall, D. (2005). *Sociology in our times* (5th ed.). Belmont, CA: Wadsworth.

Lilly, J. R., Cullen, F. T., & Ball, R. A. (2006). *Criminological theory: Context and consequences* (4th ed.). Thousand Oaks, CA: Sage.

Lynch, M. J., & Michalowski, R. (2006). *Primer in radical criminology: Critical perspectives on crime, power, and identity.* (4th ed.). Monsey, NY: Criminal Justice Press.

Lynch, M. J., Schwendinger, H. and Schwendinger, J. (2006). The status of empirical research in radical criminology. In F. T. Cullen, J. P. Wright & K. R. Blevins (Eds.), *Taking stock: The status of criminological theory, advances in criminological theory*, Vol. 15 (pp. 191-215). New Brunswick, NJ: Transaction.

Macionis, J. J. (2005). *Sociology* (10th ed.). Upper Saddle River, NJ: Pearson Prentice Hall.

Maguire, B. (1988). The applied dimension of radical criminology: A survey of prominent radical criminologists. *Sociological Spectrum, 8,* 133-151.

Martin, R., Mutchnick, R. J., & Austin, T. W. (1990). *Criminological thought: Pioneers past and present.* New York: Macmillan.

Moyer, I. L. (2001). *Criminological theories: Traditional and nontraditional voices and themes.* Thousand Oaks, CA: Sage.

Paternoster, R., & Bachman, R. (Eds.) (2001). *Explaining criminals and crime: Essays in contemporary theory.* Los Angeles: Roxbury.

Pepinsky, H. E. (1999). Peacemaking primer. In B. A. Arrigo (Ed.), *Social justice/criminal justice: The maturation of critical theory in law, crime, and deviance* (pp. 52-70). Belmont, CA: Wadsworth.

Pepinsky, H. E., & Quinney, R. (Eds.). (1991). *Criminology as peacemaking.* Bloomington: Indiana University Press.

Quinney, R. (1970). *The social reality of crime.* Boston: Little, Brown.

Quinney, R. (1973). A transcendental way of knowing. In N. M. Regush (Ed.), *Visibles and invisibles: A primer for a new sociological imagination* (pp. 168-177). Boston: Little Brown.

Quinney, R. (1974). *Critique of legal order: Crime control in capitalist society.* Boston: Little Brown.

Quinney, R. (1979, February). *The production of criminology. Criminology, 16*, 445-457.

Quinney, R. (1980). *Class, state, and crime* (2nd ed.). New York: Longman.

Quinney, R. (1982, November). *The nature of the world: Holistic vision for humanist sociology. Humanity and Society, 6*, 322-339.

Quinney, R. (1985). *Myth and art of criminology. Legal Studies Forum, 9* (3), 291-297.

Quinney, R. (1988). Beyond the interpretive: The way of awareness. *Sociological Inquiry, 58* (Winter), 101-116.

Quinney, R. (1989). *The theory and practice of peacemaking in the development of radical criminology. The Critical Criminologist*, 1 (Winter), 5.

Quinney, R. (1991a). *Journey to a far place.* Philadelphia: Temple University Press.

Quinney, R. (1991b). Oneness of all: The mystical nature of humanism. In B. D. MacLean & D. Milovanovic (Eds.), *New directions in critical criminology* (pp. 113-117). Vancouver, Canada: Collective Press.

Quinney, R. (1991c). The way of peace: On crime, suffering, and service. In H. E. Pepinsky & R. Quinney (Eds.), *Criminology as peacemaking* (pp. 3-13). Bloomington: Indiana University Press.

Quinney, R. (1993). A life of crime: Criminology and public policy as peacemaking. *Journal of Crime and Justice*, 16 (2), 3-9.

Quinney, R. (1998). *For the time being: Ethnography of everyday life*. Albany: State University of New York Press.

Quinney, R. (2000a). *Bearing witness to crime and social justice*. Albany: State University of New York Press.

Quinney, R. (2000b). Criminology as moral philosophy, criminologist as witness. In R. Quinney (Ed.), *Bearing witness to crime and social justice* (pp. 193-213). Albany: State University of New York Press.

Quinney, R. (2000c). Socialist humanism and the problem of crime: Thinking about Erich Fromm in the development of critical/peacemaking criminology. In K. Anderson and R. Quinney (Eds.), *Erich Fromm and critical criminology: Beyond the punitive society* (pp. 21-30). Urbana: University of Illinois Press.

Quinney, R. & Wildeman, J. (1991). *The problem of crime: A peace and social justice perspective* (3rd ed). Mountain View, CA: Mayfield.

Schaefer, R. T. (2005). *Sociology* (9th ed.). New York: McGraw-Hill.

Shelden, R. G., Tracy, S. K., & Brown, W. B. (2004). *Youth gangs in American society* (3rd ed.). Belmont, CA: Wadsworth.

Shelden, R. G., & Brown, W. B. (2003). *Criminal justice in America: A critical view*. Boston, MA: Allyn and Bacon.

Shoemaker, D. J. (2000). *Theories of delinquency: An examination of explanations of delinquent behavior*. New York: Oxford University Press.

Siegel, L. J. (2007). *Criminology: Theories, patterns, and typologies* (9th ed.). Belmont, CA: Wadsworth.

Sullivan, D., & Tifft, L. (1998). Criminology as peacemaking: A peace-oriented perspective on crime, punishment, and justice that takes into account the needs of all. *The Justice Professional*, *11* (1-2), 5-34.

Williams, F. P. III, & McShane, M. D. (2004). *Criminological theory* (4th ed.). Upper River, NJ: Prentice Hall.

Wozniak, J. F. (2000). The voices of peacemaking criminology: Insights into a perspective with an eye toward teaching. *Contemporary Justice Review*, 3(3), 267-289.

Wozniak, J. F. (2002a). Peacemaking criminology approaches to crime prevention. A review of successful primary, secondary, and tertiary strategies. Paper presented at the annual meeting of the American Society of Criminology, Chicago.

Wozniak, J. F. (2002b). Toward a theoretical model of peacemaking criminology: An essay in honor of Richard Quinney. *Crime & Delinquency*, 48, 204-231.

Wright, R. A. (2000). Recent changes in the most-cited scholars in criminology: A comparison of textbooks and journals. *Journal of Criminal Justice*, 28, 117-128.

Chapter 10

Reflections on Women's Crime and Mothers in Prison: A Peacemaking Approach

Polly F. Radosh

"What is important in the study of crime is everything that happens before crime occurs. The question of what precedes crime is far more significant to our understanding than the act of crime itself. Crime is a reflection of something larger and deeper." —Quinney (2000, p. 2)

Among my earliest memories of my childhood in upstate New York is learning to cut with scissors in the Irish Catholic school I attended for the first 9 years of my education. In this school the nuns were very strict and required absolute attention and adherencc to the rules and protocol of the classroom. All of the desks were in neat rows, students stood next to their desks with hands at their sides when called upon to answer a question, and when the nun looked down each row of desks she wanted to see all papers aligned at the same angle on the desk and each student holding pencils, scissors, or other implements in exactly the same way. For most students the requirements were not too difficult to master, although there were always a few stray papers that shifted, or children who held their pencils in defiance to the required norm, especially in the younger grades. Eventually everyone adhered to the protocol and there was little correction needed by about the third grade. I had a problem for most of my early education, however, because I am left-handed. It was difficult to get my paper aligned at the appropriate angle on the desk, but eventually I did master this requirement. The biggest problem for me was learning to cut with scissors. The nuns could tolerate my writing with my left hand, but they would not provide left-handed scissors and I was not permitted to use my left hand to cut.

I learned to cut with my right hand because I was not permitted to use my left hand. I eventually mastered the skill completely, and today I am perfectly competent in the use of right-handed scissors. I have so completely shifted away from my natural inclination that I am actually no longer able to maneuver my left hand to cut at all. I have transformed my innate preference for my left hand into an adaptation that is so complete that I am no longer able to revert back to my natural inclination and now I must use right-handed scissors. I have many questions about my adaptation, however: What might I have been able to accomplish if I had been able to develop my natural talents? How has my adaptation shaped my thinking or my personality? And what artistic masterpiece of cutting might I have produced if I had not been forced to shift to a more difficult means of achieving my cutting goals? Why was it so important that I conform? And, what social, organizational, or human goal was accomplished by my conformity or punishment for non-conformity?

When I think of Richard Quinney's work I think of a my educational experience. There are several parallels to my experience and the impact that Quinney has had on my thinking about crime. First, I believe that his work helps to equip those of us who are metaphorically "left-handed," in a world of "right-handed" people, with a pair of left-handed scissors. That is, he helps us to see the world as we are naturally inclined to see it, rather than as we are shaped by cultural convention or criminal justice protocol to see the world.

This is especially true with his work on peacemaking criminology. From this perspective, crime is produced by factors that are out of the control of the individual, such as political, economic, or social structures that limit human potential. To address crime with violence, or punishment, will never solve the problem of crime because violence and punishment address only the outcome, not the source of crime. From Quinney's (1991) view only "understanding, service, justice [which] flow naturally from love and compassion, from mindful attention to the reality of all that is. . . ."(p. 4) will solve the problem of crime. To focus on individual failings as the source of crime is myopic. To solve crime by punishing individual failings is unjust and will only create more suffering. What useful purpose is served by punishing, especially for those who violate laws that serve no useful social purpose? Punishing because a law-violator has broken the law, without attention to the social utility of the law or the good that could be accomplished by compliance, is to attend to the letter of law and ignore the spirit of support and communal connection that law should engender. To enforce compliance without utilitarian goals is much like forcing left-handed people to cut with right-handed scissors. We can mold most people to conform to the norms, but some people have different backgrounds, experiences, or societal impairments that make conformity differentially more difficult.

Second, he helps us to understand that adherence to laws and protocol merely for the requirement of adherence does nothing to solve social problems, address crime, or eliminate suffering. The requirement in my school that I learn to adapt to a pair of right-handed scissors was a temporary handicap for me. I eventually adapted, but the requirement did no lasting good and probably some harm to my developing skills. Quinney's insights into the criminal justice system show us that we often pay such strict attention to the requirements of control and punishment, that we miss the meaning of crime. We address the expression of crime, but we ignore the causes of crime. Quinney's work teaches us that humane, non-judgmental approaches to crime will help us to achieve a more humane society. Just as the goal of using scissors should be cutting, the goal of law should be social good. Intermediary, cumbersome, or painful obstacles to attaining the goal should be eliminated.

Third, rules, law, protocol, ordinances, and all of the other mechanisms we use to "keep peace" in our society are a means of preserving order, but we often become so focused upon the rules that we have forgotten why the rules were important in the first place. Often the requirement of adherence to law is much more important that the harm that would be done by law violation. Learning to cut with my right hand was important only because it was a rule, not because it would improve my skills, make me a better person, or cause chaos in the classroom if I did not adhere to the rule. Such is the case with enforcement of many laws. With women's crime, in particular, adherence to the law is required because it is the law, not because it promotes social justice, public order, or a better quality of life.

From his 1970s work which articulated the impact of capitalistic structures on individual action to Quinney's current work on peacemaking, love, and existentialism, the underlying structures that shape social action have been a thematic concern in his explanations of crime. Actions are shaped by forces that go beyond free will or opportunity. Events, structures, systems of oppression, and power affect human choices and predicate personal interests. Events that precede crime are as important to understanding crime as are the actual criminal events. Quinney's work is like the use of the metaphorical "left-handed scissors;" it helps us to see that law has layers of meaning that are obscured when we focus merely on the act of law violation. The true meanings of law, the life experiences of the law violator, and underlying social inequities that produce crime are not addressed. Instead, the illegal act is addressed through punishment.

From my first reading of Quinney's work when I was a student in the 1970s, I have returned innumerable times to his writings as a touchstone for my own understanding of women's crime. In no other field of inquiry do his theories make more sense. Structure, oppression, economic exploitation, and marginalized social opportunity explain almost all of women's crime. Minor drug crimes committed by women, for example, draw sentences as long as, and sometimes longer than, serious male crime. Women's crime is defined as symbolically equivalent to serious male crime, even when it is not. For many years I have returned to Quinney to help in my own understanding of this apparent injustice. It is not only patriarchy that explains this, but also the defining structures of capitalism that allocate authority for criminal definitions in the hands of the powerful. Women, who lack significant social power, are defined as criminal through definitions created to verify the existing social order. Prevailing popular views about crime and criminals, as well as public criminal justice policies, legitimate the existing system as a reflection of justice. If we use the metaphorical "left-handed scissors," Quinney's work helps us to see that women's crime is a reflection of social injustice. When we see the world as it is, rather than as we are conditioned to see it, women's crime has new meaning.

Women's crime is grounded in exploitation. Without exploitation there would not be crime. Nearly all of women's crime is related to sexual exploitation, abuse, poverty, and structural inequality. Quinney's most recent work, which explores the relationship between mature love and a world without crime, provides an especially clear lens with which to focus women's crime. A world without crime is one in which crime would not be possible because inner individual peace is reflected in peaceful coexistence (Quinney, 2000, p. 21). Crime is produced by human suffering. The connection between suffering and women's crime is widely acknowledged by academics as well as administrators of women's prisons. There is little dispute about the connections, but there is considerable disagreement about the most appropriate response to women's crime. A mature response would mean that we should move beyond the act of law violation and address the means by which the human needs of the law violator may be met. To focus on punishment of the offender ignores the fact that the crime reflects events that happened prior to the criminal action. The crime cannot be understood without attention to the prior experience, and punishment will do nothing to address the prior experience or to help the offender move beyond the pain that is reflected in crime.

Contemporary Thinking about Crime

Quinney's summary of the criminal justice system in the United States, organized around the belief that those who commit crimes deserve their punishments, is as true today as it was when he published *Class, State, and Crime* in 1977 (p. 21). Modern thinking about crime says that it results from personal failures, lack of self-control, weakness, laziness, moral lapse, or other character flaws that inhibit self-restraint. Those who commit crimes should be willing to pay the penalties for their mistakes, given the widely known "hard on crime" political ideology characterized by punitive sentencing strategies that have been well-known and highly publicized for more than twenty years. According to the predominant paradigm, one of the most important goals of criminal justice policy should be deterrence produced through sure, swift, and severe punishment. A second important goal is to restore "balance" through retribution, or to assure that the offender "pays" his or her debt to society by suffering the pains of imprisonment.[1]

Women Offenders

Criminologists are in general agreement that across time and in all cultures, women's crime is less serious and less frequent than men's. Even with significant changes in sentencing and a rapid increase in the prison population in the U.S. in recent years, women's incarceration remains a small fraction of men's.

Both arrest patterns and incarceration trends indicated that almost all of women's crime in the twentieth century has been concentrated in the area of low level property or public order (prostitution) crime.[2] In the 1980s an additional "feminine" crime surfaced, with changes in U.S. drug laws. In 2003, for example, two-thirds of women in federal and one-third of those in state prisons had been sentenced to prison for a drug crime. This compares with about half of men in federal and 20 percent in state prisons who were incarcerated for drug crimes (Harrison and Beck, 2005; Sourcebook, 2004). About 72 percent of women under correctional supervision in jail, on probation, or in prison during the decade of the 1990s had committed a property, drug, or public order offense (Greenfield & Snell 1999). This trend continues by current indicators (Harrison and Beck, 2005, p. 9).

Women's involvement in drug crime is usually low level dealing or delivery activities, although about 10 percent of federal and 15 percent of state female inmates have been incarcerated for possession (Mumola, 2000, p. 6). Limited economic circumstances motivate some non-users of drugs to sell. Of those women incarcerated during the 1990s, only 40 percent indicated that they had been employed during the months prior to their arrest (compared to 60 percent of men) and 30 percent were on welfare. Nearly 40 percent of those who were employed earned less than $600 per month (Greenfield & Snell, 1999, p. 8). Women with few economic alternatives, limited life skills, and with great economic need often participate in the drug trade as a means of supplementing their income. Risk of detection is exacerbated by their low level, high visibility positions in the drug distribution network.

In addition to difficult economic circumstances, 60 percent of incarcerated women in state prisons indicated in surveys between 1995 and 1997 that they had been physically or sexually abused in the past (Greenfield & Snell, 1999, p. 1). Women who had spent some of their childhood in foster care or institutions indicated that they had been victims of sexual or physical abuse in 87 percent of cases. Of those who grew up in homes where parents abused alcohol or drugs, 76 percent reported prior abuse; and among those who lived in homes where a family member had been incarcerated, prior abuse was reported among 64 percent of women inmates. In about 95 percent of cases among all abused women in jail, on probation, or incarcerated in a federal or state prison, the perpetrator of the abuse was someone they knew, such as a relative, their mother's boyfriend, or a family friend (Greenfield & Snell, 1999, p. 3). Not surprisingly, 80 percent of those with a history of abuse were regular users of drugs at the time of their arrest (Greenfield & Snell, 1999, p. 3).

The life circumstances of incarcerated women help to explain much of their criminal behavior. While many people who have lived in poverty or who have been victims of abuse do not commit crimes, the common thread of continuity that runs through the history of women's incarceration is that most women in prison share common life experiences. They are very likely to have been living in poverty, to have experienced prior abuse by male friends and relatives, to have had childhood experiences that included substance abuse by parents, to have been sexually abused as children, and to suffer with personal stress, trauma, and fear in many stages of their lives. According to the National Institute of Justice, the needs of women in prison are different from men and thus require different programming:

> Women in prison have some needs that are quite different from men's resulting in part from women's disproportionate victimization from sexual or physical abuse and in part from their responsibility for children. Women offenders are also more likely than men to have become addicted to drugs, to have mental illnesses, and to have been unemployed before incarceration. (Morash, Bynum, & Koons, 1998, p. 1)

Each of the special problems of women inmates may seem to be a separate issue, but they actually weave together into a complex set of problems that have been rarely addressed by the correctional system. Women whose life experiences have presented many overwhelming personal problems often seek relief in substances that ease their pain. Common backgrounds of poverty, physical and sexual abuse, and accompanying feelings of loss, betrayal, depression, and desperation spawn ongoing personal problems that are highly likely to result in recidivism if they are not addressed.

Incarceration Patterns

The number of people incarcerated in U.S. prisons and jails has increased to unprecedented levels in the last two decades. In 1980 the national rate of incarceration was 139, but this had risen to 486 by 2004 (Harrison & Beck, 2005, p.1). Table 10.1 illustrates some of the growth in incarceration rates since 1980.

Women represent a small overall proportion of the prison population, even though the percentage of women in prison is increasing faster than men (Harrison & Beck, 2005, p.1). Regardless of the rapid increase in women's incarceration, men are still fourteen times more likely to serve time in a state or federal prison. The overall greater likelihood of men to serve time in prison meant that for most of the twentieth century women's corrections received little attention. It was not until the number of women incarcerated began to rise in the early 1980s that researchers began to address either the patterns of women's incarceration or programming in women's prisons.

As research has articulated some of the unique characteristics of women inmates, patterns that differentiate women from men have become apparent. Female inmates, for example, are more likely to have been convicted of a nonviolent crime, to have a prior history of physical or sexual abuse, to be incarcerated for a drug offense, and to have been the primary caretaker for their children prior to their incarceration.

Traditionally, women received longer sentences than men for the same offenses because women offenders often deviated significantly from expected gender role restrictions that required a higher degree of self-control and lifestyle restrictions than would be typical expectations for men. Studies of sentencing, for example, have indicated that women were sentenced longer than men for the same offense because it often appeared to judges that women offenders were "worse" than male offenders. Only a few women, in comparison to men, engaged in crime, which implied that such behavior by women was an especially abhorrent anomaly to typical "female behavior" (Lanagan & Dawson, 1993, p. 2; Parisi, 1982). Patriarchal definitions of women's "proper" nurturing roles affected judicial decision-making in such a way that judges often believed that women's crime was not only law violation, but also "unnatural." The subtle, but widely dispersed, belief that women criminals were "worse" than men translated into longer average sentences for women. While all prisoners are serving longer sentences under new mandatory sentencing laws, much of the gender disparity in sentencing that had resulted in lengthy prison terms for women prior to the mid 1980s has been significantly reduced.

Table 10.1. Incarceration Trends 1980–2004: Number and Rate[a] of Incarceration

Year	Total	Rate	Males Number	Males Rate	Females Number	Females Rate
1980	315,974	139	303,643	275	12,331	11
1985	480,568	202	458,972	397	21,296	17
1990	739,980	297	699,416	575	40,564	32
1995	1,085,363	411	1,021,463	796	63,900	48
2004	2,267,787	486	1,337,700	926	96,100	64

[a] The rate of incarceration is the number of people incarcerated for every 100,000 population.

Sources: Kathleen Maguire and Ann L. Pastore eds. (1999) Sourcebook of Criminal Justice Statistics 1998. U.S. Department of Justice Statistics, Bureau of Justice Statistics, Washington DC: U.S. Government Printing Office, p. 490; Darrell K. Gilliard (1993) "Prisoners in 1992," Bureau of Justice Statistics Bulletin, Washington DC: U.S. Government Printing Office, p. 4; Harrison & Beck 2005, p.1, 9.

Sentencing reform in the mid 1980s highlighted rational criteria in sentencing, which reduced the disparity between men's and women's sentences. Factors such as prior offense history, use of a weapon in commission of the crime, whether the offense was violent, and other criteria related to the characteristics of both the offense and the offender, are now used to set the length of sentences under minimum mandatory guidelines. Women rarely commit violent crimes, and they have much lower rates of recidivism than men. As a result, women's sentences for index crimes are comparable to equally charged and convicted men.

Although objective criteria in sentencing are much more consistent than they were prior to sentencing reform, other gender differences in offending patterns, as well as gender-specific patterns related to sentencing, do work against women in drug cases. Women's involvement in the drug trade is usually at the lowest level of participation. Under federal drug conspiracy laws, participants with minor roles are sentenced as long, and often longer, than those with key roles in the distribution network. A woman who drives her boyfriend to make drug deals and waits in the car until after the deal is completed may end up serving a longer sentence than her boyfriend, who is the actual dealer. Drug convictions and sentencing rely very heavily on informant deals. The driver in the car would not have knowledge that would be beneficial to authorities and thus could not "deal" with prosecutors on her own behalf. Also, loyalty to boyfriends or husbands prevents many women from making deals, even when they have such knowledge. A review of over 60,000 federal drug cases indicates that men are much more willing to sell out women to get a shorter sentence, than women are likely to sell out men (Szalvitz, 1999, p. 43). Women are frequently convicted of drug crimes when they have had no involvement or very little knowledge of their boyfriend's involvement. Women, for example, have been convicted of "improper use of the telephone," or answering the phone for what later turned out to be a drug sale (Szalvitz, 1999, p. 43).

Inmate Mothers

In 2004 there were about 96,100 women incarcerated in prisons and jails in the United States. This represents 7 percent of the prison population (Harrison & Beck 2005, p. 1). While the exact percentage of women inmates with children is not known, most estimates indicate that about 80 percent have dependent children at the time that they are incarcerated (Watterson, 1996, p. 210; Willams, 1996, p. 80). In 1999, which is the most recent count, there were at least 126,100 children with mothers in prison, and the mean age for all children with parents in prison was 8 years (Mumola, 2000, p. 2).

There are many more children with fathers in prison than mothers, but incarcerated mothers are more likely to have been living with their children prior to incarceration (Greenfield & Snell, 1999, p. 8). Undoubtedly, the social and emotional trauma inherent in incarceration of a parent produces significant strain on all children with imprisoned parents, but the pain is especially significant for those whose families were broken by incarceration of a parent. Over 60 percent of fathers in state prisons and more than half of those in federal prisons did not live with their children in the months before arrest. But, about 60 percent of mothers in state prisons, and 73 percent of those in federal prisons, did live with their children before arrest (Mumola, 2000, p. 2).

In addition to the obvious stress created by separation, there are other concerns associated with incarceration of mothers. About 25 percent of incarcerated women are pregnant or have recently given birth at the time of their incarceration. Separation from a new-born infant creates additional stress, worry, and anxiety for an incarcerated mother. Their unique concerns are different from the typical worries of other parents who are separated from their children while in prison.

Most research on the effects of incarceration on parenting or on children have focused upon the immediate issues related to stress, anxiety, maintaining strong family ties, and other programmatic concerns. The issue is much wider than the immediate needs of inmates or families, however. Factors related to the life histories and crimes of inmate mothers both explain incarceration patterns and influence post-release family unity.

Although incarcerated women are not a monolithic group, their background characteristics are much more similar than those of incarcerated men. The overriding experience of abuse and very common pattern of substance abuse by women offenders are linked. Most incarcerated women enter prison with these problems. The fact that most also have dependent children means that many of the problems of women inmates also present problems for their children. To be effective, programming in women's prisons must address the unique characteristics of incarcerated women, as well as to promote family growth and unity. Despite widespread recognition of the unique needs of women inmates, 39 states use the same classification instrument for men and women, in 7 states the male instrument is adapted for women, and only 3 states use a special instrument for women inmates (Mumola, 2000, p. 3). By most accounts, the special needs of women inmates are met with sporadic, inconsistent, inappropriate, or inadequate programming.

Women are very likely to return to their children after release from prison. Among the many differences between male and female inmates is an overriding concern among women for the welfare of their children while they are in prison and high anxiety about how they will provide for their children when they are released. Programming in women's prisons only sporadically addresses these concerns.

But by most accounts, programming for women inmates fails to address the issues that are most important for humanistic reasons and which are most likely to reduce recidivism. As one administrator in the National Institute of Justice's survey of approaches to women's programming indicated, "Women who are victims of abuse tend to continue on as victims of abuse. Men on the other hand, tend to react to their own history of victimization by becoming abusers themselves" (Mumola, 2000, p. 10). And, as another prison administrator indicated in a private conversation, the most consistent pattern among all incarcerated women is that they "have been battered beyond belief."[3]

Women inmates have generally used more drugs and used them more frequently than men, prior to their incarceration (Morash et al., 1998, p. 1). Drugs have provided a means of escape for most women inmates. Incarceration frequently provides their first opportunity to evaluate their own lives and the effects of their decisions on their children. Women inmates' needs are different from men's and interrelated to both their prior history and their future parenting skills.

Punishment, Women's Crime, and Parenting

Current punishment strategies that focus on instilling future goals of self-restraint, personal control, and moral strength through retribution for wrongful behavior are inadequate, illogical, and futile as a response to women's crime. The prior life experiences of incarcerated women dictate more humane, and constructive approaches than characterize contemporary strategies. To use contemporary retribution models as a response to women's crime fails to recognize the prior precipitating experiences of women. Their crime does not fit the justice model for several reasons.

First, women's crime is generally non-violent, and low-level. It is often punished with serious prison time, not because of the inherent harmfulness of their criminal acts, but because of their lack of power or knowledge with which to negotiate prosecutorial deals, especially in drug cases. The punishment does not fit either the crime or the offender.

Second, women's crime commonly reflects prior life-experiences with men who clearly perpetrated serious criminal acts, such as childhood sexual molestation, rape, incest, and domestic violence. The fact that such offenders frequently were not prosecuted or punished cannot frame the defense of women in their current offense. Yet, the underlying injustice inherent in societal tolerance of suffering on one level, while over-reacting to less serious crime on another level, frames a basic violation of human rights. If the justice model, which applies a hard-on-crime strategy to combat women's drug crime, were applied evenly the issues that frame women's incarceration would be different. The dismissal or trivial reactions to the more serious actions of prior male offenders who have abused and mistreated women offenders at earlier stages of their life, however, contributes to the profound feelings of inevitable loss and hopelessness that are graphic in the stories of women offenders. Women's crime does not fit the hard-on-crime justice model because the penalties are often especially hard-on-women's-crime. While many men have been unduly sentenced to very long prison terms on the basis of this philosophy, the pattern among women is rather overwhelming.

Third, the punishment of women's relatively non-serious crime with the same vehemence with which serious male crime is addressed hurts children. Among the most consistent themes that run through the literature about inmate mothers is the intense sense of loss, betrayal, desperation, and hopelessness that accompanies their incarceration. Their children suffer the loss of their mother while the hard-on-crime political strategy publicizes justice and deterrence. Children and society would be better served by more reasonable, proportionate sentences, or no punishment at all. To perpetuate injustice into the lives of children whose mothers have been incarcerated for their boyfriends' crimes, as is frequently the case with drug crime, is inhumane, counterproductive, and futile. Women who have been victimized through multiple stages of patriarchy, exploitation, and marginalized social opportunities need understanding, support, and many therapeutic services. Punishment is the least affective way to address their crime. Among women, crime is often an obvious symptom of their suffering at another level.

Fourth, in keeping with Quinney's basic principles of peacemaking, societal response to women's crime should accommodate the unique features of their offending patterns. Women's prior experiences of exploitation should be addressed in treatment. Children of women who have committed crimes should be supported with reasonable, positive opportunities for growth and development. Punishment does not serve this end.

Prison Programs for Mothers

Mothers in prison have the same worries and concerns that all parents have about their children, but their inability to fulfill parental responsibilities for their children creates fear for their emotional and physical well-being, as well as great grief and anxiety over loss of involvement in their children's lives. Common backgrounds of abuse, high likelihood of drug involvement, and probable poverty also indicate that parenting and life-skill programs are essential for post-release success. Drug addiction treatment and therapy that helps offenders deal with problems of past sexual abuse and family violence are especially critical because these factors are linked to women's criminal behavior, as well as to their parenting skills.

The most common programming options available for inmate mothers are those that allow for special visitation. The Girls Scouts Beyond Bars program, for example, operates in 23 states and serves over 800 children (Baker, 2005, p. 1). Girl scouts with incarcerated mothers may belong to special girl scout troops that meet in prison. The purpose of the program is to enhance parenting skills for the mother and maintain involvement of mothers in their daughters' lives.

Most states provide either regular or occasional special visitation for families of inmates. Ohio and Illinois, for example, have had programs that allowed children of inmates to camp on the grounds of the prison with their mothers on some weekends during the summer. Several states, such as Arkansas, California, Connecticut, Illinois, Kentucky, Massachusetts, Mississippi, New York, Oklahoma, South Dakota, and Tennessee, allow overnight visits (Pollock 2002, p. 146). The New York Department of Corrections provides for extended overnight visits with families at 18 prisons. They also provide transportation to the prisons and operate play areas and hospitality centers for families. Texas allows for weekly contact visits between mothers and their children.[4]

The most innovative and comprehensive programs are in New York, Nebraska, Washington state, and California. Each of these states has some variation of the prison nursery program that was started in the women's prison at Bedford Hills, New York in 1901. Nebraska's program is patterned after the Bedford Hills program. In both of these programs mothers who have been convicted of an offense that did not involve their children, and who have less than two years of their sentence left to serve, may keep their babies with them in prison. Counseling, support groups, parenting classes, substance abuse treatment, and employment preparation are integral components of both programs. California offers prisoner mother/infant programs, which are operated by private agencies under contract with the state, at six locations (Christian, 2000; Ervin, 1998, p. 14; Lyke, 2006, p. 1). The best programs include substance abuse treatment, occupational counseling, and support groups in their treatment strategies.

Effectiveness of Mother Infant Programs

While comprehensive statistical analysis of four programs would not provide meaningful data, the success of mother-infant programs is accepted as definitive in those states that have funded these programs. The most common measures of success may give only vague insight into the utility of these programs, however. Recidivism, which measures the likelihood of re-offense among released inmates, is decidedly lower for women who participate in mother-infant programs. Women's recidivism is generally much lower than men's, but mother-infant programs claim a further reduction of 20 to 50 percent in recidivism. Mothers who participate, in other words, are not likely to return to prison (Christian, 2000; Ervin, 1998, p.14; Lays, 1992, pp. 44–51). Whether the recidivism results from the success of the programs or from the selection of inmates who participate in the programs is less clear. Supporters of mother infant programs claim that both the opportunity to interact with their infants in a controlled, supportive environment, and the comprehensive counseling that accompanies these programs are what lead to their success.

The success of children whose lives are enhanced by their mother's opportunity to participate in a mother-infant program are less easily studied. Researchers and advocates for more humane treatment of women prisoners have pointed out for many years that children of inmate mothers suffer tremendous loss and experience profound alteration of their lives. Critics may contend that mothers should have thought of these issues prior to committing the crime for which they were incarcerated. But, the pervasive patterns of physical and sexual abuse, drug addiction, and emotional pain characteristic of women inmates prohibits the sort of reflective thinking that would have prevented their crime, regardless of how much they love their children. And, wider structures of patriarchy and capitalism are not even imagined as sources of women's crime, by this reasoning. The result of more compassionate response to women's crime is that children who are connected in meaningful ways with their incarcerated mothers are less likely to feel abandoned, isolated, and lonely.

Prisoner programs that address the complex nature of women's confinement, which include treatment for emotional and substance abuse problems, and which help them to achieve purposeful child rearing offer the most promise for post-release success and for successful parenting. Models available in Nebraska, New York, Washington, and California may provide insight into the importance of strengthening family bonds for both inmate mothers and for their children.

Conclusions

The horrifying, heartbreaking experiences that incarcerated mothers live with, or re-live in prison, often overwhelm intentions for good parenting. Thus, prison programming that addresses only parenting skills, or which narrowly focuses on specific occupational skills, will fail to address the needs of incarcerated women. Comprehensive approaches, that treat addiction, depression, occupational skills, and parenting offer the most affective options. Women's incarceration stems not only from a conviction for a specific crime, but also from an array of social problems that affect women as a group and which permeate many facets of American culture. As Quinney tells us, what has gone on before the crime tells us more than the act itself. The life patterns of incarcerated women poignantly illustrate Quinney's point. Humane, supportive, therapeutic response to women offenders would also address what has gone on before the criminal act.

Cultural devaluation of women results in exploitation, abuse, and mistreatment. The specific illustrations of the suffering of women victims are visible in the faces of incarcerated women. To ignore the cultural problems that give rise to women's crime is to blame the victims of abuse for their own abuse. In the short-term, women who are empowered to control their own lives and to avoid men who abuse and exploit them will be the most successful after release from prison. They will also be better mothers, who may be able to break the cycles of abuse that are very commonly characteristic of their own lives and the lives of their mothers. In the long-term, ending patriarchal exploitation, economic inequality, and fostering humane, compassionate respect for human potential are essential to a peaceful society, and they are what will end women's crime.

Crime will continue until we end suffering. If we robotically adhere to laws, and models of justice, without understanding the sources of crime, we will not be able to end suffering. With Quinney's poignant explanations of what it takes to end suffering in mind, we must abandon the philosophy of punishment and find a means of supporting women offenders by responding to the sources of their suffering. We must, in other words, find a means of cutting through the arbitrary rules to find the true meaning of the actions.

Notes

1. Alternative perspectives are sometimes discussed, although they have found little representation in contemporary criminal justice policies. Liberal critics of contemporary trends suggest that education, investment in neighborhoods, community building, and jobs-training could counter crime with positive alternatives. Those who offer solutions to crime in this venue stress the importance of investment in programs to improve the quality of life among those most vulnerable to crime. Poor neighborhoods, inadequately funded schools, hopelessness fostered by urban decay, and insufficient investment in those with the fewest social opportunities produce crime, from this perspective. Solutions require investment and commitment to improve. For discussion of the underlying philosophy of criminal justice policy, see Samuel Walker (2001) *Sense and Nonsense*

about Crime and Drugs: A Policy Guide, 5th edition. Belmont, CA: Wadsworth, Chapter 1.

2. See, for example: Darrell Steffensmeier and Emillie Allan (1996) "Gender and Crime: Toward a Gendered Theory of Female Offending," *Annual Review of Sociology* Vol. 22, pp. 459-87; James Messerschmidt (1986) *Capitalism, Patriarchy, and Crime: Toward a Social Feminist Criminology*. Totowa, NJ: Rowman and Littlefield.

3. Conversation with Jane Higgins, 1989, when she was warden of Dwight Correctional Facility in Dwight, Illinois.

4. http://www.fenetwork.org/Dir98/dir98f-n.html Directory of Programs for Families of Inmates.

References

Baker, L. (2005). Inmates and daughters connect through scout troop, http://www.connectforkids.org/node/3009

Beck, A. J. (2000). Prison and jail inmates at midyear 1999, *Bureau of Justice Statistics Bulletin.* Washington DC: U.S. Government Printing Office.

Christian, S. E. (2000). Pregnant inmates get county help with MOM, *Chicago Tribune*, January 25.

Directory of Programs for Families of Inmates, http://www.fcetwork.org

Ervin, M. (1998). A center for jailed mothers, *Progressive* Vol. 62, 10.

Gilliard, D. K. (1993). Prisoners in 1992, *Bureau of Justice Statistics Bulletin*, Washington DC: U.S. Government Printing Office.

Greenfield, L. A., & Snell, T. L. (1999). Women offenders, *Bureau of Justice Statistics Special Report.* Washington DC: U.S. Government Printing Office.

Harrison, P. M., & Beck, A. J. (2005). Prisoners in 2004, *Bureau of Justice Statistics Bulletin*, p.1.

Lanagan, P., & John Dawson, J. (1993). Felony sentences in state courts, 1990, *Bureau of Justice Statistics Bulletin*, Washington DC: U.S. Government Printing Office.

Lays, J. (1992). Babies behind bars, *State Legislatures*, *18*(5), 44-51.

Lyke, M. L. (2006). Inmates keep their babies, get a grasp on responsibility. *Seattle Post-Intelligencer*, http://Seattlepl.nwsource.nwsource.com/local/111275_2purdy06.shtml

Messerschmidt, J. (1986). *Capitalism, patriarchy, and crime: Toward a social feminist criminology.* Totowa, NJ: Rowman and Littlefield.

Morash, M., Bynum, T. S., & Koons, B.A. (1998). Women offenders: Programming needs and promising approaches. *National Institute of Justice Research in Brief*, U.S. Department of Justice Office of Justice Programs, Washington DC: U.S. Government Printing Office.

Moses, M. C. (1995). Keeping incarcerated mothers and their daughters together: Girl scouts beyond bars. *National Institute of Justice Program Focus*, Washington DC: U.S. Department of Justice.

Mumola, C. (2000). Incarcerated parents and their children. *Bureau of Justice Statistics Special Report.* Washington DC: U.S. Government Printing Office.

Parisi, N. (1982). Are females treated differently? In N. H. Rafter & E. A. Stanko (Eds.), *Judge, lawyer, victim, thief* (pp. 205-220). Boston: Northeastern University Press.

Pollock, J. M. (2002). Parenting programs in women's prisons. *Women & Criminal Justice*, *14* (1), 131–155.

Quinney, R. (1977). *Class state and crime: On the theory and practice of criminal justice.* New York: David McKay Co.

Quinney, R. (1991). The way of peace: On crime, suffering, and service. In H. E. Pepinsky & R. Quinney (Eds.), *Criminology as peacemaking* (Chapter 1). Bloomington: Indiana University Press.

Quinney, R. (2000). Socialist humanism and the problem of crime: Thinking about Erich Fromm in the development of critical/peacemaking criminology. In K. Anderson & R. Quinney (Eds.), *Erich Fromm and critical criminology: Beyond the punitive society* (p. 21). Urbana: University of Illinois.

Sourcebook of criminal justice statistics. (2004). Albany, NY: Hindelang Criminal Justice Center.

Steffensmeier, D., & Allan, E. (1996). Gender and crime: Toward a gendered theory of female offending. *Annual Review of Sociology*, *22*, 459-87.

Szalvitz, M. (1999). War on drugs war on women. *On The Issues*, Winter, 42-45.

Walker, S. (2001). *Sense and nonsense about crime and drugs: A policy guide* (5th ed.). Belmont, CA: Wadsworth.

Watterson, K. (1996). *Women in prison: Inside the concrete womb.* Boston: Northeastern University Press.

Williams, E. F. (1996). Fostering the mother-child bond in a correctional setting. *Corrections Today, 58* (6), 80-81.

Chapter 11

In the Beginning was the Student: Teaching Peacemaking and Justice Issues

Michael Braswell
John T. Whitehead

This article is written in the spirit of Richard Quinney's contributions to teaching as an exploration into the contradictions, ironies, and connections (both obvious and hidden) that allow learning to unfold and show itself to teachers and students. A critique of the conflict between developing expertise and experiencing learning is offered. The value of feelings and intuition, thinking and knowledge, and imagination and creativity are examined as a way to bring teacher and student together in the process of learning into wisdom.

We live in an awkward age. Parents and politicians are demanding performance testing in public schools and universities, particularly secondary schools where the threat of vouchers looms large as parents talk of taking their children out of underachieving schools and placing them in what they perceive as more productive private schools. On the university level, the virtual age has arrived with increasing demand for Internet courses and programs, both undergraduate and graduate, where a student can complete their degree requirements without seeing the university campus or their teachers face-to-face (Thorson, 2000). Although the Internet certainly has its merits, this approach to learning and study seems the perfect mate for our "culture of convenience." As cell phone conversations become substitutes for social relationships, so too does e-mail offer itself a ready substitute for more genuine learning relationships.

Against this backdrop, Richard Quinney (1998) invites us to return to the wonder of teaching and learning. He wrote,

> My teaching has moved away from any preconceived objective to a teaching that wanders with its own pace. . . . The message of this approach, if any message need arise, is that we do not know where we are going in advance of the actual process of the going. . . . Our energies are directed to the action, not the

> fruits of the action. . . . One lives in wonder, and in the overwhelming compassion that comes from this wonder. (pp. 21–22)

To return to the experience of wonder in the classroom requires a sense of humility that challenges the certainty of our expertise as teachers. What are we to do with our course syllabus, our class schedule, and the textbooks and related materials we are to cover during the semester? Is there room within the boundaries of the time we are with our students to explore and wonder about important ideas that reveal themselves at their own pace rather than within the time limits of preconceived class schedules? Can any teachers say with certainty regarding the personality and texture of a given class, "in advance of the actual process of the going," that they know where they are going? We have our plans and preparation, and our good intentions, but the experience of the class we share with our students creates its own unique character—its own sense of moving toward a destination and conclusion.

In keeping with the spirit of wonder and exploration, our article will examine the importance of feelings and intuition, thinking and knowledge, and imagination and creativity that are central elements to experiencing learning where student and teacher may become transformed by such a process and come to see and experience a new thing. Too often, we consider experiential learning to primarily be a supplement to classroom instruction through outside, "real world" experiences such as internships and volunteer work. Although such experiences are valuable, we should also consider the classroom itself to be the real world—a community of learners exploring the issues specific to course content as well as their implications beyond the classroom, and experiencing each other in the relationship. What is learned in the real world of the classroom is joined with the personal, social, and justice context that makes up the larger mosaic that includes the real world, without which we are all connected in ways both seen and unseen. In this article, we will note some of the things we do in the classroom through which we attempt to explore this connection.

Experience and Expertise

Too often, the insecurity that drives the newly minted faculty member with Ph.D. in hand is transferred to the hapless undergraduate or graduate students who end up being students in his or her class. The most recent memories of new faculty are in too many instances the indentured servitude of 3 to 5 years of doctoral study where they learned to imitate and become extensions, sometimes enthusiastically and other times reluctantly, of sponsoring graduate faculty. Doctoral study at its best is about finding one's voice in pursuit of learning, teaching, research, and service. At its worst, it is about losing one's vision and becoming little more than an appendage to a suitable faculty host. For the new teacher who has found his or her voice, the experience of learning takes the foreground and expertise the background. Whereas the teacher may be the "student in charge," experiencing knowledge and the exchange of ideas is the priority, and all who share the class time and space are students. In such a context, ideas become as or more important than the accumulation of facts, questions more important than answers, and the journey into discovery more important than the quest for certainty.

For the new teacher who has lost or never acquired his or her own voice or vision, external validation becomes of paramount importance to quench the fires of personal and intellectual insecurity. In the classroom, a hierarchy is clearly maintained explicitly and implicitly—explicitly through academic titles like professor and doctor and student access to faculty through appointment only, and implicitly through maximizing lectures replete with dazzling descriptions of the latest studies and minimizing opportunities for student questions and discussion. In such situations, explaining takes priority over exploring. Outside the classroom, validation of the expert's assumed identity is verified by publishing in the "right" journals and serving on the "right" committees. Although doing and publishing research and serving on committees can be a good and noteworthy accomplishment, pursuing such tasks primarily for an enhanced sense of expertise can at its worst become an artificial substitute for experiencing learning. In such a case, the intimacy, spontaneity, and humor of shared learning and exploration are lost in an impressive display of intellectual exhibitionism and self-promotion, which is for the most part disconnected to the lives of students. If as teachers we are not interested in or concerned with the opinions of our students, no matter how misinformed or uninformed they might be, why should we assume that they would take to heart what we have to say? Are we inclined to respect others who show little or no respect to us?

On the balance, there is room for both experience and expertise in teaching and learning about justice and peacemaking issues. Both are important. Whereas experience would seem to take priority, expertise may provide definition and clarity to our joint process of discovery. Some of the following suggestions for enhancing the experience of learning are offered.

During the first class of the semester, introductions allow students to see each other and the teacher as persons rather than as nameless, unfamiliar faces. Questions like, What is your name? Where are you from? And What do you want to do when you grow up? can introduce personality, dimension, and humor into a new community of learners. Coming to class 5 to 10 minutes early each time allows teachers to talk informally with their students about a range of topics. Such a commitment suggests to them that we want to be there and are interested in them as persons as well as students. Conversely, teachers who are consistently 5 or 10 minutes late to class may suggest to students that they are an intrusion and that a double standard exists—students should be on time, but not those who are teaching them. Another way to encourage a sense of the individual in community regarding students is to assign them to a group of five to seven students for the duration of the semester. Although such an arrangement may not be possible for all classes, many classrooms will accommodate four or five student groups. As certain themes emerge in a given class, a greater sense of discovery and spontaneity is often gained by allowing time for group discussion first and then general class discussion. Students often feel more secure in discussing their thoughts and feelings in a smaller group. Once they are comfortable discussing ideas and issues in a smaller, more intimate setting, they are more likely to participate in broader class discussions.

Feelings and Intuition

In the beginning was the student. Before tenure, refereed journals, research grants, educational administrators—even the university itself—was the student. From feelings and intuition (sometimes superstition) about the mysteries of life in general, the student wonders about things, becomes curious, and wants to more clearly understand why things are the way they are and what can be done to make life better at least for the person in question, if not for everyone else. Ancient wisdom traditions throughout the ages have taught us that when the student is ready, the teacher will come. Perhaps it may also be true that when the teacher is ready, the students will respond. There are students who feel a strong sense of passion about justice issues. Some of their feelings are misplaced, whereas others are well-placed. Some of these students are open and ready to learn—not all of them, but enough to make a difference in our lives as teachers and in the communities where they will live and work.

When we interact with our students, it is not enough for us to hear what they are saying in terms of content. We also need to hear what they are feeling. Before their minds are conformed, their hearts are informed. Their words express feelings as well as information. A timid response based on the fear of responding with a wrong answer, an attempt to gain favor with what they think we want to hear, or an aggressive challenge to a particular lecture designed more to impress than irritate all represent responses from students that often mask genuine feelings and speak to a deep sense of insecurity and lack of confidence in our care and concern for them. As teachers, we need to try to understand where our students are with their feelings and attitudes, no matter how misguided, before we can enable them to consider where they need to be. Rollo May (1953) wrote that even rebellion "acts as a substitute for the more difficult process of struggling through to one's own autonomy, to new beliefs, to the state where one can lay new foundations on which to build" (p. 135).

We live and teach in a culture that rewards one's grade point average rather than the acquisition and utilization of knowledge, critical and original thinking, and simply doing one's best. Competition, not cooperation with others, is a contemporary priority. Education seems to be evolving into a religion based on fear. As stated previously, a high grade point average has become the goal rather than the result of the joy and wonder of learning. Of course, many students set lower goals but the focus remains on grades, the currency required to get a piece of paper after 4 to 6 years to pursue a more lucrative economic life.

Feelings and intuition point student and teacher toward the personal context of justice—how one feels inside of his or her own skin about right and wrong, good and evil, and what is just and unjust. When the teacher as student and the other students come together in the personal context, there is no real separation, at least in an existential sense. When teacher and student come together through exploration and discovery of learning, they become transparent to each other. During such moments, there is no need for the expert, as they become joined in their common shared experience and quest for the truth.

Within the hierarchy of insecurity encouraged by higher education, it is easy to confuse obedient and conforming students with disciplined ones. Discipline comes from within, obedience from without. During the 1930s, Germany had one of the best educational systems in Western Europe. Yet the land of Bach, Goethe, and Einstein gave us a holocaust that points toward the limits of education outside the realm of moral restraint. Although being educated may be of value, what one does with it is of even greater importance. For the expertise of education to become meaningful and of lasting usefulness, it must evolve into the experience of wisdom and ethical consideration. Learning into wisdom results in an experience of kindness and gratitude rather than pride, mystery rather than certainty. Sometimes the student who gets us off the subject is demonstrating a creative and independent spirit much more disciplined than the insecure and frightened overachiever who simply follows our lead and mimics our perspective. There is, of course, a balance, but staying on task should be a flexible rather than an obsessive endeavor. A disciplined student can also be on the dean's list, but such an accomplishment is not the goal but the consequence of a joy and love of learning and questioning.

Feelings and intuition often come together in the process of storytelling. Each of us has a story to tell, and in the telling of it we often come to feel more alive and more alike. Our stories include a mix of information, myth, feelings, and intuitive truth that connect us to our students through our and their suffering, hope, and joy—through the experiences we have in common. In the end, we come to find that we are more alike than different. The stories we as teachers and students tell each other are not only based on past experiences, they also speak to our hopes—the kind of persons we want to become—the kind of justice process we want to experience and be a part of. As students, we do not remember time, we remember experiences. We do not remember teaching methods and techniques, we remember teachers. The question then becomes, How do we get our students to tell their stories? In respecting where they are at with their feelings and attitudes, they are more likely to come to trust us. The more they trust us, the more likely they are to muster the courage to share who they really are—their fears, dreams, and, most important, their questions. When students tell us their stories, it is away of them raising their hands, of wanting to be recognized and remembered for who they are. Will students try harder in the classroom to earn a sought-after grade or to gain the approval of a teacher they respect and care about? Are students more likely to learn from fear of failure or from responding to the care and encouragement of a teacher who believes in their potential—even when the evidence of such potential might not be apparent?

When attempting to engage students in the learning process, a critical first step is to acknowledge their feelings and ideas no matter how disconnected or destructive they might appear to be. For example, on issues such as race, incarceration, and the death penalty, some students may express simplistic notions regarding the effectiveness of punishment as well as prejudice concerning minorities and inmates in general. Although feelings and emotions may be volatile, they are also fluid. There are a number of ways to use feelings to begin to change minds and hearts. It is possible for misplaced passions to evolve into an attitude of compassion and empathy. Telling one's stories in small groups, general class discussion, or through personal essays is away to invite students to express their beliefs and feelings. One of the authors who taught a section of a human relations course on the inmates' perspective of prison found the responses of a contingent of students frustrating when they were asked what they thought about inmates in prison. Whereas some students were sympathetic to the plight of those who were incarcerated and others had at least neutral feelings, there always seemed to be a vocal minority who were propunishment and embodied most of the ill-informed stereotypes regarding inmates. On one occasion, when asked for their opinion of those persons who were incarcerated, a vocal contingent exclaimed, "They should get what they deserved!" After reflecting for several moments, the teacher in question responded, "How many in this class would like to get what we deserved?" Not a single student raised his or her hand. The issue of deserved punishment or consequences had been moved from the criminal justice to the personal justice context. The next semester, the teacher changed his tactic for that section of the course. This time, he asked the class to imagine that they were first-time offenders beginning a five year sentence in a maximum security prison. They had been deloused, poked and prodded, and given a jumpsuit that was either too big or too small. The essentials, including a blanket, had been given to them and they were being marched single-file down a cell block to meet their cell mates in a cell built for one person but, due to overcrowding, now housed two inmates. Other inmates leered or shouted sexual obscenities at them as they were led to the cell that would be home for the next five years with someone whom they did not know. The students were asked to write a brief paragraph describing how they felt about their predicament and prospects. The change in student attitudes and response was dramatic. There were no flippant or superficial responses. The students had been placed, at least hypothetically, into the experience of being in prison for the first time. Expressions of fear, hopelessness, separation anxiety from family, and even thoughts of suicide were frequent.

Students can experience feelings of empathy by inviting a prisoner or ex-prisoner to come to class and share his or her story. Most students realize that these individuals have experienced the criminal justice process firsthand and can provide an inside view of how the justice system works. One of the most memorable prisoner visits to class involved a prisoner in a halfway house who was of college age himself. He had been a student in another university when he was arrested for drug dealing. He had sold a drug to another person he thought was a friend of his friend. Instead, the buyer was an undercover informant. Seeing and listening to someone their own age enabled students to become more aware of how real criminal justice can be—how anyone might slip into an offender role. Perhaps someone drinks and drives or uses an illegal substance and sells it to someone he or she thinks is just another student. As a result, students may come to see that criminals are not just strangers but persons we know and love. Such stories demonstrate in an experiential and intuitive way how connected we are to each other. Another example of using feelings as a springboard for identifying with persons different from ourselves involved the film, *Schindler's List* (Spielberg, 1994). After watching the film, students were asked to list all the living relatives they could think of, starting with the oldest and ending with their name at the bottom of a sheet of notebook paper. After a brief break, they were instructed to mark through or blot out all the names on the list except for their own, which they were instructed to draw a circle around. Then, the students were asked to imagine that during the past two years the U.S. government had hunted down and killed everyone on that list because of race, ethnicity, last name, region lived in, or some other reason. Now the guilty parties had been stopped and apprehended along with the murderers and were on trial for their crimes. The student in question had been saved and freed from imprisonment and certain death. They were the only one on that list who had survived. During the past two years, everyone else had been murdered. The students were instructed to write a brief essay describing how they felt about their present and their future prospects, as well as justice in general. As one can imagine they felt overwhelmed, and responses ranged from a desire for revenge to feelings of depression and suicide. This exercise provides another example of placing the student into a personal context of experience that allows them to identify with and become involved in feelings of empathy regarding persons different from themselves.

Although feelings and intuition provide a useful starting point for engaging students in the experience of learning, thinking and knowledge are a necessary next step in providing a means through which such passion can be effectively experienced and expressed.

Thinking and Knowledge

We are not only persons who possess feelings; we also think about our lives. Sometimes what feels good or right is challenged by what makes sense. "Of course there's a lot of knowledge in universities. The freshmen bring a little in; the seniors don't take much away; so knowledge sort of accumulates" (Lowell, quoted in Safransky, 1990, p. 59). Although the previous quote is obviously overstated, it does point to a certain lethargy and inertia between teachers and students. It also questions the knowledge that we as teachers hold dear but often find difficult to demonstrate the usefulness and relevance of to our students. In addition, teaching, research, and service has become a kind of educational mantra for many teachers. Unfortunately, the order of priority has changed to research (primarily, if not exclusively, publications in refereed journals), service (until one has attained tenure and/or the rank of professor), and teaching (as few classes, especially undergraduate, as possible). Of course, students may also bring little knowledge to the table of learning. They tend to be primarily focused on social learning—what they are going to do when they are not in class, which, at least in some instances, may be to their benefit.

Possessing substantial intellectual ability does not preclude us from thinking primarily about ourselves rather than the good we could do for others. In fact, the ability to think is not necessarily related to our intellectual potential. Thinking in the pursuit of knowledge as a way to achieve recognition and self-importance is not the same as thinking in service to the truth, which requires a sense of humility and wonder rather than pride and certainty. Although thinking is an important element of learning, it is at the same time a two-edged sword, particularly regarding scientific thinking. At its best, scientific thinking explores the mysteries of human behavior and the universe through developing theories and empirically testing them. At its worst, it is inclined to assume that any phenomenon that cannot be postulated and tested does not exist. Frederick Buechner (1973) compared such an attitude to a "blind man's suspecting that anything that can't be smelled, tasted, touched, or heard is probably a figment of the imagination" (p. 86). Scientific thinking faces another difficult challenge: What do we do with what we discover? Science may show us what we can do, but a myriad of ethical dilemmas arise in response to how or even whether we should apply specific scientific discoveries. For example, we possess the technology for less painful executions, abortions, or even cloning, but whether we should apply such scientific discoveries is a question of ethics rather than science. John Holt contended that "the true test of intelligence is not how much we know how to do, but how we behave when we don't know what to do" (quoted in Maggio, 1997, p. 119).

Concerning thinking and knowledge, it is important that we teach our students to develop critical thinking skills and think independently—for themselves. Such skills are essentially connected to their sense of moral beliefs and responsibility and the behavior that follows such thinking. One reality of much of modern education is that as teachers we tend to focus too much on what is, leaving little time or emphasis for what ought to be. Years of responding correctly to proper educational logic as they sit passively in our classrooms has resulted in many of our students lacking the will or ability to think about what the moral or ethical implications of what they are learning. Too often, what results is a kind of moral indifference and ignorance that allows them to ignore or, worse, ridicule the suffering of those who are less fortunate. Yehud Bacon, a sculptor who was imprisoned in Auschwitz as a boy, wrote about the moral indifference of those with whom he shared his own experience of suffering:

> As a boy I thought: "I will tell them what I saw, in the hope that people will change for the better." But people didn't change and didn't even want to know. It was much later that I really understood "the meaning of suffering." It can have a meaning if it changes oneself for the better. (quoted in Frankl, 1969, p. 39)

From thinking and knowledge building to including personal and moral responsibility in such thinking asks the question, Is it possible to integrate feelings and intuition with rational thought and scientific reasoning in a morally responsible way? and How do we begin as teachers to help our students experience such a synthesis?

An interesting way students can be encouraged to think about what they feel and believe is through their having to write a personal philosophy statement. In an ethics and justice class, students are required to write an approximately five-page typed paper espousing their personal philosophy. They are asked to respond to three questions: (a)What do they believe and what values do they hold dear? (b)Where do those values or beliefs come from and who did they learn their values from? and (c) How do they plan to translate and express their values through whatever work they choose to do? This particular assignment is identified as one of the most important assignments they will undertake during the semester. Because writing such a paper can be an intimate statement of personal feelings, beliefs, and experiences, the statements are not graded but instead are awarded 1 to 10 points added to their score of the major test on which they scored the lowest number of points. Points are awarded based on the effort that students put into writing the philosophy statement. Most students are awarded the full 10 points. In addition, because private, sometimes painful and traumatic information is contained in their personal essay, each philosophy statement is treated confidentially between student and teacher. This particular assignment is viewed by the teacher as essentially a private and privileged conversation between student and teacher. Each semester this task is assigned, a number of students indicate that it is the most challenging and difficult writing assignment they have ever had to undertake. Some students also indicate that the assignment represents the first time they have ever thought in detail about what they believed and how they might apply it to a chosen vocation. This activity is designed to help students reflect on their values, and in doing so to help them become more mindful and aware of how what they think relates to how they feel as well as how they act.

Imagination and Creativity

Imagination and creativity are inspired by the process of discovery and wonder in the face of life's mysteries. Frederick Buechner (1992) suggested that there are two different ways that we come to know something. We can find something out or it can occur to us. Finding something out follows a rational, deductive approach to learning, whereas having something occur to us, although not incompatible with reason, includes an intuitive dimension of learning. In using St. Francis of Assisi as an example, Buechner wrote, "I 'found out' that Francis of Assisi gave all his money to the poor, called the sun his brother, and preached sermons to birds. But 'it occurred to me' that he must be a saint. Or an idiot" (p. 25). It is true enough, especially concerning the diverse and often ambiguous issues surrounding the idea and process of justice, that we ought to find out what we can, but at the same time we need to be open to new ways of experiencing and nontraditional paths to knowledge. Imagination and creativity encourage us as teachers to respect the integrity and independence of students to also contribute to the process of discovery and learning. In such a context, we are more focused on being obedient to the discovery of truth in its various forms than in cultivating the status of an academic celebrity or spawning a spate of disciples. In a conversation with one of the authors, Bo Lozoff, teacher and social activist, once indicated that the way to discern between a false and genuine teacher is relatively simple: A false teacher will not let you go and a genuine teacher will not let you stay. Although teacher and student may join together in a creative community of learning in the classroom and elsewhere, the student's journey toward discovery is first a personal one that emanates from the inside out. The revealed knowledge of a creative and imagined life is not something that can be readily found in the virtual world of the Internet. It is the result of service and sacrifice. It is more about questions sought and explored than about the perceived certainty of answers found. Many of our students want a life. Instead, we offer them a career. The big questions have less to do with making a living and more to do with having a life worth living. New ideas and ways of thinking about justice and the human condition "do not spring from Policy Research reports. All cultures begin in explorations of myth in the minds of prophets, mystics, visionary scientists, artists, and crazies" (Safransky, 1990, p. 23). Arthur Koestler eloquently expressed the synthesis of the rational with the nonrational, the cognitive with the intuitive: "This oceanic feeling of wonder is the common source of religious mysticism, of pure science and art for art's sake; it is their common denominator and emotional bond" (quoted in Safransky, 1990, p. 54). The wonder Koestler wrote about reminds us as teachers to not get too mired or boxed into our fifty minute class periods. Too often, our students want to explore and discover, whereas we encourage them to settle for tentative explanations of narrow certainties. They want us to give them encouragement for their quest. We want them to give us the correct answers for the quiz.

Just as imagination and creativity can excite and inspire teacher and student, those qualities can also get us into trouble as they inevitably lead us to question and challenge sacred cultural and academic orthodoxies. Just as exploring the big questions is more essential to authentic learning than attempting to only answer the little ones, teaching our students the great virtues is more important than teaching them the small ones. Natalia Ginzburg (1985) wrote,

> Not thrift but generosity . . . ; not caution but courage and a contempt for danger; nor shrewdness but frankness and a love of truth; not tact but love for one's neighbor and self-denial; not a desire for success but a desire to be and to know. . . . And in general I think we should be very cautious about promising and providing rewards and punishments. Because life rarely has its rewards and punishments; usually sacrifices have no reward, and often evil deeds go unpunished, at times they are even richly rewarded with success and money . . . yet they must love good and hate evil, and it is not possible to give any logical explanation for this. . . . And if he suffers from injustice there or is misunderstood, it is necessary to let him see that there is nothing strange about this, because in life we have to expect to be . . . misunderstood and misinterpreted, and to be victims of injustice; and the only thing that matters is that we do not commit injustice ourselves. . . . What we must remember above all in the edu-

> cation of our children is that their love of life should never weaken. (pp. 99, 106–107)

Although exposing our students (and ourselves) to big questions and virtues is a tall order, we can begin to imagine that we all can make a difference toward a more compassionate and just world.

There are a number of ways to encourage a student's sense of imagination and creativity to more clearly and compassionately understand how people, events, and just or unjust outcomes are connected in seen and unseen ways. Stories like the following one about Nasrudin, the great Sufi teacher, can be used to explore and demonstrate such connections:

> "What is fate?" Nasrudin was asked by a scholar. "An endless succession of intertwined events, influencing each other?" "That is hardly a satisfactory answer. I believe in cause and effect." "Very well," said the Mulla, "look at that." He pointed to a procession passing in the street. "That man is being taken to be hanged. Is that because someone gave him a silver piece and enabled him to buy the knife with which he committed the murder; or because someone saw him do it; or because nobody stopped him?" (Meredith, 1984, p. 48)

No single answer to Nasrudin's teaching can capture the complete picture. Issues like gun control or ethical considerations of doing bad or failing to do the good one could do are two examples of justice themes that can be drawn and examined from this ancient teaching.

Including challenging "big" questions in the course of a class discussion is another way to encourage the process of discovery in students of deeper truths about themselves, their community, and the justice system. For example, in a particular class, students were asked to answer the following question: "If you had to choose to either be the victim in a physical assault where you would be seriously injured although you would eventually recover or be the perpetrator of the assault, which person would you choose to be and why?" Of course, students found both choices undesirable, but if forced to choose, most chose to be the perpetrator, largely out of a sense of self-preservation. A few students chose to be the victim based on deeply held religious beliefs, but a particular coed student who said very little in class offered the most profound insight. When asked why she would choose to be the victim, she responded, "Because only the victim has the power to forgive." After allowing the class to quietly consider the power of her response for several moments, we explored the ramifications of her comments, including that although we can learn and be humbled by the suffering we inflict on another person, nothing feels as good as forgiveness—of being given a second chance whether in the court of a betrayed friendship or in a court of criminal justice.

Finally, hypothetical case studies where students are encouraged to see crime and justice events through different eyes (including the offender, victim, and police officer) are useful in helping them, much as in Nasrudin's story, to understand how suffering could have been prevented, diminished, or responded to in a more restorative way (Braswell, Miller, & Fletcher, 1998). Service projects where students volunteer in soup kitchens and homeless shelters can also enable them to see the bigger picture in a more compassionate way. One of the authors used his research class to encourage students to develop a broader, more empathetic view through participant observation. Student options included visiting a religious service (if they were religious) of a religion or denomination different from their own. Some students pretended to purchase a car to see how automobile salesman treat customers. This particular assignment proved to be very popular and allowed them to see the world around them with fresh eyes. The essays they wrote about their experiences were among the best-written work in the course. The reason for the quality of their writing and the enthusiasm of their efforts was that they were engaged in what they were doing. They were allowed to choose what they wanted to observe and became a part of the learning process itself rather than simply reading about what someone else discovered.

The Example of Capital Punishment

Perhaps there is no issue in criminal justice that is more emotionally loaded than that of capital punishment. It is not uncommon for a classroom discussion to become passionate and even heated as students with opposing feelings and thoughts engage each other. One of the authors has found that exploring both the feelings, reliable information and misinformation, can have profound effects. In initial classroom polls, the majority of students tend to overwhelmingly support the use of the death penalty. When given further information, however, many say that classroom discussions have caused them to rethink their initial approval.

A number of books and films provide an excellent means of encouraging students to think about the implications of the death penalty in a more open and critical fashion. *Dead Man Walking* (Prejean, 1994; Robbins, 1996), *Deathquest* (Bohm, 2000), and *Death at Midnight* (Cabana, 1996) all put a human face on the execution experience, ranging from a Catholic nun who ministers to death row inmates, to the last 14 days in the life of an inmate who is scheduled to be executed, to a prison warden who tries to balance his duties in carrying out an execution with his personal beliefs regarding the morality of what he is doing.

More specific, one of the authors uses a particular exercise to encourage students to become more aware of the implications of executions. He starts out by asking students how many are in favor of the death penalty. A substantial number typically raise their hands. He then asks them if they know anyone who is perfect, who has never made a mistake. No one raises their hand. He proceeds to reason that because people are not perfect, it is reasonable to assume that our justice system, which is administered by imperfect people, also is not perfect. At this point in the discussion, the teacher suggests a hypothetical situation: For every 5,000 vicious killers who are executed, two innocent persons are also unfortunately executed. He continues that although it is unfortunate that two innocent persons are executed, we live in an imperfect world, and besides—think of all the vicious predators society will not have to worry about any more. He then asks all the students who consider the costs of this scenario reasonable to punish the 5,000 who are guilty to raise their hands, which those who favor the death penalty promptly do. Requesting that they keep their hands raised, the teacher then asks them what if one of the two innocents who were executed were their brother, sister, father, mother, child, or themselves? It is always interesting to observe the stunned looks on the faces of many of those who have raised their hands in support of the death penalty only to now silently drop them. To be fair, students are sometimes also asked how they would feel if a murderer who got paroled killed one of their loved ones after he or she was released. Other related questions, such as those borrowed from John Conrad (1982), are "What do the undeserving deserve?" (p. 328) and "If we dramatically increased our rate of executions, would we feel less or more secure, more pessimistic or more optimistic about our country and system of justice?"

Questions, exercises, and videos all offer ways to encourage students to become more open to different attitudes concerning such volatile issues as the death penalty. If we touch their hearts and their imaginations first, we increase the likelihood that they will genuinely seek the balance of truth.

Experiencing Whole Sight

Peacemaking goes against the grain of declaring war on crime and criminals, a theme that relies heavily on the Darwinian theory of survival of the fittest. Petr Kropotkin, a naturalist and critic of Charles Darwin, believed in a different kind of survival of the fittest:

> Yes, only the fittest survive, but the "fittest" are the ones best able to cooperate with their neighbors, to engage in mutual protection and helpfulness, not the strong ones who can overpower the weak and leave themselves with few friends and allies to help them through the winter. (quoted in Kushner, 1996, p. 176)

For cooperation and mutual aid to become more important than competition and short-term self-interest, one needs to develop whole sight.

The mind and heart, thinking and feeling, logic and intuition, and expertise and experience all point to the challenge of getting the big picture—of how persons, events, and outcomes are connected and how we can more effectively bring peace and justice to ourselves, our communities, and our criminal justice system. Parker Palmer (1983) suggested that most of us live "one-eyed" lives, relying primarily on either our heart or our head. He believed that we should bring the two elements together in a kind of synthesis he referred to as "whole sight." Whole sight encourages learning into wisdom, which focuses on compassion rather than correctness, completion rather than perfection, and opens us to the possibility to reconciling contradictions and transcending limitations. Whole sight also encourages us as teachers and students to become more mindful, which allows us to experience a deeper sense of awareness and connectedness to ourselves and others where we can come to understand that in one way or another, we are all victims and offenders, teachers and students, and incarcerators and liberators (Lozoff & Braswell, 1989). Everyone's journey toward whole sight is unique and similar: "The path is the same for everyone, but each person's footsteps are different. The most important point to remember is that no one can walk the path for you. Others can merely point the way" (Gibbs, 1990, p. 47).

We are not just teaching our students about criminal justice and criminology, we are also teaching them about the larger landscape of life—about their potential for making a difference in the world around them. This aspect of our teaching is as old as the wisdom traditions themselves. *Tikkun* is an ancient Hebrew term that means world repair:

> The spirit of tikkun is the essence of compassionate service—not "how much" good we do, but rather waking and sleeping, eating and breathing, working and playing, with an ever-present attitude of kindness to people, animals and everything else in our immediate vicinity at any given time; no time off. (Lozoff, 2000, p. 127)

In a more contemporary vein, His Holiness, the Dalai Lama, adds: "If, after trying to save the world, the world is lost. . . . No regrets" (Lozoff, 2000, p. 126). All we can do is what we can do, and more often than we realize it is enough. In reflecting on perhaps his most essential teacher, Richard Quinney (2000) wrote,

> My Mother, at least in the later years, gave me little direct advice on how to live. But I knew from the example of her life, from the way she had lived and the way she continued to live, that the instructions were clear and obvious: Be kind, be thoughtful, and be helpful whenever you can. (p. 40)

References

Bohm, R. (2000). *Deathquest.* Cincinnati, OH: Anderson.

Braswell, M., Miller, L., & Fletcher, T. (1998). *Human relations and corrections.* Cincinnati, OH: Anderson.

Buechner, F. (1973). *Wishful thinking.* New York: Harper and Row.

Buechner, F. (1992). *The clown in the belfry.* San Francisco: HarperCollins.

Cabana, D. (1996). *Death at midnight.* Boston: Northeastern University Press.

Conrad, J. (1982).What do the undeserving deserve? In R. Johnson & H. Toch (Eds.), *The pains of imprisonment* (pp. 313-330). Beverly Hills, CA: Sage.

Frankl, V. (1969). *Man's search for meaning.* New York: Touchstone.

Gibbs, J. J. (1990). *Dancing with your books.* New York: Plume.

Ginzburg, N. (1985). *Small virtues.* UK: Carcanet.

Kushner, H. (1996). *When bad things happen to good people.* New York: Schocken.

Lozoff, B. (2000). *Deep and Simple.* Durham, NC: Human Kindness Foundation.

Lozoff, B. & Braswell, M. (1989). *Inner connections.* Cincinnati, OH: Anderson.

Maggio, R. (1997). *Quotations on education.* Paramus, NJ: Prentice Hall.

May, R. (1953). *Man's search for himself.* New York: W. W. Norton.

Meredith, N. (1984, December). The murder epidemic. *Science*, p. 48.

Palmer, P. (1983). *To know as we are known.* San Francisco: Harper and Row.

Prejean, S. H. (1994). *Dead man walking.* New York: Vintage Books.

Quinney, R. (1998). *For the time being.* Albany: State University Press of New York.

Quinney, R. (2000, Spring).Went to school, went to town, to my baby bed down: The solace of words. *Wisconsin Academy Review*, 35-40.

Robbins, T. (Producer/Director) (1996). *Dead man walking* [Motion picture]. New York: Polygram Video.

Safransky, S. (1990). *Sunbeams.* Berkeley, CA: North Atlantic Books.

Spielberg, S. (Producer/Director). (1994). *Schindler's list* [Motion picture].Universal City, CA: MCA/Universal.

Thorson, M. (2000). *Campus-free college degrees* (9th ed.). Tulsa, OK: Thorson Guides.

Chapter 12

Peacemaking and Crime: Advocating Reform on the Internet

John Randolph Fuller
Amy Hembree

The internet has broadened the community of scholars that is available to peacemaking criminologists, something that can be said about any field. In the somewhat distant past, it was necessary to be at Harvard, Oxford, or Princeton in order to have access to the colleagues and library resources necessary do cutting-edge work. Later, with the advent of telephones, faxes, and interlibrary loan programs, it was possible for scholars to communicate ideas from different cities or countries. Now, the internet has taken communication to an entirely different level, making physical proximity almost unnecessary for research. Today, colleagues sitting in adjacent offices often prefer to use email rather than venture into each other's offices to discuss collaborative work. Although it is an understatement to claim that the internet has revolutionized communication, it is beyond the scope of this essay to explore this trend completely. Instead, the goal here is to relate the personal experience of one humble scholar's attempt to connect with like-minded others.

Since 1998, my wife and I have maintained one of the oldest criminology sites on the web.[1] We created Peacemaking & Crime initially as a companion website for my book *Criminal Justice: A Peacemaking Perspective*. We wanted to demonstrate that peacemaking criminology ideas could be found in the real world and were not just the naive concoctions of a few idealistic criminologists. The site has been fairly successful in spite of the failure of the book to sell enough copies for my publisher to invest in a second edition. Although *Criminal Justice: A Peacemaking Perspective* is now out of print, the website has helped me to develop a worldwide network of scholars, activists, critics, and students who have been motivated to correspond with me about peacemaking criminology. The site has taken on a life of its own, and the many links I have collected over the years serve as a major resource for my research and writing. I find myself constantly consulting the site for links to interesting and relevant material.

Although the revolutions and paradigm-shifts brought by the internet are beyond the scope of this paper, it is important to note that Peacemaking & Crime, and sites like it, would not be possible without the internet, specifically that portion of the internet known as the World Wide Web. One major reason that we produce Peacemaking & Crime is that it is relatively easy to do, and the only expense it requires is time. None of this would be possible in, say, 1975. Publishing on paper is expensive and very time-consuming, sometimes heart-rending, and, for couples, possibly divorce-causing. Peacemaking & Crime exists because it is relatively easy to produce. There are no subscribers to satisfy, no deadlines to make. The result is that—and this has been infinitely noted, especially during the internet new-economy hoopla of the late 1990s—two people can almost effortlessly collate and produce a large amount of information and serve it to a large number of people. A public database of sorts exists where none did before, and public databases make trends easy to see and ideas easy to share. This brings us back to our original stated purpose of Peacemaking & Crime: to show that peacemaking ideas exist in the real world, not just in the dusty confines of some textbook, and that they often do work.

Getting Started

I must be honest here. The idea for the site was not mine, and I do not do any technical work. My wife, Amy Hembree, is the driving force behind Peacemaking & Crime. The page was her idea, and she updates it. My modest contributions are finding links to sites and news stories and answering correspondence from those who write to praise, complain, criticize, or contribute. The collaborative work we do on the page is mutually rewarding because we share our discoveries of interesting sites and discuss what should be included in each update. Even if no one looked at the page besides us, we would continue to maintain it because we share the fun of coming up with new ways to promote the peacemaking perspective.

The first major issue that one confronts when designing a website is the development of a theme. We all have seen too many unconnected, incoherent, and self-indulgent personal web pages that we quickly skip over because they lack content and focus. I cannot imagine people really being interested in pictures of our cats, my favorite recipes, or links to my alma maters' football programs at the University of New Mexico and Florida State.[2] With peacemaking, we had a ready-made theme that was easy to define: contrast the war on crime perspective that is currently dominant in the U.S. criminal justice system with the alternative peacemaking perspective.

Features

Part of the philosophy of Peacemaking & Crime is simplicity and clarity. The site is not fancy, should load coherently on any browser, and requires no multi-media capabilities or browser plug-ins. There is no advertising. We tried to design an attractive page that would identify exactly what the site is about and what it contains. Peacemaking & Crime has a clean and unencumbered format free of animations and big graphics.

Amy updates the site by sifting through the collected stories and websites and writing headlines and one-sentence summaries. Comprehensiveness is not the aim of Peacemaking & Crime. A few wonderful sites, including Cecil Greek's Florida State University School of Criminology & Criminal Justice Criminal Justice Links and Tom O'Connor's Criminal Justice Megalinks, do this very well already, cataloging and linking to nearly every conceivable crime-related site on the web. Peacemaking & Crime, on the other hand, collects news and links specifically related to the war on crime and alternative perspectives, but does so selectively. Updates on the latest media-sensationalized trial will not be found on the site. At Peacemaking & Crime, we try to focus on the methods that society uses to deal with crime and the methods that individuals use to deal with punishment, with a special focus on methods that stand out in some fashion or events that illustrate an existing method particularly well. A final criterion is that the story be one that casual web users might miss.

For example, a few years ago, advances in DNA testing began to result in a disturbingly large number of men being freed from death row. (We use "disturbing" because the tests exonerated these men, and in the absence of late twentieth century science, they would have remained on death row and likely been executed.) At first, we included every story on the subject we could find. Then, as more and more men walked out of prison thanks to DNA testing, the stories became almost a daily occurrence, and we stopped posting them. DNA stories of that type were no longer unusual (which is also disturbing, but we will refrain from that discussion here) and could be easily found and followed by most readers on sites like CNN and MSNBC.

News Archive

The media are full of examples of how the war on crime perspective and the peacemaking perspective compete to influence criminal justice policy. This is reflected in the many tragic, humorous, and fascinating stories that appear in major publications and alternative news sources. We employ two strategies to find material for the site. The first is news feeds that are tweaked to focus on criminal justice- and criminology-related stories. The second method entails reading through several selected websites. The weakness of this method is that it is somewhat slow going and hit-and-miss and can result in wasting time on activities that have nothing to do with criminal justice or criminology. (Amy's particular weakness is a web-based Tetris game, while I once spent several hours re-playing a thirty second video of a black bear falling out of a tree onto a trampoline.) The advantage of this method is that we often unearth some obscure gems. Sites that often yield fruit for Peacemaking & Crime include Metafilter, Fark, Arts & Letters Daily, and Slate. These first four sites are much like ours in that they collect links to news stories and web activities, with Metafilter and Fark benefiting from the submissions and commentary of thousands of users. Arts & Letters Daily posts links chosen by a closed staff, with no user commentary. Slate, although web-based, is like a traditional magazine in that it offers original content written by professional journalists.

Below are three examples of stories that reflect the war on crime perspective followed by three stories that show how peacemaking criminology has become a major force in the criminal justice system.

- More mentally ill in prisons than in hospitals. This story from *Psychiatric Times* reports the disturbing trend of incarcerating the mentally ill. Prisons hold three times as many people with mental illness as do mental health hospitals, and these inmates are not only not getting minimum care, but they are subject to abuse from other inmates and the further deterioration of their mental health. The policy of many mental health institutions to refuse service to those with criminal records makes the situation even worse. Much like public housing, those convicted offenders are excluded from many mental health programs. Left untreated and at the mercy of life on the street, mentally ill offenders often have little recourse other than crime. Furthermore, according to this story, most of the mentally ill clients who end up in jail are there for misdemeanors or crimes of survival. We included this article because it provides solid data, reasonable analysis, and reveals a pressing problem for which there is a solution.
- Criminal records cripple ex-cons' new lives. This *Christian Science Monitor* story details the difficulty that former prison inmates have adjusting to life in society when their prison records continue to be held against them. This story is useful in illustrating how one mistake can have a long-term impact on a person's life. If offenders pay their dues to society by serving prison time and stay out of trouble once they are released, is it fair to continue punishing them by forever alerting prospective employers to their criminal records? This story highlights the delicate balance between the protection of society and the reclamation of the offenders' lives.

We try to balance stories about the excesses of the war on crime with selections about the alternatives to the war on crime. Amy has remarked that since starting the page in 1999, news about the peacemaking perspective in action seems to have become increasingly easy to find.

- Police study: Pre-K cuts down on crime. Peacemaking & Crime includes many small, local stories, as these often best illustrate what is happening at the ground-level war on crime. This NewsNet5.com story describes a Cleveland, Ohio, study that claims quality pre-kindergarten education reduces crime. The story also notes that there is not enough federal funding to extend quality pre-kindergarten education to all the children who need it. Although the news item does not go into how scientific or academically sound the study is (or is not), it does open a window onto local crime concerns and local ideas for dealing with them.
- Befriending your child's killer. Ultimate peacemaking? This story that appeared in Salon is one of our favorites. When teaching about peacemaking, a professor often hears questions like, "What would you do if someone murdered your daughter? Could you forgive them?" This article tells the story of Aba Gayle whose nineteen year-old daughter was murdered. Ms. Gayle now regularly visits her daughter's killer and is attempting to help him get parole. Disillusioned by the revenge motive of many victim support groups, Ms. Gayle has decided to forgive the man who murdered her daughter. Appreciating this article is a real challenge for students and professors because it shows how the abstract idea of forgiveness has been concretely applied by someone whose life was changed by a violent crime. Ms. Gayle's religious convictions have allowed her to translate into action the words that many of us profess. Also in our news archives is a story about how the father of one of the Oklahoma City bombing victims has forgiven Timothy McVeigh.
- NY court seeks to keep mentally ill out of jail. This is another story about incarceration and the mentally ill, but from an alternative perspective. "Where Justice and Mercy Meet," from the *Village Voice* describes a mental health court in Brooklyn, New York, that seeks to secure treatment for mentally ill offenders rather than sending them to prison. Like most of the subjects of our peacemaking stories, the mental health court represents a small, local or personal step toward alternatives to the war on crime approach. Although crime-control philosophies are socially and politically cyclical, updating Peacemaking & Crime has helped us to see the peacemaking methods that are seeping in around the edges of the war on crime.

Links Archive

This section is devoted to the websites of organizations, government agencies, and the like which are in some way related to the war on crime or alternative perspectives. Peacemaking & Crime provides a link and a brief description of these sites and what they offer. We prefer sites that offer original research and content and/or services rather than only lists of links.

- Civitas. Although we focus on the war on crime in the United States, sometimes a link (or news story) from a site based in a foreign country is such a good fit for Peacemaking & Crime that we cannot omit it. Civitas: The Institute for the Study of Civil Society is based in the United Kingdom and seeks "to deepen public understanding of the legal, institutional and moral framework that makes a free and democratic society possible."
- Eastern State Penitentiary. One of the great things about the web is that it offers a lot of different types of content, much of it unexpected. We discovered this haunting photo essay of Philadelphia's Eastern State Penitentiary at a site belonging to a gentleman who photographs modern ruins. Although the prison is in an extreme state of decay, it provides a good perspective on incarceration. Those who are familiar with prison interiors will notice that although much about prisons has changed throughout the twentieth century, much has not.
- Self-Arrest Form. Not all Peacemaking & Crime links have to be serious. This Citizen's Self-Arrest Form kindly provided by the East Point Police Department in East Point, Georgia, helps the civic-minded to arrest themselves if they discover that they have committed a crime. Occasionally, some of the links in our archive expire. We hope this one never does.
- Sex Offender Registries. It is important to show both perspectives on the war on crime, and this site is a good example of traditional crime-prevention methods. Basically, this site provides links to every state's sex-offender registry and registry laws, as well as the registries of individual cities and counties (when available).
- Fort Smith Police Department Crime Map. We like to include interesting features from official police department sites. This site allows Fort Smith, Arizona, citizens to see their police department's database of reported crime. As far as police department website features go, this one is pretty fancy. Like the sex-offender registries site, this crime map hews to a traditional perspective.
- Southern Poverty Law Center. Many of the sites we link to reflect the peacemaking perspective in some way, but none does so more than the Southern Poverty Law Center. This organization is a nonprofit center that combats hate, intolerance, and discrimination through education and litigation. Features at the center's site include information about legal action, its law center, Klanwatch, and Militia Task Force. One exceptional resource is its Wall of Tolerance project which identifies the thousands of supporters who have made contributions to the center's mission.

Other Stuff

Peacemaking & Crime has undergone quite a few changes in recent years. From 1999 to about the middle of 2005, the page was hosted on the servers at the University of West Georgia. Amy wrote the page in HTML and posted it via FTP. This time-consuming method meant that we updated the page only periodically when we had a critical mass of stuff to post.

Blogger has changed all that for us.[3] This nifty service, currently run by Google, allows its users to easily design and post "web logs" or, as they are more commonly known, "blogs." All a wannabe blogger has to do is sign up for the free service, choose a design scheme for their blog, and start posting.[4] Blogger-users need not be familiar with HTML or FTP or any other threatening acronym.[5]

The new format has changed how Peacemaking & Crime looks and works. We now post stories and features almost as quickly as they appear in the media because it is so easy to do. In this running format, items are categorized by date rather than by feature. Formerly, we would post each new item in its own category. For example, breaking news would go in "News," new links in "Links," and so on. Amy would manually move the very old stuff to the archive sections, which was a chore. In 2005, we did away with the categories and now post everything by date with a more detailed description of the type of item. This method pushes the older stories down the page, and Blogger automatically archives everything by month. Also, we do not worry so much about clearing out dead links anymore. By now, most web users understand that much of what is on the web, especially news, is fleeting and that the chances of a newly posted story being a live link are pretty good and the chances of an older story being a dead link are also pretty good. The page still has information about my books, as well as links to the news and links archives from the old page. Pleasantly, many of the links in the archives are still live.

Peacemaking & Crime has been around for about nine years. For a while, Amy goofed around with the format before settling on the current red logo and red-and-gray color scheme. While good webmasters can do many fancy things, we believe it is important to keep the Peacemaking & Crime interface as simple as possible. Those who would like to follow Peacemaking & Crime's evolution can check with the Wayback Machine, which has archived selected versions of the site back to 1999.[6]

Maintaining a site such as this brings one into contact with a variety of individuals who make challenging requests. One young man serving time in prison wanted us to act as attorneys and manage the appeal of his case. One mother of a delinquent requested that we see to it that the juvenile justice laws in California be immediately changed. Countless students have asked that we write their term papers. Most interesting, however, are visitors to the site who write to debate the merits of the peacemaking perspective. These range from the single-issue oriented extremists who declare that this country is being ruined by supporters of gun control, feminists, immigrants, godless atheists, anyone with a religion different from their own, environmentalists, pro-choice activists, or anti-death penalty proponents. We have found that the most effective way to respond is to treat these visitors' ideas with respect and deflect their prejudices by promoting tolerance, empathy, and equality.

Most rewarding, however, are those correspondences that deal with the substantives issues of peacemaking. Several visitors have been intrigued by peacemaking and suggested other links or discussed ways to connect peacemaking to the everyday problems of life. We have made many connections to other scholars who have become friends. For example a doctoral student at Sam Houston State University was intrigued with the site and wrote to us. This has led to my including him on some roundtable discussions at the American Society of Criminology meetings where his contributions were thoughtful and enlightening. Today, this student, Dale Brooker, is a friend with whom I hope to one day collaborate on an article about the peacemaking perspective.

Conclusion

Peacemaking criminology is an emerging perspective that is gaining legitimacy in the national conversation about the problems of crime and delinquency. Peacemaking & Crime has been our modest attempt to advance this alternative to the war on crime philosophy that has so dominated the policies of the criminal justice system. Sometimes, it is easy to get discouraged by the lack of universal acceptance to the way of peace. However, we persist because the cause is so important. We are heartened by the wisdom of Gandhi:

> First they ignore you.
> Then they laugh at you.
> Then they fight you.
> Then you win.
> These days, we are hearing less and less of the laughter.

Notes

1. Peacemaking and Crime, http://peacemakingandcrime.blogspot.com/
2. Just in case you are interested: seminoles.cstv.com/ and golobos.cstv.com/.
3. www.blogger.com
4. blogger (noun)—One who blogs.
5. We're not unapologetic Google-boosters. Blogger just happened to be a very convenient way for us to do the page. Other developer-hosted blog publishing systems include: TypePad, LiveJournal, WordPress, and Xanga. See en.wikipedia.org/wiki/Blog_hosting_service for more information.
6. The Wayback Machine, located at http://www.archive.org, appears to have archived an impressive portion of the web. Enter the URL of the site you would like to see in the search box.

Chapter 13

The Future of the Peacemaking Perspective

John T. Whitehead
Wayne Gillespie
Michael Braswell

Peacemaking represents one recent development in criminology. This paper is an effort to assess the current status of peacemaking as a paradigm and make some comments about the directions it will take in the next decade. One area of concern is the relationship of peacemaking to secular humanism. Specifically, the paper will look at the writings of Fromm, Marx, and Habermas in an effort to offer secular alternatives to the typical ancient religious traditions as sources of peacemaking principles. The paper also raises the issue of whether peacemaking should offer specific ethical guidelines or just general foundational principles such as mindfulness, caring, and connectedness. A related issue is the balance between the individual and the socio-cultural. Relying on Parsons, this section specifies each peacemaking principle at a specific analytic level. The paper also explores some apparent problems with capitalism. The writings of both Quinney and Catholic social justice advocates are examined in order to clarify peacemaking's stance concerning capitalism.

Peacemaking is becoming a more influential voice in criminal justice. From humble beginnings, it has grown to the point where it is included as one of the current branches of criminological theory (e.g., see Schmalleger 2001). Given the growth of peacemaking, now may be a good time to take stock. What are the theoretical underpinnings of peacemaking, what might be missing, and where might peacemaking go from here? This essay is an attempt to assess where peacemaking is, what problems or clarifications need attention, and what directions it could take in the next few years.

Secular Humanism and Peacemaking Criminology

Peacemaking, in a larger context, has its roots in the ancient wisdom traditions. Specifically, peacemaking is said to originate from Judaism, Christianity, Islam, Hinduism, Buddhism, and Native American customs (Braswell, Fuller, and Lozoff 2001). These are venerable traditions that offer much too modern humanity. One issue concerning the traditions, however, is that they do not necessarily speak to all of contemporary society. Significant proportions of modern minds are either agnostic or atheist or simply a-religious.

Many individuals in modern Western societies are secularists. They do not form decisions or engage in social interaction on the basis of traditional or conventional values. As such, many do not necessarily respect or adhere to ancient wisdom traditions. If peacemaking is to appeal to as broad a spectrum as possible, one necessity is to justify the viewpoint to the nonbeliever.

In other words, the tenets of peacemaking may need justification beyond saying that they stem from ancient wisdom traditions. For many, that is sufficient justification. Even some nonbelievers will be impressed and convinced by the centuries of consensus behind such traditions or by the manifest wisdom contained in those traditions. Some nonbelievers will find it impressive that so many human beings have agreed to follow such principles as to love one's neighbor as oneself, to forgive trespasses and serve the poor. Others, however, will ask for proof for such principles, proof apart from the revelations of a deity or prophet to whom they do not subscribe. Such individuals may find nonreligious language more convincing.

One possible approach in this direction is to use humanistic literature as well as ancient wisdom traditions to support a peacemaking approach. One such thinker from the humanist paradigm is Erich Fromm. Fromm (1947) distinguishes between authoritarian and humanistic ethics. Authoritarian ethics could refer to a religious-based ethic in which the source of the ethical command is the authority of the divinity or the church interpreting a divine command. Catholicism, for example, through its official teaching authority claims that bortion and artificial birth control are both unethical. Humanistic ethics, on the other hand, relies on the human conscience which is "the reaction of our total personality to its proper functioning or dysfunctioning; to the totality of capacities which constitute our human and our individual existence" (Fromm 1947, p. 158). Going further:

> Actions, thoughts, and feelings which are conducive to the proper functioning and unfolding of our total personality produce a feeling of inner approval, of "rightness," characteristic of the humanistic "good conscience." On the other hand, acts, thoughts, and feeling injurious to our total personality produce a feeling of uneasiness and discomfort, characteristic of the "guilty conscience." (Fromm 1947, p. 159)

Fromm gives the instructive example of a man in therapy who had wanted to become a musician but whose father wanted him to become a businessman. The man became depressed and went to therapy to deal with the depression. The problem was that the man in question was not following his "conscience"; he was not being productive in the sense of becoming all that he could become.

The notion of happiness is integral to understanding this perspective:

> Happiness is the indication that man has found the answer to the problem of human existence: the productive realization of his potentialities and thus, simultaneously, being one with the world and reserving the integrity of his self. In spending his energy productively he increases his powers, he "burns without being consumed." (Fromm 1947, p. 189)

Parenthetically, Fromm along with many peacemaking advocates throughout the ages, would thus differ with the famous Biblical story of Adam and Eve that made work a curse for humans. Fromm would argue that productive work-work that allows a person to realize her or his potential-is, in fact, activity that makes one feel like they are in the Garden of Eden because it brings joy and completion!

Fromm's concept of productive work is also consistent with Marx's early treatise on labor and alienation. According to Marx, the essence of human beings may be expressed through their labor. Through labor, the creative potential of a man or woman may be unleashed. He wrote that "as individuals express their life, so they are. What they are, therefore, coincides with their production, both with what they produce and with how they produce" (Marx 1965, p. 32). However, a condition known as alienation develops in modern Western societies as a result of forces associated with capitalism (e.g., commodification, private property, wage labor, etc.). In particular, capitalism converts labor into labor-power; by selling this labor-power for wages, human beings become alienated or disconnected from the very products of their work. Work becomes externally rewarded rather than internally gratifying. Through capitalism, people become alienated from the product they produce, the creative act of production, their inner self, and their community.

Fromm also thinks that work has become distorted in modern society:

> People work to make money or to save time. People work in order to make more money; they use this money in order to make still more money, and the end-the enjoyment of life-is lost sight of. People are in a hurry and invent things in order to have more time. Then they use the time saved to rush about again to save more time until they are so exhausted that they can not use the time they saved. (Fromm 1947, p. 194)

The condition that Fromm describes is very similar to Marx's notion of alienation. The worker becomes estranged from the creative process and his or her own product:

> The more the worker produces, the less he has to consume; the more value he creates, the more worthless he becomes; the more his product is shaped, the more misshapen the worker; the more civilized his object, the more barbarous the worker; the more powerful the work, the more powerless the worker; the

> more intelligent the work, the duller the worker and the more he becomes a slave of nature. (Marx 1884)

The distortions in work and labor that both Fromm and Marx described are also related to Max Weber's concept of Zweck-rational social action. It is based on instrumental or purposive rationality that developed in the modern Western world through the capitalist economy. In short, Zweck-rational social action is akin to "economic thinking." Weber implied that this form of action was more sophisticated than behavior associated with spiritual or traditional reasoning; he believed that only this purposive-rational action was meaningful in the modern age.

It is possible to link Weber's theory of social action with Marx's theory of labor. Neo-Marxian scholars, such as Jürgen Habermas, have attempted a grand synthesis of Weberian and Marxist theory. Habermas' work is extensive. Most notably is his reformulation of Marx's historical materialism, his integration of Weber with Marx, and his development of the theory of communicative action.

Habermas first intends to correct the economic determinism that he believed was inherent in Marx's later writing. There are two basic elements in Habermas' reconstruction of Marx's historical materialism: "the history of human society cannot be framed in a narrow way as an economically determined progress through five different modes of production" (Pusey 1987, p. 28). Habermas set about developing a theory of social evolution that is defensible against criticisms concerning economic reductionism.

Habermas expands the original economic base to include interaction. In fact, he claims that interaction is based on communicative rationality, and that this communicative action is the most basic human phenomenon. It is another form of rationality, distinct from those identified by Weber, that seeks to establish understanding through communication. In short, communicative action is the foundation of sociocultural life.

In order to arrive at this newfound type of social action, Habermas incorporates the ideas of Weber. Habermas builds upon Weber's notions of social action and rationality. In fact, Habermas devotes much of his Reason and the Rationalization of Society to the resurrection and modification of Weber's Protestant Ethic. However, Habermas opposes Weber's contention that only purposive-rational action can result in meaningful social action; he maintains that value-rational action may have structure-forming effects as well. For example, Weber proposed that interaction based on a means-end rationality (i.e., where an individual behaves in a particular way to receive a desired result) forms the basis for dominant social institutions like the economy. Habermas notes that this way of thinking is not inherently superior to others. In fact, communication is the basis for achieving all goals. Habermas argues that communication must be oriented toward achieving mutual understanding rather than realizing a self-serving goal or desired end result. He advances a form of communicative rationality where human interaction is not based on "getting what one wants" but rather on "mutual understanding."

Habermas extracts the positivistic elements from Weber's cultural theory and attempts to make the process of rationalization compatible with a cognitivist theory of ethical development. According to Pusey (1987), Habermas "gives greater prominence to rationalization as a world-historical process construed as a cultural process that is grounded in a progress of ideas with its own partially independent dynamic, its own internal 'logic,' and with its own potential for rationalization in the positive, emancipatory sense" (p. 31). Finally, Habermas connects Weber's social action with rationalization in order to develop a positive outcome to the institutionalization of reason in society. Habermas hopes that the rationalization of communicative action will lead to interaction free from domination and oppression. By positively linking social action with rationality and rationalization, Habermas develops his theory of communicative action (Pusey 1987). As with other variants of radical sociology, Habermasian critical theory takes as its broad goal human emancipation (Flacks and Turkel 1978). In particular, the main objective of communicative action is to achieve communicative understanding, or when the actions of agents are coordinated through acts of reaching understanding (Habermas 1984).

Habermas' theory of communicative action, with its emphasis on reaching understanding and consensus through uncoerced communication, might appeal to humanists who are interested in exploring normative issues from a decidedly secular perspective. In a similar vein, existentialism may be another possible approach. Existentialism implies that humans must take responsibility for the creation of their own meaning and rules. Such meaning is enhanced to the extent one can "live in the moment." May et al. (1958) writes, ". . . the symptoms of isolation and alienation reflect the state of a person whose relation to the world has become broken (p.56)." Here the peacemaking perspective could argue that its principles offer the most hope for peace on the planet. Habermas' theory of communicative action also enhances this perspective by offering that principles of peace can only be promulgated by first realizing that an implicit demand for freedom and equality is contained within communication itself. Furthermore, pointing to the centuries of human experience behind the principles, the peacemaking theorist can make the pragmatic argument that peacemaking principles work. They prevent war, killing, injury, and even property damage. Thus the peacemaking theorist could suggest to the existentialist that peacemaking principles have utilitarian value and thereby justify their adoption.[1]

The Need for Specific Guidelines for Peacemaking Criminology

An area of concern in peacemaking is the need for more explicit guidelines. In particular, how do principles from secular humanism translate into specific guidelines and theoretical development for peacemaking criminology? Some critics might contend that mindfulness, caring, and connectedness are legitimate as overarching principles. It is hard to argue that humans should be mindful of one another and nature, care for fellow humans, and realize that all of us are interdependent and interconnected.

The critical question is not whether peacemaking offers broad general principles. The critical question is whether peacemaking offers sufficient instructive guidance in troubling situations. Philosopher John Hardwig (1997) provides a challenging example: If a woman is eighty-seven years old and is diagnosed with a terminal illness, does peacemaking offer her helpful advice on what to do next? Does she fight to live as long as possible at whatever cost? For example, assume that fighting the disease has a 50 percent chance of success but will cost thousands of dollars. Assume further that fighting the disease will involve care-giving by the woman's fifty-five year-old daughter. The daughter will have to take time out of her business or career. The care-giving will cost the daughter in terms of her own financial and other success. In turn, it will affect the ability of the daughter to provide for her own family, including the college education of her son, the subject's grandson.

What is the course of action that best embodies the peacemaking principles of caring and connectedness? On the one hand, it could be argued that caring for the sick mother would be a concrete instance of caring and also a demonstration of the connectedness of the generations. Others could contend that the caring thing to do is not to fight to the end, or perhaps as Hardwig suggests, even commit suicide out of a "duty to die." Such a suicide would allow the daughter to pursue her career and support her family. It would allow the grandchildren the opportunity to go to a better college and then make greater contributions in their lives.

Other traditions make rather specific declarations regarding guidelines. The U.S. Catholic bishops, for example, have issued a policy statement on capital punishment. They condemned the practice and offer a detailed explanation of their rationale for doing so. The Catholic Church has also issued a specific directive on euthanasia:

> Whatever its motives and means, direct euthanasia consists in putting an end to the lives of handicapped, sick, or dying persons. It is *morally unacceptable* (emphasis added). (Catechism 1994, p. 549)

Going further, the Catholic Church distinguishes such active euthanasia from discontinuing medical procedures that are "burdensome, dangerous, extraordinary, or disproportionate to the expected outcome" and says that these "can be legitimate" as the "refusal of 'over-zealous' treatment" (Catechism 1994, p. 49).

The point is not whether or not the Catholic teaching on euthanasia is the correct one. The issue is whether peacemaking needs to offer more explicit ethical guidelines or simply offer broad principles such as the principles of caring, mindfulness, and connectedness (Braswell and Gold 1998).

Granted, peacemaking is not a church or even a religious ideology, but even individual philosophers can make rather concrete recommendations. Peter Singer, for example, argues that all of us should contribute 20 percent of our income to the needy. Singer thinks that we are so interconnected, one human to another, that we should demonstrate our connectedness by this double tithe.

Peter Singer has also devised a list of "new commandments" to replace the old commandments. For example, compared to the first old commandment

("Treat all human life as of equal worth"), Singer offers the first new commandment: Recognize that the worth of human life varies. Specifically, Singer contends that "life without consciousness is of no worth at all" (Singer 1994, p. 190). Thus preserving someone's life who is merely in a vegetative state is wrong. His third new commandment is to "Respect a person's desire to live or die" versus the old third commandment to "Never take your own life, and always try to prevent others taking theirs" (Singer 1994, pp. 196–197).

Singer's principles are considerably more specific and concrete than the principles of connectedness, caring, and mindfulness (Braswell and Gold 1998). So his challenge to peacemaking might be to grow and develop, to move beyond initial, foundational principles and begin to offer more instructive guidebooks for living. A worthy caveat regarding Singer's bold "new commandments" is that while prescriptive guidelines may be interesting and intellectually stimulating, the prescriptive may well be more dangerous than the descriptive which is more fluid and flexible. Prescriptions almost always demand a sacrifice, human or otherwise.

Given Hardwig's example of the eighty-seven year-old who is dying, is the economic measure of the decision the only form of measurement needed? Does one's life or death come down to a loss/profit statement? Perhaps the daughter doesn't want to care for her dying mother for a variety of economic and other reasons. Whatever the daughter's choice, will her actions affect her children's (the grandchildren's) ability to feel compassion? Is sacrifice whether on the part of the dying mother, her daughter, or the grandchildren a good or bad thing? Should sacrifice be born out of love and compassion or economic gain? Can economic advantage buy peace of mind? Can even a dying mother/grandmother have something important to teach her daughter and grandchildren?

Another example is welfare reform. Conservatives tout welfare reform because they claim that welfare rolls are down. What they fail to note is that poverty is not being reduced and the needy are not being helped. In 1998 the poverty threshold was $1095 yet welfare leavers were earning only between $665 to $1083 a month. About half of leavers were reporting that food did not last until the end of the month and about 40 percent were unable to pay rent, mortgage, or utility bills (Schram and Soss 2001).

What is the peacemaking response? It is not enough to say that caring is a basic principle. Both former President Clinton and current President Bush claim to be caring individuals (Bush touts "compassionate conservatism"). Caring as a principle needs to be translated into actions and policies that result in measurable benefits.

Does peacemaking simply endorse the compassionate conservatism of President Bush and thus rely on individuals and faith-based organizations to deal with poverty and the poor? Do we just write checks to Mother Teresa's nuns so they can clean up Calcutta and Mott Haven in New York City? Or do we need to reform or reinvent welfare so that it is a government program that actually delivers benefits instead of scape-goating the poor?

One option is to say that only the foundational principles are possible. Prescriptive guidelines above and beyond those principles will not be forthcoming because such guidelines are limiting. It is up to the individual, immersed in the spirit of the foundational principles, to decide what is the peaceful/peacemaking course of action.

This response makes the individual the ultimate arbiter of right and wrong. If the individual proceeds out of a belief that she or he is acting in light of the three basic principles, then that individual's choice is an ethical choice.

Another perspective is that peacemaking in the context of the wisdom traditions, would disagree that the individual is the final arbiter of right and wrong, but would acknowledge that it is the individual who makes the choice to do right or wrong. Peacemaking in this sense is more about a person's attitude and the "intentions" of his or her actions. Since outcomes of actions continue to have consequences and cannot be fully realized, intentional acts of compassion and loving kindness would be consistent with ancient standards of accountability.

So peacemaking must make a choice. Let the individual be the ultimate arbiter of ethics or offer more specific guidelines than mere foundational principles.

Another possible response for peacemaking is to say that it is not a school of ethics and thus does not offer solutions for all ethical issues. Peacemaking can argue that it is just a criminal justice and criminological school of thought and thus it only offers criminal justice solutions. Thus peacemaking can suggest such criminal justice solutions as victim-offender reconciliation, family group conferencing, victim-offender panels, reintegrative shaming, and faith-based corrections (Braswell, Fuller, and Lozoff 2001). Peacemakers do not offer, however, and need not apologize for not offering a comprehensive set of ethical principles that apply to the broad spectrum of human conundrums.

One problem with this response is that most human problems do, at least tangentially, become criminal justice problems. Euthanasia, for example, is illegal in the United States. The State of Michigan prosecuted Dr. Kevorkian as a criminal. So what at first seems like only an ethical issue, euthanasia, very quickly becomes a criminal justice issue. To claim that peacemaking is only concerned with criminal justice issues is to avoid the reality that most human issues often become criminal justice issues.

The Individual, Systemic, and Cultural Contexts of Peacemaking

A related issue is for peacemaking to recognize the balance between the individual and the social-cultural. On the one hand, peacemaking subscribes to the need to balance the individual or personal and the institutional (e.g., see Braswell, Fuller, and Lozoff 2001, especially the fifth chapter). On the other hand, there appears to be a sense that the individual is primary, that we need to go from the inside out, from the individual to the collective:

> Ultimately, it does come back to the individual; the one who experiences personal transformation and, as a result, engages others in peacemaking activities. (Braswell, Fuller, and Lozoff 2001, pp. 6–7)

Sometimes, however, we need to go in both directions simultaneously, from the inside out and from the outside in.

As unit theory arises from metatheory, methodology inevitably emerges. Filmer (1998) notes that "theory implies method as a form of practice" (p. 228). He continues to suggest that methodology is concerned with the basic underlying logical, practical, and philosophical issues regarding the application and testing of theories. Filmer refers to method as "a specialist form of theory." However, no one methodological practice is appropriate to every type of social phenomena. In fact, most scholars match their method to their theory by examining the level of analysis at which their theory is poised to explain.

Speaking very generally, most criminologists limit their levels of analyses to two levels: the micro and the macro. The micro-level is concerned with assessing individual characteristics and phenomena such as age, self-control, delinquent peer associations, intelligence, hormonal balances, and blocked opportunities. The macro-level addresses group or aggregate qualities such as poverty rates, degrees of ethnic heterogeneity, and proportions of residential mobility. Likewise, certain theoretical concepts are best suited to the micro or macro level. For instance, Messner and Rosenfeld (1997) restrict social learning theory, social control theory, and strain theory to the individual-level whereas they specify cultural deviance, social disorganization, and anomie at the group level.

Perhaps this strict dichotomy between the individual and group levels is false, or at least misleading. It seems to have resulted in artificially constructed intra-disciplinary boundaries that restrict theories of crime causation. However, even the classical sociological theorists struggled with similar analytic questions. Weber concentrated on social action at the individual level and emphasized the quest for understanding and ideal types. Durkheim maintained that aggregated behavior and groups, specifically institutions, were the appropriate subject of sociological inquiry. He stressed uncovering social facts. In short, the macro-micro dichotomy has plagued sociological inquiry since its inception.

Parsons (1968) engaged this troublesome topic throughout his career. He essentially distinguished three levels of analysis: the cultural system, the social system, and the individual personality:

> A system of action, at the most general level, may be conceived as differentiated into four analytically distinct primary subsystems. Three of these are clear and well known: cultural system, social system, and individual personality. I have suggested further that the behavioral organism must be carefully distinguished analytically from the personality. (Parsons 1968, p. 17)

Parsons delineated social phenomena into three spheres. However, at the individual level, he seemed to sub-divide social phenomena into either action or behavior. This is a subtle point. Using Parsons' analytic division, it is possible to specify each broad peacemaking principle (i.e., caring, connectedness, and mindfulness) at a specific analytic level (i.e., cultural system, social system, individual personality).

As previously mentioned, three metatheoretical concepts within the peacemaking paradigm are connectedness, caring, and mindfulness (Braswell and Gold 1998). Connectedness arises when we realize that "people are not isolated, disconnected beings. Rather we are earthly beings and social beings . . . what we do has direct consequences on those to whom we are connected" (Braswell and Gold 1998, p. 29). Caring involves the notion that "ethical caring is ultimately grounded in natural caring—for example, the natural caring a mother has for her child" (p. 31). Nel Noddings goes as far as to assert that traditional morality has reflected only masculine reasoning (one grounded in principles and instrumental rationality); feminine reasoning places a greater emphasis on discourse and understanding. And finally, mindfulness can persuade us "to move from the passion of single-minded self-interest to a growing sense of compassion that includes others and their needs" (p. 34). Although other legitimate specifications may exist, we believe that—in order for peacemaking criminology to develop into a general theory—it should be specified in a particular manner.

Peacemaking could be examined from three analytic levels. For example, the ethic of care could be studied and promoted at the level of culture. American culture is currently not organized around an ethic of care; we live in a capitalist, consumer culture where everything and everyone has a price. Welfare states seem to have a stronger commitment to the ethic of care and, consequently, they enjoy lower rates of poverty, unemployment, and crime. Second, the concept of connectedness is inherent at the institutional (social system) level. In fact, crime might result from institutional imbalance and institutional insubordination to the ethic of care. The economy is the dominant institution in the American system, and its superordinate position most likely creates crime and suffering. Third, mindfulness arises from communicative social action at the individual level. Mindfulness requires individuals to consider the consequences of their actions; it is a rational-choice based concept. However, the notion of mindfulness also implies a form of meaningful human interaction where individuals are geared toward communicative action rather than self-serving, strategic action. Communication based on mutual understanding is essential to peacemaking. Thus, our version of peacemaking theory calls for an end to crime and suffering by increasing mindful interaction, strengthening connectedness through non-economic social institutions, and adhering to a cultural ethic of care.

This specification seems most consistent with Parsonian theory. Parsons (1968) carefully indicated the principal agents by which each level can be referenced as follows:

> I think it is legitimate to consider the pattern-maintenance systems in action as centering at the level of codes in which particularized and concrete meanings

> (information) are organized and articulated. For the cultural system itself, which is paramount in action, these codes are classifiable as religious, evaluative (moral), aesthetic (expressive), and empirical-cognitive. For the social system they are basically evaluative, normative in the narrower sense (legal), political, and economic. It seems to me appropriate to use the term "identity" to designate the pattern-maintenance code-system of the individual personality. (Parsons 1968,: p. 20)

Parsons adds that identity is learned through social interaction. He maintains that identity has the highest level of stability once established and that it cannot be altered by environmental rewards. Interestingly, Parsons noted that identity controls processes of action.

Kaplan (1964) proposed the term explanatory shell as an umbrella concept under which the object domain of a given theory is located. In this sense, the explanatory shell of peacemaking includes the individual, the social system, and the cultural system. Specifically, the ethic of care is reproduced at the cultural level; connectedness is integrated at the institutional level; and mindfulness is socialized at the individual level.

Peacemaking and the Tenacity of a Capitalist Ethos

The peacemaking model offered above involves a hierarchical structure where mindful individuals are connected through social institutions that operate according to the cultural ethic of care. This vision of the world contrasts quite dramatically with early twenty-first century modernity. In fact, it is important to note how the peacemaking model differs from the system of globalized capitalism that is currently in place.

Capitalism has displaced all social institutions in the modern world. For example, consider the response of the Catholic Church to socialism. Several popes, for example, have argued for economic systems that respect the right to own property (capitalism) but still strive for a just living wage. Leo XIII, for example, condemned socialism in its attempt to end private property, a remedy he labeled as "manifestly against justice" (Fremantle 1963, p. 168).

More completely, Pope Leo XIII condemned socialism because:

> the fact that the remedy they propose is manifestly against justice. For every man has by nature the right to possess property as his own. This is one of the chief points of distinction between man and the animal creation. . . . (Fremantle 1963, p. 168)

Building on the encyclicals, the Catechism of the Catholic Church (1994) goes further. It advocates a just wage which guarantees each man "the opportunity to provide a dignified livelihood for himself and his family on the material, social, cultural, and spiritual level" (Catechism 1994, p. 584). It also notes that owners "have an obligation to consider the good of persons and not only the increase of profits" (Catechism 1994, p. 584). Concerning workers, the Catechism says that "Recourse to a strike is morally legitimate when it cannot be avoided, or at least when it is necessary to obtain a proportionate benefit" (Catechism 1994, p. 584).

Yet the Church often seems to be at odds with those clergy who attempt to realize such benefits for impoverished workers in third world countries through their support of "liberation theology." Sometimes what is written is designed to lead to meaningful action, sometimes it is designed to be read, considered, but not carried out.

One peacemaker, Quinney, on the other hand, points to the Marxist critique of capitalism as "a system of exploitation. The servitude of the wage laborer to capital is essential to the capitalist mode of production" (Quinney 2000a, p. 201). Elsewhere, Quinney approves of a "radical rejection of Western capitalist civilization" in search of "a socialist humanism" (Quinney 2000b, p. 27).

Quinney does not explicitly say that he is against private property, but he does say that he opposes exploitation and aims for positive peace. Positive peace, he explains, "exists when the sources of crime-including poverty, inequality, racism and alienation-are not present. There can be no peace-no positive peace-without social justice" (Quinney 2000a, p. 205). Going further, he points to the need for positive social programs "that eliminate the structural sources of violence and crime" (Quinney 2000a, p. 206). Quinney's critique could be viewed in the spirit of "structural Marxism."

Braswell, Fuller, and Lozoff (2001) criticize our consumer culture for being a chase "after all the 'stuff' that's supposed to make us happy but never will" (p. 65). Lozoff specifically notes that:

> consumerism encourages us from the time we're born to have ceaseless desires. To put it simply, we want so much, all the time, that we have not even noticed how much quality of life we give up in the process of buying, comparing, repairing, safeguarding, discarding and replacing. Our lives run us instead of us running our lives." (Lozoff, 2000, p. 154)

Elsewhere he says that the United States is

> tied to a consumer mode of life's purpose that never brings us the wholehearted satisfaction we inwardly crave, because consumerism-while promising satisfaction at every turn-relies on our never being satisfied. (Lozoff 2000, p.: 26)

Critics of Quinney and Braswell, Fuller and Lozoff may suggest that they carry their conclusions to their logical conclusion. Since we live in a consumer society, would abdication of private property and calls for communal sharing of goods, if adopted in sufficient numbers, wreak havoc on the American economy? Witness the recent terrorist actions against the World Trade Center towers in New York City. People—consumers—stopped flying out of fear. Immediately, airlines laid off thousands of workers and asked for a federal bailout of their troubled industry.

The peacemakers may be right. Perhaps we do live in a consumer society gone astray. But what is their solution? It is one thing to say band together with your neighbors and share resources. A handful of people demonstrating such communal intimacy would probably not affect the economy in a substantial way. But if taken seriously and adopted by millions, could it have a negative impact on the American and global economy? So what is the next step? How do we accomplish peacemaking and not bring down the economy? How do we make the transition from a consumer society to a peacemaking society?

The terrorist attack of September 11th showed that any consumer slowdown can have dramatic effects on the economy. Thousand of workers were laid off, conventions were canceled, automakers started offering zero percent financing on brand new 2002 model cars, and retailers were searching for customers. Some wealthy Americans started a new fad called "patriotic shopping."

If capitalism is indeed irredeemably wedded to the exploitation of the workers, then what do we do next? Marxism led to communism, but communism, at least the brand practiced in the Soviet Union, failed. So what, for example, do the peacemaking theorists have to suggest for the direction of the American economy.

There may be remedies that are less drastic than dismantling our capitalist economy. For example, there are new companies that park cars in busy areas and you pay to drive one whenever and as long as you need it. So here is a capitalist venture that addresses some of the concerns raised by Lozoff.

Erich Fromm apparently called for a new type of state which does not obliterate capitalism but which is mainly socialistic. In Wozniak's terms, Fromm calls for a sane society in which all humans "work toward restructuring the economic, political, and cultural levels of society" (Wozniak 2000, p. 53).

Since Fromm died at the beginning of the process of globalization, it falls to current peacemakers to spell out their prescriptions for not just a sane society or sane state, but a sane global economy. What will it look like? How can it be implemented? It is not enough to decry our consumer culture and call for neighbors to share resources. If we are serious about the need for change, it is necessary to outline our vision and how to achieve it.

Parenthetically, it is interesting to note that even as a child Fromm claimed that he rejected capitalism. In an interview shortly before he died, Fromm said that as a child he "found it . . . very strange that people devote their life to making money, and I was very embarrassed when a man had to admit in my presence that he was a businessman, in other words, that he spent his whole time making money. . . ." (cited in Funk 2000, p. 3)

This raises a fundamental question: Are businessmen in business just to make money? The answer is Yes and No. Yes, they are in business to make money in the sense that if they do not make a profit over a period of time, they will go out of business. But, no, they are not in business solely to make money. They are in business to make a product or offer a service—a product or service that people will demand. Ideally, such products and services benefit society. Realistically, some products and services are frivolous or harmful. Fast food, for example, appears to contribute to the growing problem of teenage obesity (Schlosser 2002).

In fact, in the current economy it goes further than this. In today's highly competitive marketplace, businesses must provide quality products and quality service. Management consultant Tom Peters (1988), for example, argues that in the automobile market it is no mystery why Japanese automakers have done well—they provide a quality product, down to the cupholders.

So, contrary to Fromm's discomfort with business persons as single-minded devotees of making money, Peters and others would argue that businesses are providing quality products and/or services that attract and continue to attract customers. Of course, the "supply and demand" catechism of Peters is essentially an amoral principle which requires no altruism or compassion and in the end, may result in little if any peace. And when underperforming or corrupt businesses are found out, they do not necessarily go out of business as Peters implies. They are often bought out and merge with other more powerful businesses of similar ilk in a kind of corporate mutation. Perhaps there are too many products driven primarily by greed and profitability with too little concern for the environment and the people who buy and use them. The "One Minute Manager" may prove to be one minute too much. Does it really matter if we are "going to hell in a hand-basket," that we go more efficiently? What may be effective in the long-run, may not be very efficient in the short-term.

Perhaps it is more "spiritual" to be a minister, teach college, or run a prison ministry. But not everyone can or wants to do these things. Some have to staff the publishing houses that provide the textbooks for the university. Some have to work at the auto plants that produce the cars that the ministers and college professors and psychoanalysts drive. Of course, it can also be pointed out that unbridled capitalism has and is wreaking havoc on the American economy.

From the Great Depression to Enron, the dark side of capitalism continues to remind us that contrary to Gordon Gekko in the film, *Wallstreet*, "Greed is not good." We know physical resources are finite. What do we produce and acquire once all material is used up? Some resources can be replenished, but can for example, the Amazon Rainforest be replenished in its natural state notwithstanding a new exhibit at Epcot Center in Disney World? There may be enough economic and natural resources to take care of our needs, but can (and should) there be enough to take care all that we want? Motives other than money can encourage innovation and development. Innovators like Albert Einstein weren't motivated primarily by money. Some producers would appear to be more motivated by economic gain. Does the happiness and joy that Fromm identifies come more from the work itself or more from the monetary and status rewards which result from the work? While the two are obviously not mutually exclusive, the one which takes priority is an essential clue to our personal and collective future.

One point of view is that peacemaking will not bring down the economy because its goal is to transform the economy. When is enough enough? Peacemaking is more long-term, capitalism more short-term. The same technology can be used for either conservation or consumerism. The more resources we conserve (not hoard), the more we have to help others. Bo Lozoff seems to strike a balance in the debate when he suggests that all work is worthy and honorable as long as it "benefits the world instead of harms it," (Lozoff 2000, p. 136).

Peacemaking and the American Dream

Another problem critics note in a rejection of capitalism and consumerism is that it is too simplistic. They would contend that American culture is more than a consumer culture.

Messner and Rosenfeld (2001), for example, note that the American Dream actually has multiple components. One value is an achievement orientation: "People are encouraged to make something of themselves, to set goals, and to strive to reach them" (Messner and Rosenfeld 2001, p. 62). A second value is individualism that focuses on thinking for yourself and making your own decisions. A third value is universalism in which all are encouraged to achieve. They label the fourth value "the fetishism of money" by which they mean that money has the key role "as the 'metric' of success" (Messner and Rosenfeld 2001, p. 63). Achievement, individualism, universalism, and materialism compel individuals to acquire personal success that is quantified in a standard, exchangeable form: money. However, their conduct is usually moderated through social institutions.

Messner and Rosenfeld focus on the economy, the polity, the family, and education as the four primary institutions that regulate human behavior and social action. These institutions are inter-connected and dependent upon one another. Yet, in capitalist societies, like the United States, the polity, the family, and education are subordinate to the economy. Messner and Rosenfeld (1997) state that "what is distinctive about the United States, however, is the exaggerated emphasis on monetary success and the unrestrained receptivity to innovation" (p. 69). The dominance of the economy devalues non-economic institutions, forcing them to accommodate economic requirements, and thereby allowing the economy to penetrate education, the family, and the polity. Individuals become most attached to the economy, which is the institution with the least restraint. Higher crime rates may result from the aggregate combination of weakened non-economic, institutional bonds and a lack of institutional (social) control.

More simplistically, the American Dream can become "a sales slogan for he material comforts and individual opportunities of a middle-class lifestyle: a car, a house, education for the children, a secure retirement" (Messner and Rosenfeld 2001, p. 6). Individuals in society feel an intense pressure to achieve these material comforts by any means necessary.

In his condemnation of consumerism, Lozoff is probably right to criticize the negative aspects of the American Dream. Consumerism can become shallow and people can spend much of their time working longer hours to buy time-saving devices with the end result that people actually have less time to spend on things that have deeper significance than the latest fashion or media driven trend. But, as Messner and Rosenfeld point out, the American Dream also has positive features. The American Dream has also inspired economic and technological development. Certainly, television and the Web can be used for frittering away countless hours on QVC, the Home Shopping Network or eBay. But they can also be used to connect to libraries, view documentaries or serious articles on important issues, and communicate with people all over the world.

Habermas, too, discusses the problems associated with capitalist economy. In particular, he notes that certain features of capitalism such as money distort the ability to achieve consensus in the lifeworld. Habermas (1987) re-introduces the phenomenological concepts of lifeworld and system. Specifically, the lifeworld represents the (internal) views of acting subjects on society, whereas the system signifies an external or observational orientation. Habermas is concerned with what he calls the colonization of the lifeworld by the system. In terms of social action, when colonization occurs, formal instrumental social action displaces substantive and communicative action in everyday life. Colonization occurs when the system and lifeworld are uncoupled and in a state of disequilibrium. Steering media such as money and power invade the consensus producing processes in language. During uncoupling, Habermas (1987) maintains that the system "unleashes system imperatives that burst the capacity of the lifeworld they instrumentalize" (p. 155). Uncoupling also disturbs reproduction processes in the domains of culture, society, and personality. Manifestations of such disturbances include loss of meaning, anomie, and psychopathologies. Evidence of Habermas' contention can be found in the rapid growth of psychological depression in our culture and the legitimization of violence as entertainment.

Habermas, unlike Marx or Quinney, does not demonize the capitalist system directly. Rather, he shows how capitalism can distort the primary medium of social life (i.e., communication). In *Between Facts and Norms*, Habermas develops a discourse theory of law and democracy that is based on his earlier theory of communicative action. Here, he discusses communication in terms of a discourse principle that underlies both morality and law. According to Habermas (1999), the discourse principle holds that "just those action norms are valid to which all possibly affected persons could agree as participants in rational discourse" (p. 107). In terms of discourse theory, the threat that steering media like money have upon communicative processes becomes more dire. Capitalism has the potential to not only distort social interaction in the lifeworld but also to compromise the legitimacy of positive law. In addition to proffering a critical theory based on Neo-Marxian principles, Habermas also elaborates on the safeguards that may be taken to limit the influence of the economy on formal law. Again, pragmatic demonstrations of his concern for safeguards seem apparent in such current legal developments as those calling for malpractice protection for medical doctors and health management organizations and the suspension of civil rights in the fight against terrorism. Although his theoretical discussion is quite extensive, Habermas sees the solution in democratic procedure.

The lesson for peacemaking is that the solution, then, is not a total rejection of American culture, economy, and society—the American Dream. For one thing, a total rejection is unrealistic because "the beliefs, values, and goals associated with the American Dream are firmly entrenched in the American historical experience and consciousness" (Messner and Rosenfeld 2001, p. 108). Also, many of the features of the American Dream are functional and even beneficial. For example, it is hard to say that setting goals and striving to reach them (see above) is undesirable. So the solution seems to point toward trying to transform the American Dream. We do not need to reform or recapitalize the Dream. We need to use the best of capitalism—individual initiative and innovation—to transcend its limitations. The wisdom traditions indicate that our lasting judgment will be found in how we treat the "least of those"; those who are in prison, who are hungry and naked. Will they also be a part of the transformed American Dream? Will they be visited, fed, and clothed?

Thich Nhat Hanh (1999) exhorts us to look more deeply and become more aware of how our dreams and the dreams of others are interconnected, the worst of and the best of humanity that comprise our culture. In discussing Christianity, he writes, ". . . when you love God you have to love your neighbor, otherwise you cannot say that you love God. Then you have to go further. You have to love your enemy. . . . If you say, 'I have to try to love him,' this is nonsense. You have to understand him and by doing so you will love him (pp. 33–36)." For human beings living in our culture to feel they are included in the best aspects of the American Dream, they will need to feel they belong in a larger sense of community. We all need a sense of home and belonging in order not to lose hope that our lives and the life of our culture improve and be more just. Otherwise, we will lose hope. It is not just about the economic context, a place to live. It is also about the relational context, a place to belong (e.g., see Sullivan and Tiff 2001). Thich Nhat Hanh provides an insight into such a distinction. "Every one of us needs a home. The world needs a home. There are so many . . . people who are homeless. They may have a building to live in, but they are homeless in their hearts (p. 52)."

Conclusion

Peacemaking is a viable theory in criminology. Moreover, it is a realistic approach to addressing crime and suffering in the United States and abroad. Although peacemaking is a valid and valuable frame of reference, it also needs to be examined to see if there are deficiencies. Given that the foundations of peacemaking were first based on ancient wisdom traditions, it seems time to incorporate elements from humanism into its framework. Peacemaking needs to be reified from a secular standpoint and, as with any theoretical perspective, continues its evolution into full maturity. It is suggested that the peacemaking principles of caring, connectedness, and mindfulness operate at distinct analytic levels. In order to reduce crime and suffering, mindfulness must be promoted at the individual level with integration and connectedness occurring through noneconomic social institutions; an ethic of care must be cultivated at the cultural level. Capitalist economy, particularly a globalized capitalist economy that supercedes the nation-state system, is a predominate source of crime and suffering in the modern world. As such, capitalism is a problem that must be addressed by peacemaking. Since a complete dismantling of the capitalist world economy is untenable and would probably prove to be detrimental, solutions that restructure the underlying mechanics of the system must be advanced. This essay has tried to point out the current status of the peacemaking perspective, what it answers and what it does not answer, and where it needs to go next. Given the positive start of peacemaking and the ground it has already covered, we are hopeful that the next steps will be taken and the answers to many of the questions we have raised in this discussion will emerge.

Note

1. Still another possibility is to pursue Rawls and his writing on justice. Rawls contends that there are two principles of justice: First, each person is to have an equal right of the most extensive scheme of equal basic liberties compatible with a similar scheme of liberties for others. Second, social and economic inequalities are to be arranged so that they are both (a) reasonably expected to be to everyone's advantage, and (b) attached to positions and offices open to all (Rawls 1999, p. 53).

References

Alexander, J. (1994). *Twenty lectures: Sociological theory since World War II.* New York: Columbia University Press.

Antonio, R. J. (1990). The decline of the grand narrative of emancipatory modernity: Crisis or renewal in Neo-marxian theory? In G. Ritzer (Ed.), *Frontiers of social theory: The new syntheses* (pp. 88–116). New York: Columbia University Press.

Bales, K. (1999). *Disposable people: New slavery in the global economy.* Berkeley, CA: University of California Press.

Braswell, M. C., Fuller, J., & Lozoff, B. (2001). *Corrections, peacemaking, and restorative justice: Transforming individuals and institutions.* Cincinnati, OH: Anderson Publishing Company.

Braswell, M. C., & Gold, J. (1998). Peacemaking, justice and ethics. In *Justice, crime and ethics*, 3rd ed. (pp. 23–40). Cincinnati, OH: Anderson.

Commission for the Catechism of the Catholic Church. (1994). Catechism of the Catholic Church. Liguori, MO: Liguori Publications.

Eysenck, H. J. (1977). *Crime and personality.* (Revised ed.) Frogmore, St. Albans: Paladin.

Filmer, P. (1998). Theory/practice. In C. Jenks (Ed.), *Core sociological dichotomies* (pp. 227–245). London: Sage Publications.

Flacks, R., & Turkel, G. (1978). Radical sociology: The emergence of Neo-Marxian perspectives in U.S. sociology. *Annual Review of Sociology*, 4, 193–238.
Fremantle, A. J. (1963). *The papal encyclicals in their historical context.* NewYork: New American Library.

Fromm, E. (1947). *Man for himself: An inquiry into the psychology of ethics.* New York: Holt, Rinehart and Winston.

Fromm, E. (1956). *The art of loving.* New York: Harper and Row.

Funk, R. (2000). Erich Fromm's life and work. In K. Anderson & R. Quinney, *Erich Fromm and critical criminology: Beyond the punitive society* (pp. 3–18). Urbana: University of Illinois Press.

Habermas, J. (1984). *The theory of communicative action: Reason and the rationalization of society* (Volume 1). Boston, MA: Beacon Press.

Habermas, J. (1987). *The theory of communicative action: Lifeworld and system* (Vol. 2). Boston, MA: Beacon Press.

Habermas, J. (1999). *Between facts and norms: Contributions to a discourse theory of law and democracy* (3rd ed.). Cambridge, MA: The MIT Press.

Hanh, T. N. (1999). *Going home: Jesus and Buddha as brothers.* New York: Penguin.

Hardwig, J. (1997). Dying at the right time: Reflections on (un)assisted suicide. In H. Lafollette (Ed.), *Ethics in practice* (pp. 53–65). New York: Blackwell.

Hardwig, J. (1997). Is there a duty to die. *Hastings Center Report* 27, (2), 34–42.

Kaplan, A. (1964). *The conduct of inquiry.* Scranton, PA: Chandler Publishing Company.

Lozoff, B. (2000). *It's a meaningful life—It just takes practice.* New York: Viking Arkana.

Marx, K. (1884). *The economic and philosophical manuscripts.* [On-line] Available: http://csf.colorado.edu/psn/marx/Archive/1844-EPM/1st.htm#s4.

Marx, K. (1965). *The German ideology.* London: Lawrence & Wishart.

May, R., Angel, E., & Ellenberger, H. (Eds.). (1958). *Existence: A new dimension in psychiatry and psychology.* New York: Basic Books.

Messner, S. F., & Rosenfeld, R. (2001). *Crime and the American dream* (3rd ed.). Belmont, CA: Wadsworth.

Messner, S. F., & Rosenfeld, R. (1997). *Crime and the American dream* (2nd ed.). Belmont, CA: Wadsworth.

Parsons, T. (1968). The position of identity in the general theory of action. In C. Gordon & K. J. Green (Eds.), *The self in social interaction* (pp. 11–23). New York: John Wiley & Sons, Inc.

Peters, T. (1988). *Thriving on chaos: Handbook for a management revolution*. New York: Knopf.

Pusey, M. (1987). *Jorgen Habermas*. New York: Tavistock Publications.

Quinney, R. (2000a). *Bearing witness to crime and social justice*. Albany, NY: State University of New York Press.

Quinney, R. (2000b). Socialist humanism and the problem of crime: Thinking about Erich Fromm in the development of critical/peacemaking criminology. In K. Anderson & R. Quinney (Eds.), *Erich Fromm and critical criminology: Beyond the punitive society* (pp. 21–30). Urbana: University of Illinois Press.

Rawls, J. (1999). *A theory of justice* (Revised ed.). Cambridge, MA: Belknap Press.

Schlosser, E. (2002). *Fast food nation: The dark side of the all-American meal*. New York: Harper Collins.

Schmalleger, F. (2001). *Criminology today*. Upper Saddle River, NJ: Prentice Hall.

Schram, S. F., & Soss, J. (2001). Success stories: Welfare reform, policy discourse, and the politics of research. *Annals of the American Academy of Political and Social Sciences*, 577, 49–65.

Sheleff, L. S. (1997). *Social cohesion and legal coercion: A critique of Weber, Durkheim, and Marx*. Amsterdam: Rodopi B. V.

Singer, P. (1994). *Rethinking life and death: The collapse of our traditional ethics*. New York: St. Martin's Griffin.

Snow, D. A., & Oliver, P. E. (1995). Social movements and collective behavior. In K. S. Cook, G. A. Fine, & J. S. House (Eds.), *Sociological perspectives on social psychology* (pp. 571–600). Needham Heights, MA: Allyn and Bacon.

Sullivan, D., & Tiff, L. (2001). *Restorative justice: Healing the foundations of our everyday lives*. Monsey, NY: Willow Tree Press.

Weber, M. (1964). *The theory of social and economic organization*. New York: The Free Press.

Wozniak, J. F. (2000). Alienation and crime: Lessons from Erich Fromm. In K. Anderson & R. Quinney (Eds.), *Erich Fromm and critical criminology: Beyond the punitive society* (pp. 43–58). Urbana: University of Illinois Press.

Index

Contributors

Kevin B. Anderson worked with Richard Quinney as professors in the Department of Sociology at Northern Illinois University. They coedited *Erich Fromm and Critical Criminology: Beyond the Punitive Society*. Currently, Kevin is a professor of political science, sociology, and women's studies at Purdue University and his teaching and research interests are in political and social theory.

Michael C. Braswell is a professor of criminal justice and criminology at East Tennessee State University. His current interests include original fiction addressing social justice issues and ways peacemaking can influence ethics.

John Randolph Fuller is a professor of criminology at the University of West Georgia. His latest book is *Juvenile Delinquency: Mainstream and Crosscurrents*.

Wayne Gillespie is an associate professor of criminology and assistant dean of graduate studies at East Tennessee State University. His research interests include substance use/abuse, violent behavior, and criminological/sociological theory.

Amy Hembree is a freelance writer and editor. She has written supplementary materials for a number of texts.

David Kauzlarich is associate professor and chair of the Sociology and Criminal Justice Studies Department at Southern Illinois University, Edwardsville. His research interests include state crime, peace studies, and criminological theory. He is the author or coauthor of several scholarly articles and book chapters and has written three books, *Crimes of the American Nuclear State* (with Ronald C. Kramer); *Introduction to Criminology*, 8th Edition (with Hugh D. Barlow); and *Sociological Classics*.

Ronald C. Kramer is professor of sociology and director of the criminal justice program at Western Michigan University. His published works include *Crimes of the American Nuclear State; State-Corporate Crime: Wrongdoing at the Intersection of Business and Government,* and a number of articles on international law and state crime.

M. Joan McDermott is currently an associate professor of criminal justice in the Center for the Study of Crime, Delinquency, and Corrections, and director of Women's Studies at Southern Illinois University, Carbondale. Her current research interests are in intimate partner violence, feminist theory, and interdisciplinary approaches to the study of girls' violence.

Raymond J. Michalowski is Arizona Regents Professor of Criminal Justice at Northern Arizona University. His published works include *Order, Law and Crime; Radikale Kriminologie; Crime, Power and Identity; Run for the Wall: Remembering Vietnam on a Motorcycle Pilgrimage;* and *State-Corporate Crime: Wrongdoing at the Intersection of Business and Government.*

Alan Mobley is a criminal justice professor in the School of Public Affairs at San Diego State University. He coauthored "The Corrections Corporation of America: AKA The Prison Reality Trust" in David Schichor and Michael J. Gilbert (eds.) *Privatization in Criminal Justice: Past, Present, and Future* and authored "Convict Criminology: The Two-Legged Data Dilemma" in Jeffrey Ian Ross and Stephen C. Richards (eds.), *Convict Criminology.*

Harold "Hal" Pepinsky is professor of criminal justice at Indiana University and coauthor of *Myths that Cause Crime* and coeditor of *Criminology as Peacemaking* and *We Who Would Take No Prisoners*. He has also written the *Geometry of Violence and Democracy; Peacemaking: Reflections of a Radical Criminologist,* and many journal articles and book chapters focusing upon varieties of criminal justice policy issues.

Polly F. Radosh is chair of the Department of Women's Studies at Western Illinois University. Dr. Radosh has published numerous articles on women in the criminal justice system. She continues to teach, research and write about issues affecting women in prison and has recently begun a new trajectory of research on Irish immigrant women.

Randall G. Shelden is professor of criminal justice, University of Nevada–Las Vegas. He is also a Senior Research Fellow with the Center on Juvenile and Criminal Justice in San Francisco. He is the author or coauthor of *Criminal Justice in America: A Sociological Approach*; *Girls, Delinquency and Juvenile Justice* (3rd edition), with Meda Chesney-Lind); *Youth Gangs in American Society* (3rd ed.), with Sharon Tracy and William B. Brown (both third editions); *Controlling the Dangerous Classes: The History of Criminal Justice* (2nd edition); *Delinquency and Juvenile Justice in American Society* (Waveland Press); *Juvenile Justice in America: Problems and Prospects* (Waveland Press, coedited with Daniel Macallair). He is also the author of more than fifty journal articles and book chapters on the subject of crime and justice.

Chuck Terry is a lecturer in the sociology department at the University of California, Santa Barbara. He authored *Overcoming Prison and Addiction* and "From C-Block to Academia: You Can't Get There from Here" in Jeffrey Ian Ross and Stephen C. Richards (eds.), *Convict Criminology*.

Larry L. Tifft is professor of sociology at Central Michigan University where he has taught for thirty-two years. His motivation for writing has been to keep the ideas and ideals of Peter Kropotkin alive for future generations. Much of his writing has been a collaboration with Dennis Sullivan. Together they have written the cult classic, *The Struggle to be Human: Crime, Criminology, & Anarchism* (1980); *Restorative Justice: Healing the Foundations of our Everyday Lives* (2001; 2005), and the edited work, *Handbook of Restorative Justice: A Global Perspective* (2006). Together they also founded the journal, *Contemporary Justice Review*, and were instrumental in establishing the Justice Studies Association. Larry lives in Mt. Pleasant, MI with his wife/partner, Lyn Markham, and their son, Skye.

John T. Whitehead is professor of criminal justice and criminology at East Tennessee State University. He has published many articles on death penalty opinion and on correctional worker stress, and he is coauthor of *Juvenile Justice* (5th ed.) published by Lexis-Nexis.

John F. Wozniak is a professor of sociology and chair of the Department of Sociology and Anthropology at Western Illinois University. He has coauthored articles on correctional policies; public attitudes toward crime; functions and social supports of police; and elderly offenders. His current research interests include textbook coverage of corporate crime; progressive social activism on crime and justice; application of C. Wright Mills's theory toward the study of crime; and the rise of peacemaking criminology.